CLINTON BUSH AND CIA CONSPIRACIES
FROM THE BOYS ON THE TRACKS TO JEFFREY EPSTEIN

WAR ON DRUGS BOOK 4

SHAUN ATTWOOD

ACKNOWLEDGEMENTS

A big thank you to Mark Swift (editing),
Jane Dixon-Smith (typesetting and book-jacket design),
Mark Luscombe (additional cover work)

SPELLING DIFFERENCES: UK V USA

This book was written in British English, hence USA readers may notice some spelling differences with American English: e.g. color = colour, meter = metre and = jewelry = jewellery

SHAUN'S BOOKS

English Shaun Trilogy
Party Time
Hard Time
Prison Time

War on Drugs Series
Pablo Escobar: Beyond Narcos
American Made: Who Killed Barry Seal? Pablo Escobar or George HW Bush
The Cali Cartel: Beyond Narcos
The War Against Weed (Expected 2020)

Un-Making a Murderer: The Framing of Steven Avery and Brendan Dassey
The Mafia Philosopher: Two Tonys
Life Lessons

Pablo Escobar's Story (4-book series 2019-20)
T-Bone (Expected 2022)

SOCIAL-MEDIA LINKS

Email: attwood.shaun@hotmail.co.uk
YouTube: Shaun Attwood
Blog: Jon's Jail Journal
Website: shaunattwood.com
Instagram: @shaunattwood
Twitter: @shaunattwood
LinkedIn: Shaun Attwood
Goodreads: Shaun Attwood
Facebook: Shaun Attwood, Jon's Jail Journal, T-Bone Appreciation Society

Shaun welcomes feedback on any of his books.
Thank you for the Amazon and Goodreads reviews!

CONTENTS

CHAPTER 1
THE BOYS ON THE TRACKS

On August 22, 1987, seventeen-year-old Kevin Ives went to spend the night at the house of his friend, sixteen-year-old Don Henry. The two fresh-faced boys with big eyes and smiles, and their hair blow-dried into quiffs, lived in Saline County, Arkansas. The next day at 10 AM, Kevin's mother received a call.

"Linda, are Kevin and Don with you?" Don's dad asked.

"No, Curtis, I thought they were with you."

"That's strange. I gave the boys permission to go out hunting after midnight. Haven't seen them since, but don't worry, Linda. They're OK. Don knows his way around those woods."

"Did they take guns?"

"Of course they took guns. You don't go hunting without guns." Curtis promised to look for the boys and get back to Linda. Having already searched for them at 4 AM, he feared that something bad had happened. Driving around in the darkness, he had encountered a deputy in a police car.

"Have you seen two boys?"

"Who specifically are you looking for?"

Wary of volunteering information because the boys had been hunting illegally, Curtis had kept quiet, thanked the deputy and continued his search. After driving around for hours, he had returned home to call Linda.

Alone at home after receiving the call from Curtis, Linda was feeling uneasy. While washing laundry, she wondered where the boys could be. When Kevin had sought permission to sleep over, she had initially said no. Only after calling Curtis – who had reassured her – had she consented. Convincing herself that Kevin would arrive home at any moment, she resisted calling the police.

1

At noon, her phone rang. "Get over here quick!" Curtis said. "They've been shot and tied to the railroad tracks and run over by a train."

Linda felt her world turn upside down. In a daze, she listened to Curtis, disbelieving anything he said because it was impossible. He must have lost his mind. As Curtis gave directions to his house, she found herself unable to write anything down. In a trance, she trudged next door, and said to a married couple, "Call this man and get directions to his house."

"Why are we going over there?" the woman asked.

"I have to go straighten out something about Kevin."

"What's wrong with Kevin?"

"Curtis Henry said he's been shot and tied to the railroad tracks."

The woman collapsed. Her husband transported Linda in his car. When she spotted Kevin's car outside of the house, she knew that her son was OK. As she approached the house, a policeman emerged.

"Where are Kevin and Don?" she asked.

"Why don't you come inside, Mrs Ives?"

"Curtis said they've been shot and tied to the railroad tracks."

"We don't have any indication that they were shot or tied."

Don's stepmother was inside with Curtis.

"What had Kevin been wearing?" the policeman asked.

"Jeans, a T-shirt, a gold chain, Nike sneakers and socks."

"There's no reason to go to the tracks or to view the bodies. It would be in your best interest to go home."

At her residence, friends consoled Linda. Her daughter arrived. She called the dispatcher at the railroad where her husband worked and left a message for him to contact her and come home.

Larry called. "Linda, has something happened to your mom? Is it one of the kids? Is it Alicia?"

"No. No. No."

"Is it Kevin? Did something happen to Kevin?"

"Larry, I think he's dead."

"I'll be home as soon as I can."

As the identities of the corpses had not officially been confirmed, Linda clung to the belief that Kevin was OK. It was all a case of mistaken identity.

Pale and trembling, Larry arrived in a car, which he almost fell out of. Friends propped him up and helped him into the house. For privacy, the couple went into a bedroom with their daughter.

"What are we going to do?" Larry asked.

Feeling completely helpless, but knowing that she had to be strong for her husband, whom she had never seen in such a state, she said, "I don't know, Larry, but we'll get through this somehow. We can do it."

Throughout the night, Larry sobbed and cried for help. Unable to sleep or to comprehend what was going on, Linda remained numb with shock.

In the following days, the authorities explained that the boys had been fatally run over by a train at approximately 4 AM. Travelling at 50 mph, the train had dragged their bodies for over half a mile. As 1.9 grams of cannabis had been found in Kevin's trousers, the police theorised that the stoned boys had either died accidentally or had killed themselves in a suicide pact.

Having raised Kevin to always be aware of trains, Larry doubted the accident theory. Two months earlier, Larry had been the engineer on the train that had now run over the boys. If he hadn't been transferred, he would have seen the tragedy. As for suicide: Kevin didn't suffer from depression. In fact, both boys loved life.

Curtis instinctively felt that the police had missed something, either accidentally or perhaps they were withholding information. If the police had done such a thorough investigation, why had they left Kevin's foot out there for two days in plain sight? Don's parents dismissed both theories. Getting stoned didn't drive people to suicide or any such extremes of behaviour.

Curtis asked a friend, a hunter, to examine the tracks. The

friend returned dismayed. He had found little blood, which didn't happen at the scene of freshly killed animals. Linda didn't yet know about the lack of blood, but it had been spotted by the medical staff who had attended the tragedy, the train crew and the police. The tiny amount of blood found ten minutes after the impact of the train was purple not red, and the body parts were pale. If the boys had been dismembered, fresh red blood should have been everywhere.

The Emergency Medical Technician's report stated: "Blood from the bodies and on the body parts we observed was a dark color in nature. Due to our training, this would indicate a lack of oxygen in the blood and could pose a question as to how long the victims had been dead."

Not only was the blood telling a different story than the police, but the witnesses on the train had reported that the boys were frozen still as if they were already dead.

"Our headlight was on the bright position," said Danny DeLamar, the conductor, "and I noticed down the rail in front of me, some ten or fifteen cars away, there was a dark spot on the rail. I looked hard at it, and towards the last, I stood up to see what it was. When we were approximately one-hundred feet from this dark spot, Engineer Shroyer yelled out, 'Oh my God!' He hit the whistle and the emergency brakes at the same time. We could tell there were two young men lying between the rails just north of the bridge, and we also saw there was a gun beyond the boy who was lying to the north. There was something covering these boys from their waist to just below their knees, and I'm not sure what this object was. They were both in-between the rails, heads up against the west rail, and their feet were over the east rail. Both were right beside each other and their arms and hands were to their sides, heads facing straight up. I never noticed any movement at all."

While the police circulated rumours that the boys were suicidal drug addicts, Linda grew more suspicious. The evidence suggested a homicide, but three weeks later, the Arkansas medical examiner,

Dr Malak, ruled the deaths were an accident. He claimed the boys had fallen into a cannabis-induced psychedelic trance, and lay down side by side, where they were killed in a state of deep sleep.

Present at the ruling, both sets of parents were flabbergasted. They had travelled to Little Rock convinced that a medical professional would have ascertained the truth, and they would get answers to all of the questions that had been haunting them. Even though they didn't understand the properties of cannabis, the ruling made no sense – it raised even more questions.

"THC intoxication. Dr Malak, what exactly does that mean?" Linda inquired.

"The level of marijuana in the children's blood was very, very high," Dr Malak said conclusively, speaking in an almost incomprehensible Egyptian accent.

"How high?" Linda asked.

Reluctantly, Dr Malak drew a vertical line on a blackboard with 5 at the bottom and 100 at the top. He said 5 corresponded to being under the influence of cannabis. "Your children's levels were here," he said, pointing at 100. "This is how stoned they were."

"What kind of measurement is that?" Linda said. Even the nurse in the room shook her head.

Gazing dismissively at the parents through thick glasses, Dr Malak launched into a lecture about the hallucinogenic properties of cannabis. "You want to know?" he said, reaching for the envelope with the autopsy photos.

"No," they said, shocked that he would resort to such a tactic. Pressing for answers only vexed Dr Malak, who repeatedly threatened to reveal the photos.

"They don't want to look at those," said a chief deputy. He removed the envelope from the table and whispered to Linda, "He told me twenty, Linda. They would have had to smoke about twenty joints."

"Who told you twenty?" Linda asked.

"Malak."

"Well, Dr Malak," Curtis said, "we know that they were lying in identical positions, soldier style, on the tracks. If they were so stoned, so intoxicated and in a psychedelic stupor, how could they have done that?"

"I've seen stranger things in my career." He lectured about the effects of hashish on camels. He never mentioned the lack of blood at the crime scene or its purplish colour.

The state crime lab didn't test the levels of drugs in the boys' blood. It was told to back Malak's ruling, which was ridiculed by the media and locals. The only people pretending to believe the ruling were the police. "We are satisfied with the ruling," the chief deputy of the Saline County Sheriff's Office told a reporter.

Linda started to hear that the paramedics at the scene were concerned about the lack of blood. She reached out to them. Only one agreed to talk. A hospital worker friend arranged a meeting. Linda and her friend arrived to find the paramedic with three deputies.

"I've changed my mind," he said, trembling. "I can't speak to you."

"Billy, we've been hearing rumours about the appearance of the blood," Linda said. "Please talk to me for a minute in a private room."

"I can't talk to you, Mrs Ives. Just get my report. I spent five hours writing that report. I knew I would need to have total recall about the events of that day. It's all in my report."

"Billy, have the deputies intimidated you?"

"No, ma'am. They haven't."

With Billy obviously terrified, Linda gave up.

"I've never seen three deputies in the hospital together, especially after nine at night," Linda's friend said as they exited.

With the facts provided by Dr Malak not adding up, Linda demanded a second opinion and hired a private investigator. Local law enforcement and the state crime lab tried to sabotage her efforts. After she requested the report that had taken five hours for Billy to write, the hospital said that it didn't exist. Linda got court orders requesting samples of everything the crime lab had. Dr Malak refused to obey the court orders.

With the public outraged by the injustice and the stonewalling by Dr Malak, the media started to investigate his track record. In 1982, a man's body was found with five bullet wounds, which Dr Malak ruled a suicide. In 1985, a North Arkansas man was fatally shot. He ruled it a suicide even though the victim had four shotgun wounds to the chest. In 1986, he ruled accidental drowning in a case of a victim who had been shot in the head. When a depressed patient was found hung in the shower of a hospital, he ruled it a suicide. When the wife sued the hospital for negligence, he changed the cause of death to an accident that had happened during a voluntary act of strangulation and masturbation designed to increase sexual pleasure. His most far-fetched ruling was that of James Mylam, whom Dr Malak claimed had died from ulcer-related natural causes. When Mylam's skull was recovered, it was determined that he had been decapitated with a sharp knife.

After Linda held a press conference, various experts came forward, who found faults with the police investigation and Dr Malak's claims, including about the psychedelic effects of cannabis. Linda demanded a grand jury investigation into the deaths.

The bodies were exhumed. Dr Joseph Burton, an Atlanta medical examiner, performed a second examination. He concluded that the boys had only smoked a few joints before their deaths. With the concurrence of six of his peers, he stated that Don Henry had been stabbed in the back, and Kevin Ives' skull had been crushed prior to him being placed on the tracks – a type of injury associated with being smashed in the head with a rifle butt. A grand jury concluded that the deaths were the result of foul play, and urged further investigation.

A year after the boys had been found on the tracks, Linda was thankful that a murder hunt had finally begun. Some locals had told her that an airstrip in the area the bodies were found was rumoured to be receiving cocaine drops. Small planes flying low with their lights off had been sighted. She wondered whether the boys had seen some illegal activity, and been murdered by a criminal gang.

CHAPTER 2
FROM POVERTY TO MILLIONAIRE
CRACK KINGPIN

Twenty-seven years before the death of Linda's son, Rick Ross was born to a black maid in Texas, a state where people of colour still had to address white men as "Sir." Abandoned by his father – a sharecropper and pig farmer – Rick spent his first three years in Arp, a little town in the sticks. With his mother and older brother – who protected him from rats and snakes – he lived in a tiny two-bedroom house overlooking a highway with the occasional car roaring by. Beyond a patch of weeds next to the house was a run-down gas station with two rarely used pumps. Away from the trappings of city life, the family – including their dog, Pooch – bonded. Sitting on an old couch, they watched cartoons, which their mother only allowed after the completion of their chores.

In 1963, Rick, at age three, started to accompany his brother to school. Tiny Rick had to climb onto a school chair. The brothers returned home from school one day to find their mother in a stern mood.

"Go to your room and pack your clothes and toys. We're moving to California."

Limited to cleaning houses, she hoped that California would have better opportunities for her family. After she revealed that his brother had to stay in Texas, Rick sobbed. She would send for his brother after they had settled in. His brother, Pooch and all of Rick's toys went to his father's house. To California, Rick and his mother only took fried chicken and some clothes.

The first few months in California, Rick and his mother lived on a couch at his aunt and uncle's house. He enjoyed playing with his five cousins. In-between spending time on welfare, his mother did odd jobs. After she started working full-time, they moved into a bedroom at another family member's house, belonging to Uncle George and Aunt Bobbi Jo, who had two kids.

Uncle George would get drunk and turn abusive. One night in 1966, he came home in a jealous rage. Aunt Bobbi Jo protested that she had not been unfaithful. "Don't lie to me, bitch!" he screamed back. With a steak knife, George stabbed Bobbi Jo in her left breast and shoulder, cutting them both wide open.

Rick's mother urged George to leave. He refused, so she pulled out a small pistol, which George had bought her to protect herself in the dangerous neighbourhood. "You done lost your mind if you think I'm gonna stand here and let you kill that girl. Just go, George."

"It's not over, Bobbi Jo. I'll be back," George threatened, before leaving.

They took Bobbi Jo, with blood gushing from her wounds, to a neighbour's house, and bandaged her. With George stalking the area, they moved Bobbi Jo to Rick's mother's boyfriend's house. They were preparing to take Bobbi Jo to a hospital to get stitches when Uncle George kicked the door in.

"Get over here, Bobbi Jo! Don't make me tell you again!" He knocked the boyfriend out of the way, and was about to continue beating Bobbi Jo.

"Please, Jesus. Please, Jesus," Bobbi Jo whimpered.

Rick's mother pushed Bobbi Jo and Rick away from Uncle George.

Bang!

She shot her brother, Uncle George, in the chest. He fell dead. She was arrested, but released after a week when the investigators decided it had been self-defence.

A few years later, Rick and his mother moved into a three-bedroom house in South Central Los Angeles, by the Harbor Freeway. His mother enrolled him in St Lawrence of Brindisi

Parish Catholic School in Watts. After getting into a fight with a student two years his senior, who had weaselled out of paying a marbles' debt, Rick was expelled. The injustice ended his interest in school work.

In Manchester Elementary School, located in a gang-infested neighbourhood, Rick dreamt about becoming a policeman, a fire fighter or a pilot. Even though he was having difficulty reading and writing, he enjoyed the new school. One day, walking to school with his cousins and friends, he noticed a crowd around the swimming pool in Manchester Park. He and the others pushed their way to the front of the throng and saw a bloated corpse in the water. Immediately, he suffered a flashback to Uncle George, dead, his eyes wide open. After that, he had nightmares about his mother abandoning him. When his older brother joined them in 1972, he started feeling safer.

At Bret Harte Junior High School, Rick struggled academically. He built alliances with gang members that he would later use. By 1973, two Crip gangs prevailed in his school: 92nd Street Crips and 102nd Street Crips. With the majority of his friends already gang members, it wasn't long before Rick was fantasising about joining.

As one of the most violent gangs in LA, the Crips were involved in murders, extortion, robberies and drugs. Members traditionally wore blue clothing, and had their own tattoos and gang hand signs. As well as peer pressure and the desire to make money from selling drugs, young people aspired to be Crips because of their affiliation with superstar rappers such as Snoop Dogg, Ice Cube and Ice-T. Although Rick built relationships with Crips, he credits one particular incident for steering him away from becoming a full member.

At the end of a school day, he put his books in his locker. He turned around to a pistol aimed at him, held by a member of the Denver Lane Bloods, rivals of the Crips. With the gun near his forehead, he thought he would be killed like Uncle George. The Blood had a bandanna over his face, so Rick could only see his eyes. The Blood and an accomplice held him at gunpoint for several seconds. When they finally walked away, he was shaking with terror. He hurried home. In the safety of his house, he visualised the death of Uncle George and the bloated corpse in the pool. Trembling, he decided not to go join a gang.

After he started acting like the class clown, his mother punished him by whipping him with belts and ironing chords. He began to channel his energy into tennis, which he enjoyed and excelled at. He trained with Dorsey High School's team, spending his meagre allowance on the bus fare to get there. Using his aunt's address in the Dorsey School district, he applied to and was accepted by Dorsey High, even though he was still failing academically.

A friendly coach bought him tennis clothes and gear. By practising three hours daily, he earned a place on the varsity team. The matches took him out of South Central Los Angeles after school, which helped distance him from the gangs. In 1976, his team almost won the city championship. He was offered a college sports scholarship. Surely tennis would get him out of the ghetto. Unable to read or write, he lost his scholarship and was unable to realise his dream of going to college. After schoolkids found out about his illiteracy, they teased him mercilessly. Before the end of his senior year, he quit school.

On the streets of South Central, Rick explained to employers that he was a hard worker, willing to roll up his sleeves and wash cars or dump trash, but he was unable to get a job or to move out of his mother's house.

In 1979, he received a grant to enrol in Los Angeles Trade–Technical College. He wanted to learn about auto upholstery and to work on low-riders. Instead, he ended up attending bookbinding classes and he joined the tennis team.

In his second year, he stopped going to classes to hang around the neighbourhood. He went to low-rider carhops, parties where booze and drugs flowed freely, fancy stereo systems blasted music and young women dressed to tease. He blamed his lack of success with the opposite sex on not having a low-rider. By acting as a lookout for street prostitutes, he earned $100 from pimps. He bought an old car, which his friends helped him to repair. Getting deeper into the carhop scene, he stole cars and earned money from chop shops. He was arrested for grand theft auto, but the judge dismissed the case.

Free from jail, he sat on his porch, contemplating what to do with his life. A friend invited him over to chat. The friend wasn't making enough money from painting cars to pay for college, so he had started selling cocaine to white students at San Jose State University. He extracted a bag of white powder. "It's a new thing, man. I can sell this for $50."

Having seen the movie *Super Fly* about a black cocaine dealer trying to quit the underworld drug business, Rick was interested in selling cocaine because the movie had glamorised the lifestyle. In his book, *Freeway Rick Ross*, he stated, "I barely heard the word 'students' or 'San Jose' or even 'cocaine.' I was totally focused on 'extra money.' I wanted in on the game."

Around the neighbourhood, he took $50 worth of cocaine from his friend, wrapped in paper folded into a tiny envelope. Nobody knew what it was in South Central LA. Cocaine was considered a drug reserved for rich white people. Finally, a PCP addict confirmed that it was pure. Rick sold it for twice the price, which convinced him that cocaine was his ticket to riches. To raise capital to buy cocaine, he and a friend stole the wheels off a Buick. He bought $300 worth of cocaine from the college friend who had introduced him to it.

From a growing customer base, he saved up almost $10,000 from cocaine proceeds, and tried his own cocaine. While he was high, someone stole his money. He swore never to use it again because it would stop him from getting rich. Over four years, he went from making $50 a week to million-dollar deals by the age of 23. The contacts he had built with gang members since childhood were used for protection, debt collection and settling disputes.

Some nights, dozens of kilos of cocaine were cooked into

crack, which he marketed as Ready Rock. Buyers drove up to his crack houses, which served drugs like a drive-in fast-food restaurant. He had money-counting houses, drug-cooking houses, crack-storage houses, apartment buildings, a laundromat and an auto-body shop. Record company executives urged him to invest in their artists. By 1985, he was the biggest cocaine dealer on the West Coast.

By 1988, he feared getting arrested. The police were closing in. They raided his accomplices and robbed them. Sometimes they planted drugs to make arrests. He had heard that one policeman was going to kill him on sight. The policeman tracked him down and fired at him, but he fled.

As well as the increased danger, the consequences of the drugs he had sold had become increasingly apparent in his neighbourhood: women prostituting, destitute addicts pushing shopping carts … After rethinking his occupation, he quit to concentrate on the businesses he had invested in, but the government indicted him for drug crimes. Under the statute of limitations, drug charges can be prosecuted for a number of years after the crimes are committed. He served five years.

Immediately after his release, Oscar Danilo Blandón, one of Rick's former cocaine suppliers, tried to entice him back into the game. At first, he resisted, but the Nicaraguan hounded him for six months. Feeling indebted to Blandón for past favours, he agreed to introduce Blandón to a purchaser. It was a sting operation. Rick was arrested for brokering a deal.

In November 1996, aged 36, he received a life sentence. With no possibility of parole, he was going to die inside. Devastated by the severity of the sentence, he was escorted from the courtroom by federal marshals. While he shuffled along in shackles, his eyes found his mother's. She broke down and sobbed hysterically. As he left the courtroom, all he could hear was her crying.

In prison, Rick eventually shook off the sense of hopelessness and decided to fight back. He needed to get the Ninth Circuit Court of Appeals to agree that he had been over sentenced. To communicate with the court, he had to be able to read and write, so he started to educate himself.

CHAPTER 3
JOURNALIST UNCOVERS
CIA DRUG TRAFFICKING

Gary Webb attended a community college in Indianapolis, where a student newspaper published his music reviews. For four years, he studied journalism at Northern Kentucky University. In 1980, he co-wrote a series for the *Kentucky Post* called "The Coal Connection," about the murder of a coal company president linked to organised crime. It won the national Investigative Reporters and Editors Award for reporting from a small newspaper.

In 1988, the year after the death of Linda Ives' son, Gary started to work at the *San Jose Mercury News*. After winning numerous regional awards, he contributed to an article about the 1989 Loma Prieta earthquake. It won the *Mercury News'* staff the Pulitzer Prize for General News Reporting in 1990.

While at Northern Kentucky University, Gary had maintained a long-distance relationship with Sue, whom he had met in Indianapolis. On February 10, 1979, they had married at a Unitarian church. Gary had been living the Californian dream with Sue, but early symptoms of depression emerged after their family expanded to three kids and he received complaints about a series of articles he had written claiming that the California Department of Motor Vehicles had spent millions on software that wasn't working properly.

In 1994, he wrote "The Forfeiture Racket," an exposé of drug-asset-forfeiture laws, which enabled police departments to profit from confiscating houses, cars, cash and property belonging to anyone they suspected of dealing drugs. Due to the War on

Drugs, these confiscations had taken on a life of their own, and seemed to violate property rights. They did not require a criminal conviction and it was extremely difficult and costly in terms of legal expenses for people to get their property back.

The story included an inmate serving life without parole in United States Penitentiary Lompoc for cocaine trafficking. The inmate had found a loophole that could potentially have caused the annulment of the Justice Department's asset forfeitures that had taken place since 1991. After visiting the inmate, Gary published the story in the *Mercury News*. It caused lawmakers in California to rescind the forfeiture laws, and Gary won the H L Mencken Award for reporting from the Free Press Association.

Intrigued by the story, a woman calling herself Coral rang Gary in July 1995. She claimed to have contacted the inmate in Lompoc prison to ascertain whether Gary was trustworthy. The inmate had vouched for Gary. She pitched him the story of her boyfriend, Rafael Cornejo, a Nicaraguan drug trafficker stuck in jail for three years without a trial, whose house had been seized and sold by the government. Having finished writing about forfeiture laws, Gary wasn't interested.

"There's something about Rafael's case that I don't think you would have done before," Coral said. "One of the government witnesses is a guy who used to work with the CIA selling drugs. Tons of it ... And now he's working for the government again." She added that Rafael's case would never go to trial because he had imported four tons of cocaine for the US government, and she had copies of all of the legal documents to verify her claims.

Intrigued, Gary researched Rafael. Articles described him as a cocaine kingpin with ties to the Cali Cartel in Colombia and money launderers in Panama. When Gary met Coral, she showed him numerous reports, including a grand-jury transcript pertaining to Oscar Danilo Blandón, a US government witness scheduled to testify against Rafael, whom she alleged sold drugs for the CIA. She asked Gary to attend Rafael's court hearing the next day.

"I don't know how she got those things," Gary said. "I've been doing this type of work for nineteen years and I've only seen federal grand-jury transcripts once in my life." As part of the legal process, the government had released transcripts, DEA and FBI documents and other information disclosing Blandón's link to the CIA. "Somebody fucked up somewhere. But when I saw those documents, I thought, this is a different story. We're not doing a story about some poor guy in jail with his property taken away. We're doing a story about some CIA-connected drug dealer."

Before the hearing, he asked the prosecutor about Blandón. In a nervous tone, the prosecutor denied any knowledge of Blandón, which increased his curiosity. Wondering why the government was protecting such a big player, he took the story to his editor at the *Mercury News*, who requested more info on Blandón.

At the next court hearing, the case against the trafficker was dismissed because Blandón's name had been struck off the witness list. Realising that he had been used by Coral to get Rafael released, Gary watched Blandón exit the courtroom. Coral said that Rafael and Blandón had both worked for Norwin Meneses, a big fish for a CIA drug ring.

Gary threw himself into more research. He found a story about Meneses having drug charges in Nicaragua in 1992, and another story from 1986 linking Meneses with the Nicaraguan rebels. He obtained lists of names, court records and interviewed police and prosecutors.

In December 1995, he was authorised by his managing editor to travel to San Diego and Nicaragua to try to locate Meneses and Blandón. Unable to speak Spanish, he teamed up with a Swiss reporter living in Nicaragua who had married a Nicaraguan. The Swiss reporter was already familiar with the key players. They searched court records and interviewed Meneses, but couldn't find Blandón. Meneses confirmed that the CIA had facilitated the operation, using American pilots. He warned Gary about the gravity of the story. If he exposed the truth, then not only his life, but also the lives of his family, would be put at risk.

In California, he went to San Diego, where he found Blandón's name in a court case from 1992. "I just started going down the list of attorneys who had represented Blandón and his co-defendants. I just started calling them up and asking, 'Have you seen Blandón? Do you know where he is? Have you heard from him?'" Nobody would reveal anything about him.

Eventually, a lawyer told him, "Blandón's testifying as a government witness. He's working for the DEA now."

"Are you sure this is the same guy?"

"Yeah. I represented his wife and then he disappeared out of the case and turned up working for the government. Now he's set up one of his old customers in a sting operation."

The old customer was Rick Ross, who Gary had previously read about when he had researched his original drug-forfeiture story that had led to the CIA story. The *LA Times* had described Rick as "South Central's first multimillionaire crack lord." The lawyer continued, "Blandón was one of Rick's biggest suppliers. He's been supplying Rick for a long time. My impression is that Blandón may have started Rick out in the business."

Gary studied Rick's rap sheet. Rick had been busted, but had never lost his assets. This seemed like a re-occurring pattern. The smaller players would get wiped out by the legal system but the larger ones were able to stay in business. He sent a letter to Rick, on remand in the Metropolitan Correctional Center in San Diego, requesting an interview.

"Then the weirdest thing happened." Gary said he got a call from Jesse Katz at the *Los Angeles Times*, who had written a 2,400-word report back on December 20, 1994: "Deposed King of Crack Now Freed After Five Years in Prison. This Master Marketer Was Key to the Drugs Spread in LA."

Katz stated, "If there was an eye to the storm, if there was a criminal mastermind behind crack's decade-long reign, if there was an outlaw capitalist most responsible for flooding Los Angeles streets with mass-marketed cocaine, his name was Freeway Rick … Rick did more than anyone else to democratise it, boosting volume, slashing prices, and spreading disease on a scale never before conceived ... His coast-to-coast conglomerate was selling more than $500,000 a day, a staggering turnover that put the drug within reach of anyone with a few dollars."

Katz asked Gary what he wanted to talk to Rick about. Upon receiving Gary's letter requesting an interview, Rick had contacted Katz to find out whether Gary was sincere and if Rick should allow the interview.

At the office of Rick's lawyer, Gary asked about Blandón. The lawyer was under the impression that Blandón was going to testify on Rick's behalf. Gary said that the opposite was true and produced paperwork that showed Blandón was a US government witness. The lawyer protested that his request for documents had been blocked by the prosecutor in the interest of national security. Gary offered to help if he could visit Rick in prison.

"Who's this?" Rick said, shuffling into a sparse prison visitation room, restricted by handcuffs and leg chains.

"He's a reporter," the lawyer said. Rick joined the two men sat on steel stools at a table bolted to the floor.

"So what do you know about Blandón?" Gary asked.

"I don't know him," Rick said, sat in an orange jumpsuit and chains.

"C'mon, Rick," Gary said. "Blandón is gonna testify against you tomorrow."

"He's the witness they've been hiding," the lawyer said.

"Man! Ain't no way they flipped Blandón, man!" Rick stood.

"Sit down, and listen to what he has to say," the lawyer said.

"They didn't flip anyone," Gary said. "Blandón was working for the government the entire time."

"You for real?" Rick asked.

"Yeah."

"Blandón's a snitch!" Rick said. "Look, man, he was a thousand times heavier than I'll ever be. He LA, New York, Atlanta, everywhere. I couldn't sell it fast enough to keep up with supply."

"Wait a minute," Gary said. "You mean demand."

"I mean supply. I was buying a hundred kilos a week, selling $3 million a day, and I still couldn't get rid of the inventory fast enough. It was raining coke. I gave him [Blandón] $6 million a week allegedly."

"That's impossible," Gary said.

"Is it?" Rick replied.

"How did you sell that much cocaine on the street?"

"We used to cook it with baking soda, and called it Ready Rock. The powder was for rich folks."

"Holy shit!" Gary said.

"Look, I was just an elf. Blandón was Santa Claus." Rick returned to his cell certain that he had been used by the CIA.

Gary left the jail convinced that the CIA-run drug ring had flooded Los Angeles with cocaine through Rick, whose relationships with the Crips and Bloods had made Rick "the biggest gang wholesaler in south-central LA." Gary visited Rick's neighbourhood, and witnessed the devastation cocaine had caused.

A few weeks later, he attended Rick's court hearing in San Diego, the purpose of which was to determine whether Rick's lawyer could question Blandón about his relationship with the CIA. Motions had been filed by the prosecutors seeking to prevent any such questions from arising. The few people in the court room included Jesse Katz from the *Los Angeles Times*.

The US Assistant District Attorney prosecuting the case saw the two journalists, spoke with his colleagues, approached the judge and whispered something to her.

"Please approach the bench," the judge said to Rick's lawyer.

For almost an hour, the lawyers and judge discussed whether the CIA could be mentioned.

"All this time Katz was going crazy," Gary said. "He was straining to hear what they were saying. But it was impossible. Finally, he got pissed off and left. He never came back to cover the trial."

At Rick's trial in San Diego, Gary heard Blandón testify against Rick. Afterwards, Rick's lawyer told Gary that he lacked the knowledge to launch an effective cross-examination of Blandón. "The prosecution hasn't told me anything about this Contra stuff. They haven't said anything about the CIA. I don't know enough to even raise any of this shit in court."

"Man, I'd ask him a lot of questions." Gary instructed the lawyer to examine the DEA records and grand-jury transcripts that had been turned over inadvertently in the case of the trafficker whose girlfriend had contacted him in the first place.

In court, the lawyer went on the attack. The startled prosecutor kept leaping up to object to every question, but the judge overruled him. Blandón explained how he had got into cocaine trafficking. He described where the cocaine was sourced, how much he sold and how much money he raised. The lawyer asked Blandón about the extent of his involvement with the US government. Blandón said the government knew everything.

"Mr Blandón, how much money did you take in from cocaine sales while working for the US government?"

"One and a half billion dollars." When asked who in the US government he had been working with, he replied the CIA.

"Mr Blandón, what did the CIA have you do?" Blandón admitted that the CIA had asked him to send the money to a rebel group fighting a war in Nicaragua. "Mr Blandón, did the CIA specifically know you were selling cocaine to buy guns and supplies to support its cause?"

"They knew who we were. Why else would they come to us?" Under oath, Blandón admitted that everything he had done was at the behest of a Nicaraguan colonel who was a paid agent of the CIA.

Gary took the information to his bosses, who admitted it was potentially the biggest story they had ever had. At that time, the CIA was operating under the presidency of Ronald Reagan and Vice President George HW Bush. They had launched an unprecedented expansion of the War on Drugs declared by President Richard Nixon.

Reagan's anti-drugs campaign had the slogan, "Just say no."

His wife, Nancy, was a leading spokesperson. She said, "If you're a casual drug user, you're an accomplice to murder." This, in combination with media headlines about rabid crack users, had resulted in a dramatic shift in public opinion about drugs, which had paved the way for the zero tolerance policies introduced in the mid to late 1980s.

"Casual drug users should be taken out and shot," said LA Police Chief Daryl Gates. It was the beginning of the ballooning of the prison population with non-violent drug offenders, which increased from 50,000 in 1980 to over 400,000 by 1997, greatly assisted during the latter part by the policies of President Bill Clinton. How could a government spearheading the War on Drugs get away with flooding the US with cocaine?

By March 1996, Gary had submitted 25,000 words to the editors. "The story went through, it seems like, 50,000 rewrites," he said. No objections to the content were raised. "I wrote a memo saying this story has a very high unbelievability factor built into it. The best way to protect it is to release other source documents and we can do this easily with hyperlinks on the Net. And management of the paper had been drumming into reporters that they should always think of ways to use the vast resources of the Internet to interface with the reader. They saw the *Mercury News* as Silicon Valley's newspaper." He insisted on the website making available all of his source material – court papers, grand-jury transcripts, FBI and DEA reports – and links to government documents, a detailed timeline, photos, biographies of the key players and sound clips of Blandón's testimony at Rick's trial.

On August 18, 1996, it was published as the cover story. At first, interest built slowly until Gary went on a talk show on KABC out of LA. When the people of south-central LA heard that the CIA was behind the cocaine deluge that had devastated their community, the uproar commenced. "It was suddenly on radio shows all over the country. When I was on the talk shows I gave out the website address, so that anybody across the country could read the story. The furore really started when people began reading this for themselves." The website began getting over a million hits a day.

Numerous constituents started calling the office of Representative Maxine Waters, South Central Los Angeles district, demanding that she investigate Gary's story. He accepted her invitation to speak at a town meeting.

The coverage so far had all been in Gary's favour. He was invited onto talk shows. His superiors congratulated him on his success and on being named the National Press Association Journalist of the Year. Finally, he had realised his dream of publishing a story that would put him on the map – but how long would the praise last?

CHAPTER 4
DEA AGENT DISRUPTS THE
GUADALAJARA CARTEL

In 1981, DEA agent Kiki Camarena relocated to Guadalajara, which was under the control of a Mexican cartel. While the Colombian kingpins had ascended noisily, their Mexican counterparts had refrained from making news headlines. Most of them had come from the state of Sinaloa, where cannabis and opium grew in the mountains, and where the law of the gun prevailed. Raids by the police and the army had only made the clannish hill people more determined and brutal. In Guadalajara, they travelled around with bodyguards toting weapons and cash in suitcases.

The heads of the Guadalajara Cartel included Miguel Ángel Félix Gallardo a.k.a. El Padrino or the Godfather. Formerly a member of the Sinaloa State Police, Félix Gallardo learned the drug business by absorbing the methods of the smugglers he arrested. As they lacked organisation, he contacted their bosses and guaranteed them protection provided that they worked for him. Those who refused were murdered. He built powerful contacts during his time as a bodyguard for the governor of Sinaloa. Tailored suits gave him the veneer of a well-educated entrepreneur even though he was a cold and calculated killer. As well as restructuring Mexico's trafficking industry, he had brokered the protection agreements between the government officials and the other bosses, which gave him a leadership role.

Every route into America, he knew intricately. He organised a distribution network in the American Southwest, which enabled the industrial-scale distribution of cannabis, opium and later on, cocaine – which put him into business with Pablo Escobar, whose shipments were increasingly getting seized as they entered Florida's coast. When the Colombians looked at diversifying their supply routes, they turned to Félix Gallardo, who guaranteed Escobar that he could get his loads into America. While initially prioritising the Medellín Cartel, Félix Gallardo refused to give Escobar exclusivity. Mexico was open for business with all of the Colombian cartels, including Escobar's enemy, Cali. Félix Gallardo believed that Escobar would never establish enough power in Mexico to challenge his dominance, and he wanted to maximise his profits by doing business with everyone. Those flying from Colombia to Southern California and refuelling in Northern Mexico took a route that became known as the Trampoline.

In the beginning, Pablo paid Félix Gallardo in cash, but the Mexicans soon coveted the profit margin on cocaine that US drug laws kept so high. As the shipments from Colombia increased in size, Félix Gallardo began to demand payment in drugs rather than currency, which could depreciate. What seemed like a great deal to Pablo at the time would lead to Mexican dominance in the trade. On the normal simple routes with the drugs hidden in trucks and trains, 35 percent of Colombian cocaine went to the Mexican Cartel. On more difficult routes, including using tunnels, the Mexicans got 50 percent. Entering distribution put the Mexicans into competition with the Colombians.

Running his business like a corporation, thirty-five-year-old Félix Gallardo was always seeking to expand quietly. By the early 1980s, he controlled banks, hotels, radio, media, an air force and cocaine refineries, whereas Kiki was operating on a tight budget, out of an office with a handful of men, two secretaries and weather-worn cars and radios. Requests to headquarters for replacements and reinforcements were mostly ignored.

Félix Gallardo's business partners included twenty-nine-year-old Rafael Caro Quintero, who came from a clan of smugglers based in rough and ready mountain towns. He developed industrial-sized plantations of cannabis without seeds called sensimilla, which had been cultivated in Oregon and California. Using modern agricultural techniques and cheap labour, he converted thousands of acres of barren desert into gigantic weed farms. As his wealth and legend grew, so did his psychopathic behaviour, which put him on a collision course with Kiki, who heard a story about Caro Quintero.

The Federales had shared the story because it was typical of how the senior police interacted with the traffickers across Mexico. In the Mexican Federal Judicial Police (MFJP), a new commander arrived for work, surrounded by subservient police-men who fed his ego. One day, boots stomped into his reception and his door burst open to reveal a charismatic curly haired cowboy in slim jeans, high-heeled boots and an unbuttoned shirt showing off gold chains. While hit men with submachine guns positioned themselves strategically, the commander watched his colleagues shrivel with fear.

While he glowered, Caro Quintero approached his desk. "Are you with us?"

Although he had been expecting a visit and was looking forward to supplementing his income, the commander felt disre-spected by his visitor's insolence.

"What do you want? Silver or lead?"

While his face turned crimson, his underlings gazed know-ingly. "Silver." He nodded. After the visit, he lived luxuriously and he never ordered any raids on the traffickers.

Born in 1930, the oldest Guadalajara Cartel boss was Ernesto Fonseca Carrillo a.k.a. Don Neto, who had pioneered cocaine routes through South America. The Ecuadorian Army had captured him with thirty kilos. Skinny and with eagle eyes, the countrified bandit had fathered hordes of children with various wives and mistresses. He financed opium and cannabis plantations and shipped cocaine to Los Angeles, San Diego and Tijuana. He contracted out his hit men to other traffickers.

Formerly a US Marine, thirty-three-year-old Kiki had moved

to Guadalajara with his wife Mika. Both were from Calexico, a town on the border of California and Mexico. As a teenager, Kiki had idolised the FBI and dreamt of becoming an agent. With the US ramping up the drug war, he had decided against the FBI to become a narcotics agent. He soon became addicted to the undercover lifestyle. Throwing himself into work, his mind never left his job, even during his time off, especially when socialising with his colleagues. Rather than discuss sports, he preferred talking about their ongoing cases. No matter how many arrests he made, he noticed that the drugs never stopped, so when he got a call inviting him to the Guadalajara office, he viewed it as an opportunity to make a difference by going after the suppliers.

Up in the mountains, cannabis and opium fields were flourishing and in Guadalajara, traffickers were spending a fortune purchasing everything from aircraft to entire police forces. Due to the recent murder of a policeman, Kiki knew the risks were high. As a commander of the Federales, Rafael Davila had been moved to Guadalajara. Having refused bribery, he was gunned down outside of a popular disco. Whereas many traditional Mafia killings were done quietly with little evidence, the brazen nature of the slaying of Davila suggested that the hit men knew that they could do whatever they wanted and face no consequences. Addicted to the adrenaline from undercover work, Kiki looked forward to the danger in Guadalajara.

As it was illegal for American agents to work undercover in Mexico, Kiki's wife thought that would bring about an improvement. She assumed that her husband would spend weekends and nights at home, and the family would be more unified. Pregnant with their third son, she had withheld her anguish over Kiki's long hours because of the passion he expressed for his work. Over dinner, he became animated when a case was nearing conclusion. She knew that there would always be risks in his profession, and the agents' wives just had to accept that. In June 1980, Kiki received his transfer from Fresno. His colleagues gave him a sombrero and a Mexican emergency ration kit, which included a dead chicken and a six-pack of beer.

In 1982, James 'Jaime' Kuykendall arrived to run the Guadalajara office. Having become a federal agent in 1957, he was the oldest agent there. From Texas, the forty-eight-year-old had learned Spanish from his wife and his tequila intake was legendary with the saloon cowboys. Believing that the shooting of the car had been an attempt to run the agents out of town, he wanted to demonstrate that they would not be intimidated. In cowboy boots, he paced the office, saying, "Next time something worse is going to happen."

Jaime found Kiki overworked and so stressed out that he had punched a supervisor in the jaw. Pressure came from the constant requirement to produce arrest and seizure statistics to justify the War on Drugs. From his previous work, Kiki knew that arresting low-level people was easily done to earn medals and to satisfy the DEA headquarters, but that never made any difference to the drug trade. Going after the big boys required patience and long-range thinking. Information coming in painted a picture of protection provided to the traffickers by officials on a wide scale. The kingpins were insulated by so many levels below, it was impossible to determine who was protecting who, where the money went and how the components of the cartel interacted. If he were to make a difference, concentrating on low-level arrests was out of the question.

Even though there were more DEA agents in Mexico than any other country, a Mexican drug lord had never been indicted in America. Hoping to dismantle the Guadalajara Cartel, the DEA launched Operation Padrino, named after Félix Gallardo, but the agency's attempts to draw the cartel's structure ended up looking like spiderwebs. Félix Gallardo was estimated to be shipping up to two tons of cocaine monthly, putting him on par with the bosses of the Medellín Cartel.

Jaime decided to gather intelligence on the relationships between the kingpins and the political and business elite. This approach went against the orders from headquarters, but he was ready to handle complaints. Determined to capture the kingpins, he was tired of agents posing for photos with drugs in one hand and a low-level dealer in the other.

In May 1982, an informant told Kiki about a giant cannabis plantation, 220 acres, in the State of San Luis Potosí, 200 miles away from Guadalajara. He doubted that anything of that size could grow in the desert. The informant insisted that underground wells had nourished cannabis plants that were over five foot tall. The kingpins running the operation were Caro Quintero, Don Neto and El Azul, and a commander of the Federales was providing protection and weapons.

A field of that size would prove Kiki's point that the eradication programme was a hoax. Aircraft provided by America was supposed to regularly fly over different zones of Mexico. It would be impossible not to see 220 green acres on the desert. What was the point of America providing financial assistance and aircraft if everybody involved in the eradication programme was being bribed? To find out for himself, he would need to fly over the area, which would require an official Mexican escort.

DEA bosses expressed scepticism over the existence of the plantation and refused Jaime's suggestion of shutting down the Mexican–American border to halt commerce. Such an act of economic warfare would strain relations and provoke anti-US sentiment. The US embassy wanted concrete evidence before it would request a flyover with a DEA agent. In response, Kiki obtained photos, which he submitted to the embassy, which forwarded them to the Attorney General's Office in Mexico.

Backed into a corner by the Americans, Mexican officials launched a raid to destroy the crops. On a clear September morning, army and police took off in helicopters, with Jaime and Kiki aboard. Years later, Jaime commented on how astounded they were by the dark green spot on the desert that became more visible as the clouds cleared. After they had landed in the middle of the plantation, he and Kiki gazed at each other, overwhelmed, frozen by the magnitude of the problem. As it was below an airline route and three miles from a railroad, the government must have known.

The Mexican government claimed to have busted 4,000 tons of quality sensimilla, with some plants up to eight feet high, flourishing from modern agricultural techniques, including wells and tons of fertiliser. The plantation supported a little village. The authorities found a barracks with bunks for one hundred people. Although the kitchen stocked fresh food, people were absent for miles around, so the bosses must have been tipped off.

Kiki tried to obtain ownership papers for the property, but the local officials were evasive. Not only was he up against the police, the army and the Mexican government, but his own bosses insisted that the raid was insignificant, it was a unique case and there wouldn't be any more like it. After he responded that the plantations were prevalent, another 170 acres of cannabis were found in Sonora, also owned by Caro Quintero. Mexican police delayed the raid, so that the fields could be harvested. Some seizures were made to satisfy the illusion of the War on Drugs.

Jaime filed a report about the size of the plantations: "Now, the only question is, what are we going to do about it?" He said that the large-scale operation was only possible because of the approval of high-level government officials. Such flagrant criminality meant that the government was negligent or corrupt and it should be forced to take drastic action by the American president, senior politicians and US Congress. "What the hell can 25 agents do in Mexico that 2,000 agents can't do in the States? We shouldn't be making busts abroad. A DEA agent should be overseas to gather intelligence and make enough cases to make the point, to tell the US government what is going on, so that the government can take the appropriate political action."

While Kiki was satisfied with the raids and looking forward to more progress, his actions were putting him on the radar of the cartel and the senior government officials who were making millions from cocaine.

CHAPTER 5
RICK ROSS LEARNS THE RACIST
HISTORY OF DRUG LAWS

Stuck in prison on a life sentence, Rick Ross hadn't benefited from Gary Webb shining the spotlight on his cocaine business and its ties to the CIA. Motivated by the desire to obtain his freedom through legal action, he had learned to read and write. As well as studying case law, he read about the history of drug laws.

He discovered that on July 17, 1971, President Richard Nixon had declared what is now known as the War on Drugs. "America's public enemy number one in the United States is drug abuse. In order to fight and defeat this enemy it is necessary to wage a new all-out offensive."

But a few things didn't add up. The majority of the prisoners incarcerated for drug crimes whom he was housed with were black, over 50 percent of them. As blacks were approximately 12 percent of the US population, where were all of the white drug users? His grandparents had been slaves, so he couldn't help but make a comparison. He decided to dig deeper through reading. Just like he had suspected, he learned that the earliest drug laws were designed to put minorities behind bars. They were introduced by politicians harnessing racism to get votes and to protect business interests. Before these laws were introduced, drugs such as heroin and cocaine were legal, and drug abusers were treated by doctors.

Chinese labourers working for a pittance were the first to suffer. After the Civil War, fought from 1861 to 1865, the Chinese were shipped over to build railroads and to work at goldmines. In the south, they replaced slaves on cotton and rice plantations. Many were addicted to smoking opium, a habit cultivated by the biggest trafficker of opium in the world: the British government.

When the US economy slowed in the 1870s, the Chinese became scapegoats. In San Francisco, exclusion laws targeted the large Chinese community of male labourers. It became illegal to wear a ponytail down your back, to carry water suspended by poles or to possess a particular kind of laundry. On November 15, 1875, the San Francisco Board of Supervisors passed an ordinance making it a misdemeanour to keep or to frequent opium dens. It targeted Chinese opium smokers, but not the whites who regularly consumed medicinal opium in tonics such as laudanum, which were gaining popularity. Around the same time that Queen Victoria was taking laudanum and cannabis to alleviate menstrual cramps, newspapers claimed opium smoking was a tool used by the Chinese to stimulate uncontrollable sexual desire in white women. Images were circulated of pale-skinned beauties lured to opium dens run by evil-eyed Chinamen eager to indoctrinate them into sex slavery. Incarcerating the foreign devils enabled politicians to increase their popularity with white voters.

Similar anti-Chinese sentiment surged in Canada in the 1920s. The media told stories of cunning Asian traffickers converting innocent young locals into rabid dope fiends. The victims were mostly white women suffering from the illness of drug addiction. The villains were immoral yet highly intelligent Chinese who drugged white women and forced them into prostitution to pay for opium. While out contracting sexually transmitted diseases, these women would end up abandoning their long-suffering children. These stories were accompanied by spooky pictures of wizened Asians with long fingernails casting evil eyes on addicts with bodies ravaged by needle marks.

The *Vancouver Daily World* claimed that opium was a weapon the Chinese were using in an attempt to annihilate the white race and that "actual attempts have been made on the lives of government officials engaged in the fight against the big influences at work behind the scenes." The *World* published stories about Chinese dealers who boasted to their white customers about "their superiority at being able to sell the dope without using it. Taunted him by telling him that the yellow race would rule the world. That they were too wise to attempt to win in battle but that they would win by wits. That they would introduce drugs into the homes of the Caucasians; would strike at the white race through 'dope,' and that when the time was ripe they would take command of the world."

At a meeting to introduce prison sentences for drug trafficking of not less than six months and not more than ten years, with lashes, and the deportation of aliens, the *World* reported that women sobbed while listening to a drug investigator describe "girls in their teens" from some of the best families in Vancouver who had prostituted themselves to Chinese, Japanese and "Hindoos" to earn money for drugs.

Four days after the meeting, an anti-drugs activist, Mrs James O'Brien, "touched on the degradation of young girls who fell into the tolls of the Orientals once they became drug addicts." She mentioned a white boy in jail for stealing and administering drugs to a young girl. "I could not forget the sight of that young fellow behind bars. I keep on remembering his big blue eyes, filled with tears. I asked him if there was anything I could do. 'Just tell mother I'm hungry,' he said. And then I went to Stanley Park and saw Orientals driving by in their big limousines, rich through the gains that had put that poor boy behind the bars."

Reality was better expressed in the memoirs of CW Harvison, a former commissioner of the Royal Canadian Mounted Police, assigned to drug enforcement in Montréal during the early 1920s. "These were not the luxurious 'opium dens' of the movies, wherein smokers sprawl in comfort on plush divans while scantily clad maidens flit across deep Oriental rugs to serve their every want … The furnishings were simple: a wooden shelf covered with straw matting … The premises used for smoking were usually on the upper floor of buildings, over shops, restaurants, or other business premises. Three or four of the larger and most frequented places were upstairs over gambling rooms ... The Chinese opium smokers were almost invariably peaceful and docile. Many of them were older citizens who had had the habit for years and could not understand why, suddenly, a fuss was being made."

Decades after the inception of US drug laws that had targeted the Chinese, cocaine laws were introduced to incarcerate blacks. After slavery was abolished in 1865, many blacks migrated north to work in factories. They settled in urban areas, mostly confined to ghettos. In the early 1900s, the whites felt threatened by black labourers, so cocaine – which hadn't been viewed as a problem until then – was criminalised to incarcerate black users.

In the late 1880s, the Parke-Davis Company was mass-marketing cocaine. The Sears, Roebuck & Co. catalogue advertised cocaine and a syringe for $1.50. But in 1890, the *Journal of the American Medical Association* printed: "Negroes in the South are reported as being addicted to a new form of vice – that of 'cocaine sniffing' or the 'coke habit.'" In response, President Theodore Roosevelt created the first drug czar, Dr Hamilton Wright, who said, "[it's] been authoritatively stated that cocaine is often the direct incentive to the crime of rape by the Negroes of the South and other regions." Dr Wright procured an expert, Dr Christopher Koch, who testified to Congress, "Most of the attacks upon the white women of the South are the direct result of a cocaine-crazed Negro brain." The press followed suit claiming that drugs gave blacks superhuman strength to commit crimes and to resist white authority.

In black-and-white-striped prison garb, blacks on chain gangs were forced to work for free, reinstituting the slavery that they had escaped. All perfectly legal under Section 1 of the Thirteenth Amendment to the US Constitution: "Neither slavery nor involuntary servitude, *except as a punishment for crime whereof the party shall have been duly convicted*, shall exist within the United States, or any place subject to their jurisdiction."

The earliest lobbying to make cannabis illegal came from

the pharmaceutical societies of the 1860s who wanted it to be categorised as a poison, so they could eliminate their competition. By 1906, most drugs, including cannabis, were still available as medicine, but a law was introduced requiring the labelling of the contents and dosage. In the 1930s, a movement called chemurgy started to harness agricultural output into industrial production. They wanted to use cannabis as a raw material for industry.

Its founders included Henry Ford – the architect of the modern auto industry – who grew up on a farm outside of Detroit, and believed that industry should be linked to agriculture: "Why use up the forests which were centuries in the making and the mines which required ages to lay down, when we can get the equivalent of forest and mineral products in the annual growth of the hemp fields."

Ford believed that hemp was a more efficient source of the materials to make cars and the fuel to run them. He had constructed a prototype car with biodegradable engine parts and its body made from hemp. Weighing six times less than a standard car, the bioplastic car could withstand blows ten times harder than steel without denting. He produced two biofuels: corn ethanol and hemp biodiesel, which ran his prototype car. In the early 1900s, his ethanol captured 25 percent of fuel sales in the Midwest, which was upsetting the oil companies. He knew that anything made from the hydrocarbons of the oil molecule could be made from domestically produced carbohydrates and hemp. Hemp polymers would be the building blocks of all industrial products. His organic car was just a glimpse of that.

Previously, the obstacle to making cannabis competitive on an industrial scale was that the separation of the fibre from the stalk needed to be done by hand, a slow and costly process. The invention of the decorticator solved that. *Popular Mechanics* featured an article: "New Billion-Dollar Crop," envisioning the revival of cannabis plantations worldwide.

Around that time, William Randolph Hearst had built the largest newspaper and magazine business in the world. His advertising boasted that twenty-eight Hearst newspapers were read by more than twenty million people in eighteen key cities of the United States. To supply paper for his tabloids, he had invested in millions of acres of timber forest and wood-pulp paper mills. The onset of mass-produced hemp paper, much cheaper than forest paper, was a threat to his empire.

Big in the chemical-based synthetic field, Lammot du Pont II also felt threatened. In 1935, du Pont's company had produced nylon, and had bought the patents to create dozens of products from oil, ranging from stockings to car tyres, all easily displaced by hemp products.

Hearst and du Pont were funded by Mellon National Bank, later known as The Bank of New York Mellon. The bank's president, Andrew W. Mellon, also owned Gulf Oil. Oil companies were expanding, but cannabis would have provided a cleaner and more economical fuel. The owner of Standard Oil, John D Rockefeller – who said, "Competition is a sin," – contributed $4 million to the campaign for alcohol prohibition as a strategy to eliminate the competition posed by Henry Ford's biofuels. When prohibition took effect in 1918, it included a ban on ethanol, rendering its production illegal. Ford was forced to abandon the production of cars he had grown from the soil. Prohibition created a surge in the production of hard liquor by organised crime, and violence and corruption swept the country, so it was repealed in 1933.

Andrew Carnegie and Rockefeller wanted to eliminate herbal treatments, including cannabis, because they were bankrolling the fledgling pharmaceutical industry. They didn't want people growing cheap medicine such as cannabis in their own backyards. They wanted people to buy drugs created in laboratories instead of natural remedies.

These business leaders brought their industries – synthetic textiles, oil, pharmaceuticals, plastics and its derivatives – into an alliance against cannabis. Liquor distilleries pitched in, too, because they viewed cannabis as competition. Fortunately for the business leaders, the banker, Andrew W. Mellon, was the

Secretary of the Treasury for the US federal government. In 1930, he appointed his future son-in-law, Harry Anslinger, a law-and-order evangelist, to head the Bureau of Narcotics. Harry's heavy-handed attempts to stop people from drinking during Prohibition hadn't gone so well. His department was facing budget cuts and his agents were idle. They needed a new enemy to declare war on.

Back then, most Americans hadn't even heard of cannabis. They were concerned with the health problems associated with heroin, opium and morphine. Instead of treating drugs as a medical issue, Harry announced, "The Treasury Department intends to pursue a relentless warfare against the despicable dope-peddling culture who preys on the weakness of his fellow man."

Believing that prohibition would contain the depraved impulses of the masses, he turned his bureau into a weapon to eradicate cannabis from America, and eventually, worldwide. As federal agents went about raiding people's homes for narcotics, he boasted about eliminating major drug rings. But with his limited budget, he was unable to police all forty-eight states. He tried to convince the states to get the local police to crack down on drugs. Despite his sales pitch, only eight states signed on; the rest saw it as federal interference in their affairs. He set out to destroy the public's perception of the cannabis plant: it was loved and respected by the majority, and for good reasons.

In ancient times, cannabis was known as the miracle plant. Going back 5,000 years, it was used medicinally to treat ailments ranging from rheumatism to malaria. The oldest cannabis paper dates back to China in 4000 BC. From Asian societies, it made its way to Europe, where it was used as an industrial crop. It produced paper, oil, wax, resin, rope, cloth, pulp, fuel, plastic and food in the form of edible oil or flour from grinding the seeds. It's rich in protein carbohydrates and essential fatty acids such as omega 3 and 6. In the eighth century, the Emperor Charlemagne encouraged its cultivation. It was used by monks to transcribe the Holy Scriptures, and it provided the parchments for the first Bible printed by Gutenberg. Millions of miles of ropes were produced from cannabis fibre, which comes from the outer wrapping of the stem.

About 300 years ago, it arrived in America. Back then, England needed a lot of hemp, so it was grown in the colonies. For centuries prior to 1850, most ships were rigged with hemp rope and sails. A forty-four-gun frigate used over sixty tons of hemp for rigging, including an anchor cable twenty-five inches in circumference. There is a virtually limitless range of fabrics that can be produced with the fibre of cannabis, from carpet backings to fine linens almost indistinguishable from natural silk. Its oil can provide a clean-burning fuel for domestic lighting and heating or fuel for cars. There are over 5,000 items that can be produced with cannabis ranging from crackers to surfboards. The cannabis plant grows at almost any latitude and requires no herbicides or pesticides to be cultivated. It grows faster than almost all other crops. It can produce up to twenty-five tons of biomass per year per cultivated acre, which is phenomenal. Two of the Founding Fathers, George Washington, the first president, and Thomas Jefferson, the third president, grew it on their farms. The drafts of the Declaration of Independence were written on hemp paper. Some citizens paid their taxes with hemp.

With so much going for hemp, Harry Anslinger's racist businessmen came up with a cunning strategy. Having lost 800,000 acres of timberland to the Revolutionary General Pancho Villa, William Randolph Hearst hated Mexicans. At only 23, he wrote to his mother, "I really don't see what is to prevent us from owning all Mexico and running it to suit ourselves." Hearst proposed using the Mexican name, marijuana, which was mostly unknown to Americans. Using his vast empire, he demonised hemp in articles like this one in *The San Francisco Examiner*: "By the tons it is coming into this country – the deadly, dreadful poison that racks and tears not only the body, but the very heart and soul of every human being who once becomes a slave to it in any of its cruel and devastating forms … Marijuana is a shortcut to the insane asylum. Smoke marijuana cigarettes for a month and what was once your brain will be nothing but a storehouse of horrid specters. Hasheesh makes a murderer who kills for the love of killing out of the mildest mannered man who ever laughed at the idea that any habit could ever get him …"

Hearst's other nationwide publications stated, "Users of marijuana become STIMULATED as they inhale the drug and are LIKELY TO DO ANYTHING. Most crimes of violence in this section, especially in country districts are laid to users of that drug."

"Was it marijuana, the new Mexican drug, that nerved the murderous arm of Clara Phillips when she hammered out her victim's life in Los Angeles? … THREE-FOURTHS OF THE CRIMES of violence in this country today are committed by DOPE SLAVES — that is a matter of cold record." This strategy disguised the true objectives of the corporate alliance, while stoking the fear of blacks and Mexicans.

During the Mexican Revolution of 1910 to 1920, many Mexicans moved to America to avoid the violence. They worked hard, performing jobs that many whites felt were beneath them. The backlash against the Chinese at the end of the previous century had reduced the supply of cheap immigrant labour, so the Mexicans were welcomed. To fill shortages, direct requests were sent to the President of Mexico for more workers and recruiters travelled to Mexico.

The stock market crash of 1929 and depression led to job shortages. President Herbert Hoover deflected the blame onto the Mexicans, claiming they had come over to steal jobs and to use social services. Hearst's tabloids stereotyped Mexicans as an evil group of alien beings. In the cities, whites started rounding up Mexicans, just like they had with the Chinese. They crammed them into buses, trains and ships for deportation. Signs went up, such as MEXICANS KEEP GOING – WE CAN'T TAKE CARE OF OUR OWN – CHAMBER OF COMMERCE and WE SERVE WHITES ONLY – NO SPANISH OR MEXICANS.

During Mexican Repatriation, two million were deported between 1929 and 1936, more than half of whom were US citizens who had been counted as white on the US census until 1930. The federal government relished the ease of deporting Mexicans versus other immigrants due to the proximity of Mexico to the United States.

Although people around the world had been smoking cannabis for centuries, the habit didn't arrive in America until the early twentieth century. It was brought over by Mexicans who used it to relax at the end of a tiring day working in the fields. Other poor minorities followed suit.

By feeding the media with fabricated stories of blacks and Mexicans embarking on killing and raping rampages while under the influence of Mexican loco weed, Harry easily demonised cannabis, and received plenty of funding for his department to fight the scourge. He said cannabis, "can arouse in blacks and Hispanics a state of menacing fury or homicidal attack. During this period, addicts have perpetrated some of the most bizarre and fantastic offences and sex crimes known to police annals."

He testified to Congress that, "coloureds with big lips lure white women with jazz and marijuana." He said, "There are 100,000 total marijuana smokers in the US, and most are Negroes, Hispanics, Filipinos and their entertainers. Their Satanic music, jazz and swing, result from marijuana use. This marijuana causes white women to seek sexual relations with Negroes, entertainers, and any others." He said, "Reefer makes darkies think they're as good as white men," and, "the primary reason to outlaw marijuana is its effect on the degenerate races."

The mainstream media, including Hearst's *Cosmopolitan* magazine, flooded the market with publications linking cannabis to deviant behaviour such as white women running away with blacks and Latinos, sex crimes, insanity, suicide and even murder. Smoking reefers caused instant addiction and possibly death within weeks. One TV programme showed a weed-crazed teenager beating his mother to death with a frying pan and going on the rampage with an axe.

The propaganda exceeded Harry's expectations. The public believed that cannabis was the greatest threat to humanity. Every state signed on to his Uniform State Narcotic Act. Frightened out of their minds, the public clamoured for even more protection from Harry, who was constantly posing in photos in Hearst's publications in the act of smashing one drug ring after another.

In 1937, Harry introduced the Marihuana Tax Act. During congressional hearings, he insisted that cannabis caused insanity and made people commit violent crimes, including rape and murder, which he backed up with a scrapbook of articles from Hearst's publications, including marijuana-crazed axe murderers.

Only one person contested Harry's claims: Dr William C Woodward, the Legislative Counsel of the American Medical Association (AMA). He slammed Harry and the Bureau of Narcotics for distorting earlier AMA statements that had nothing to do with cannabis and making them appear to be AMA endorsements for Anslinger's view. He said Harry lacked any evidence to support his claims:

"It has surprised me, however, that the facts on which these statements have been based have not been brought before this committee by competent primary evidence. We are referred to newspaper publications concerning the prevalence of marijuana addiction. We are told that the use of marijuana causes crime.

"But yet no one has been produced from the Bureau of Prisons to show the number of prisoners who have been found addicted to the marijuana habit. An informed inquiry shows that the Bureau of Prisons has no evidence on that point.

"You have been told that schoolchildren are great users of marijuana cigarettes. No one has been summoned from the Children's Bureau to show the nature and extent of the habit, among children.

"Inquiry of the Children's Bureau shows that they have had no occasion to investigate it and know nothing particularly of it.

"Inquiry of the Office of Education – and they certainly should know something of the prevalence of the habit among the schoolchildren of the country, if there is a prevalent habit – indicates that they have had no occasion to investigate and know nothing of it.

"Moreover, there is in the Treasury Department itself, the Public Health Service, with its Division of Mental Hygiene. The Division of Mental Hygiene was, in the first place, the Division of Narcotics. It was converted into the Division of Mental Hygiene, I think, about 1930. That particular Bureau has control at the present time of the narcotics farms that were created about 1929 or 1930 and came into operation a few years later. No one has been summoned from that Bureau to give evidence on that point.

"Informal inquiry by me indicates that they have had no record of any marijuana or cannabis addicts who have ever been committed to those farms.

"The bureau of Public Health Service has also a Division of Pharmacology. If you desire evidence as to the pharmacology of marijuana, that obviously is the place where you can get direct and primary evidence, rather than the indirect hearsay evidence."

Harry insisted that cannabis had no medicinal use, and that it should be taxed out of existence. Doctor Woodward said, "To say, however, as has been proposed here, that the use of the drug should be prevented by a prohibitive tax, loses sight of the fact that future investigation may show that there are substantial medical uses for marijuana." He added, "We cannot understand yet, Mr Chairman, why this bill should have been prepared in secret for two years without any intimation, even, to the profession, that it was being prepared." After that, it was insinuated that the doctor had wasted his time attending the hearing because he didn't have anything awful to say about cannabis.

Dr James C Munch, a pharmacologist at Temple University, Philadelphia, was more accommodating. His expertise was based on injecting an extract of cannabis into the brains of 300 dogs, two of which had died. He stated that cannabis completely disintegrates a human's personality and causes violent irritability, while admitting that he had never done experiments with humans, only animals, and he wasn't actually a dog psychologist. The government liked his testimony so much that they made him the US Official Expert on cannabis for the Bureau of Narcotics, from 1938 to 1962.

Dr Munch admitted in court that he had smoked cannabis once to test its dangerous effects. Under oath, he said, "After two puffs on a marijuana cigarette, I was turned into a bat." The public was so convinced about the demonic properties of cannabis espoused by Harry and Dr Munch that people were able to get out of military conscription by admitting cannabis use, and murderers were able to mitigate their sentences by stating that they were under the influence of "an addictive drug which produces in its users insanity, criminality and death." Called in as an expert witness, Dr Munch ended up saving so many murderers from the death penalty that Harry asked him to stop testifying.

After the congressional hearings for the Marihuana Tax Act of 1937, the bill went to the floor of the House of Representatives for a debate. Harry and Andrew W. Mellon stuffed the place with their confederates. Harry presented his gore files of fabricated news stories published in Hearst's newspapers. The Speaker of the House stated that the American Medical Association was in favour of the bill, which was a lie. The debate lasted ninety seconds. On June 14, 1937, President Roosevelt signed it into law. The industrialists profiting from all of the products rivalling hemp – clothing, paper, plastics and pharmaceuticals – had achieved the first federal prohibition.

At the time of the approval of the Marihuana Tax Act, the federal government knew it had no authority to make drugs illegal. It was operating outside of the powers granted to it by the Constitution as stated in the Tenth Amendment, part of the Bill of Rights, ratified in 1791: "The powers not delegated to the United States by the Constitution, nor prohibited by it to the States, are reserved to the States respectively, or to the people."

When the federal government made alcohol illegal in 1919, they had to amend the Constitution. To get around that, the

Marihuana Tax Act didn't make cannabis illegal. It levied a tax on it. Anyone buying, selling, possessing or distributing cannabis was required to pay a tax, but there was a catch: to obtain the tax stamp, the cannabis had to be submitted to be weighed, so that the tax could be determined. But anyone presenting cannabis to be weighed without a tax stamp was in violation of the law and subject to imprisonment for tax evasion.

The entire cultivation of cannabis nationwide was prohibited even though the psychotropic compounds are only found in the flower and the leaf. The majority of the representatives who voted didn't even know that marijuana and cannabis were the same thing, and that they had just annihilated the production of hemp, which had been used profitably for centuries.

Overnight, a new class of criminals was created. Prisons, which were designed to contain people who harmed other people – murderers, robbers, rapists, paedophiles – started to fill with those who were choosing to hurt themselves: addicts. The first to be convicted under the Marihuana Tax Act was fifty-eight-year-old Samuel R Caldwell from Denver. Sentencing him to four years' hard labour in Leavenworth, the judge said, "I consider marijuana the worst of all narcotics. Under its influence, men become beasts. In the future, I will impose the heaviest penalties. The government is going to enforce this new law to the letter."

Sceptical about the government's claims that cannabis was causing murder, rape, insanity and the annihilation of young people, the Mayor of New York commissioned the first scientific study on its use. Thirty-one independent scientists worked for over five years. In 1944, the LaGuardia Committee Report concluded that smoking cannabis did not cause aggressive or anti-social behaviour or an increase in sexual depravity or alter the fundamental aspects of personality. It demolished all of Harry's claims.

Harry discredited the report in the media and dispatched his agents nationwide to hunt down and destroy every copy they could find. He prevented any more cannabis from being available for research. At his behest, the media smeared anyone who disagreed with him, especially musicians and actors. Fearing his wrath, Hollywood studios gave him personal control over all movie scripts that mentioned drugs. He banned movies he felt were sending the wrong message.

During World War II, hemp received respite from Harry when it was deemed vital to the Allies' war effort. In 1942, the United States Department of Agriculture released a film aimed at farmers, "Hemp for Victory," in which the narrator stated:

Long ago, when these ancient Grecian temples were new, hemp was already old in the service of mankind. For thousands of years, even then, this plant had been grown for cordage and cloth in China and elsewhere in the East. For centuries prior to about 1850 all the ships that sailed the western seas were rigged with hempen rope and sails. For the sailor, no less than the hangman, hemp was indispensable.

A forty-four-gun frigate like our cherished *Old Ironsides* took over sixty tons of hemp for rigging, including an anchor cable twenty-five inches in circumference. The Conestoga wagons and prairie schooners of pioneer days were covered with hemp canvas. Indeed the very word canvas comes from the Arabic word for hemp. In those days hemp was an important crop in Kentucky and Missouri. Then came cheaper imported fibers for cordage, like jute, sisal and Manila hemp, and the culture of hemp in America declined.

But now with Philippine and East Indian sources of hemp in the hands of the Japanese, and shipment of jute from India curtailed, American hemp must meet the needs of our Army and Navy as well as of our industry. In 1942, patriotic farmers at the government's request planted 36,000 acres of seed hemp, an increase of several thousand percent. The goal for 1943 is 50,000 acres of seed hemp.

In Kentucky, much of the seed hemp acreage is on river bottom land such as this. Some of these fields are inaccessible except by boat. Thus plans are afoot for a great expansion of a hemp industry as a part of the war program. This film is designed to tell farmers how to handle this ancient crop now little known outside Kentucky and Wisconsin.

This is hemp seed. Be careful how you use it. For to grow hemp legally you must have a federal registration and tax stamp. This is provided for in your contract. Ask your county agent about it. Don't forget.

Hemp demands a rich, well-drained soil such as is found here in the Blue Grass region of Kentucky or in central Wisconsin. It must be loose and rich in organic matter. Poor soils won't do. Soil that will grow good corn will usually grow hemp.

Hemp is not hard on the soil. In Kentucky it has been grown for several years on the same ground, though this practice is not recommended. A dense and shady crop, hemp tends to choke out weeds. Here's a Canada thistle that couldn't stand the competition, dead as a dodo. Thus hemp leaves the ground in good condition for the following crop.

For fiber, hemp should be sewn closely, the closer the rows, the better. These rows are spaced about four inches. This hemp has been broadcast. Either way it should be sewn thick enough to grow a slender stalk. Here's an ideal stand: the right height to be harvested easily, thick enough to grow slender stalks that are easy to cut and process.

Stalks like these here on the left wield the most fiber and the best. Those on the right are too coarse and woody. For seed, hemp is planted in hills like corn. Sometimes by hand. Hemp is a dioecious plant. The female flower is inconspicuous. But the male flower is easily spotted. In seed production after the pollen has been shed, these male plants are cut out. These are the seeds on a female plant.

Hemp for fiber is ready to harvest when the pollen is shedding and the leaves are falling. In Kentucky, hemp harvest comes in August. Here the old standby has been the self-rake reaper, which has been used for a generation or more.

Hemp grows so luxuriantly in Kentucky that harvesting is sometimes difficult, which may account for the popularity of the self-rake with its lateral stroke. A modified rice binder has been used to some extent. This machine works well on average hemp. Recently, the improved hemp harvester, used for many years in Wisconsin, has been introduced in Kentucky. This machine spreads the hemp in a continuous swath. It is a far cry from this fast and efficient modern harvester, that doesn't stall in the heaviest hemp.

In Kentucky, hand cutting is practicing in opening fields for the machine. In Kentucky, hemp is shucked as soon as safe, after cutting, to be spread out for retting later in the fall.

In Wisconsin, hemp is harvested in September. Here the hemp harvester with automatic spreader is standard equipment. Note how smoothly the rotating apron lays the swaths preparatory to retting. Here it is a common and essential practice to leave headlands around hemp fields. These strips may be planted with other crops, preferably small grain. Thus the harvester has room to make its first round without preparatory hand cutting. The other machine is running over corn stubble. When the cutter bar is much shorter than the hemp is tall, overlapping occurs. Not so good for retting. The standard cut is eight to nine feet.

The length of time hemp is left on the ground to ret depends on the weather. The swaths must be turned to get a uniform ret. When the woody core breaks away readily like this, the hemp is about ready to pick up and bind into bundles. Well-retted hemp is light to dark gray. The fiber tends to pull away from the stalks. The presence of stalks in the bough-string stage indicates that retting is well underway. When hemp is short or tangled or when the ground is too wet for machines, it's bound by hand. A wooden bucket is used. Twine will do for tying, but the hemp itself makes a good band.

When conditions are favorable, the pickup binder is commonly used. The swaths should lie smooth and even with the stalks parallel. The picker won't work well in tangled hemp. After binding, hemp is shucked as soon as possible to stop further retting. In 1942, 14,000 acres of fiber hemp were harvested in the United States. The goal for the old standby cordage fiber, is staging a strong comeback.

This is Kentucky hemp going into the dryer over mill at Versailles. In the old days braking was done by hand. One of the hardest jobs known to man. Now the power braker makes quick work of it.

Spinning American hemp into rope yarn or twine in the old Kentucky river mill at Frankfort, Kentucky. Another pioneer plant that has been making cordage for more than a century. All such plants will presently be turning out products spun from American-grown hemp: twine of various kinds for tying and upholsters work; rope for marine rigging and towing; for hay forks, derricks, and heavy duty tackle; light duty fire hose; thread for shoes for millions of American soldiers; and parachute webbing for our paratroopers.

As for the United States Navy, every battleship requires 34,000 feet of rope. Here in the Boston Navy Yard, where cables for frigates were made long ago, crews are now working night and day making cordage for the fleet. In the old days rope yarn was spun by hand. The rope yarn feeds through holes in an iron plate. This is Manila hemp from the Navy's rapidly dwindling reserves. When it is gone, American hemp will go on duty again: hemp for mooring ships; hemp for towlines; hemp for tackle and gear; hemp for countless naval uses both on ship and shore. Just as in the days when *Old Ironsides* sailed the seas victorious with her hempen shrouds and hempen sails. Hemp for victory!

As soon as World War II ended, hemp became evil again and Harry changed his scare tactics. In 1937, testifying before a congressional committee, he said that cannabis users specifically did not progress to heroin: "I have not heard of a case of that kind ... The marijuana addict does not go in that direction." Tapping into a growing fear of young people using hard drugs, he backtracked on his earlier claim by now stating that cannabis created a large appetite for heroin, morphine and cocaine. Without a shred of proof, the media promoted a myth that 95 percent of narcotic addicts had started with cannabis. With smoking cannabis clearly now a direct stepping stone to heroin addiction, Harry demanded legislation from Congress to classify and punish smokers of cannabis as severely as users of heroin and cocaine.

Prior to the war, Harry had claimed that cannabis made you extremely violent. After the war, he stated that it made you so passive that you were subject to the influence of Communism. In 1951, at the Senate Crime Hearings, he backed a proposal to increase the penalties for all drug crimes because behind every narcotics peddler lurked a Communist, who was scheming to incapacitate all of the cannabis smokers and to overthrow the US government. High on cannabis, members of the military would be incapable of fighting wars. On TV, he said, "According to all the documents that we have been examining, today, a major source is red China."

"Have you seen a marked increase in the amount of drugs circulating in this country, which you believe come from red China since China went Communist in 1949?" asked the host.

"Oh, very much so. Under the Nationalists, they had the situation pretty well under control. About a thousand executions a year under the Nationalist Chinese government," he said, smirking slyly as if desiring the introduction of the death penalty for drug criminals.

With the country in the grip of Cold War hysteria, the public lapped up his claims that Communists were plotting to intoxicate America. No politicians could appear to be soft on Communism. President Truman signed the Boggs Act of 1951, increasing sentences for possession and requiring minimum mandatory sentences. Agitating for even tougher laws, Harry got President Eisenhower to push the Narcotic Control Act of 1956 through Congress. Cannabis now carried the same penalties as heroin. Getting arrested for possession of cannabis in 1956 carried a mandatory sentence of two to ten years. In states like Missouri, a second arrest for cannabis possession was punishable by life in prison.

After the legal extermination of cannabis in America, Harry turned his attention worldwide. He used America's growing economic power to bully other nations into signing onto his philosophy. If they refused, America wouldn't support them economically. He used the United Nations to strong-arm the rest of the world. As the largest funder of the UN, the US had more control over UN activity. Through the UN in 1961, he codified his drug policy into the Single Convention on Narcotic Drugs, which 150 countries agreed to. They were required to combat and eradicate the cultivation of cannabis. With cannabis production illegal worldwide, the petrochemical industry thrived and produced the ecological carnage we have today. Air pollution. Water contamination. Deforestation. Animal extinction. Wars over oil.

After working under five presidents and finally retiring from the Bureau of Narcotics, he warned his successors about an impending drug revolution that would be nothing less than an assault on the foundation of Western civilisation. But according to Johann Hari in *Chasing the Scream*, Harry ended up a drug dealer and an addict. Before retiring, he had procured heroin for an addict in Congress called Senator Joe McCarthy, a powerful hunter of Communists. To prevent McCarthy from having to buy drugs in the black market, which may have caused a public scandal, he had provided McCarthy with a legal supply of heroin. Having relished arresting people addicted to morphine earlier in his career, Harry, in his twilight years, relied on daily doses of morphine to relieve his angina.

Despite prohibition, the amount of young people smoking cannabis continued to grow. The hippie revolution in the late 1960s brought its use into the open. Smoking it became a symbol of rebellion and an affirmation of individual rights. The potheads preaching peace and love didn't represent the sex-crazed deviants and axe murderers Harry had portrayed. Hollywood stars demanded legalisation.

This troubled the new head of the Federal Bureau of Narcotics, Henry Giordano. He developed a campaign aimed at young people. The pitch was that anyone who smoked cannabis would become an unmotivated dysfunctional loser. With pot use widespread, the public demanded independent research. For the first time, the federal government approved scientific testing.

Doctor Leo Hollister of Palo Alto Veterans Hospital said, "We found out that the drug makes people happy. It makes them intoxicated, and finally, makes them sleepy, which is about what marijuana users were telling us was happening all the time."

According to Dr Stanley Yolles, testifying at the Senate Hearing on Marijuana Legislation in 1969, the amount of young Americans who had used cannabis at least once was estimated to be anywhere from eight to twelve million. He added, "Can you imagine what would happen to the law enforcement and the corrections system of this country if each of these twelve million people had been caught by a policeman when smoking his first marijuana cigarette? The first place in which legal reforms can be made is in the removal of mandatory minimum penalties for all cases of drug abuse." To capitalise on the public's mood, Congress passed the Controlled Substances Act in 1970, which eliminated minimum mandatory sentences and reduced penalties for possession.

With conservative Republicans aghast at the hippie generation, they looked to President Nixon to restore moral order. Repulsed by the idea of the federal government softening its stance on cannabis, Nixon stated that nothing further would be enacted until more was known about its dangers. On White House tapes, Nixon was recorded venting on the Jews: "Every one of the bastards that are out for legalising marijuana are Jewish. What the Christ is the matter with the Jews?"

Biding his time, Nixon authorised a commission to do new research, which he filled with right-wingers, including a conservative Republican governor as its chairperson. He instructed them to take a hard line, so that he could justify ramping up his war against the peace-loving activists opposing the Vietnam War, many of whom smoked weed. By criminalising them, they could be arrested, the anti-war movement would collapse and once in prison, they wouldn't be able to vote for people running against his party.

From the Richard Nixon White House tapes: "I want a goddam strong statement on marijuana from this son-of-a-bitchin' counsel. I mean one that tears the ass off'em. I want to hit the marijuana thing, and, by God, I wanna hit it right square in the puss. I want to find a way of putting more on that."

Millions of dollars were allocated to ascertain cannabis's most evil properties. It was the most in-depth investigation ever conducted by the federal government.

When the results came in, the National Commission on Marijuana and Drug Abuse's spokesperson said, "The recommendation of the commission in its first report is that we do not feel that private use or private possession in one's own home should have the stigma of criminalisation. That people who experiment should not be criminalised for that particular behaviour." The commission found that cannabis use alone did not cause crime, that the existing laws led to the selective prosecution and arrest of people with objectionable politics, hair styles and skin colour, and that the enormous cost of enforcing cannabis laws overwhelmingly outweighed any benefit of the laws. It was the most comprehensive and publicised research on cannabis ever done.

The results enraged Nixon. He threw the report in a waste-paper basket without reading it. He had the reports recalled and destroyed. Determined to oppose the results of the report, he went on TV: "I shall continue to oppose efforts to legalise marijuana." Building on Harry Anslinger's narratives, Nixon declared a new all-out offensive.

In 1970 the Marihuana Tax Act of 1937 was repealed as being unconstitutional because to obtain a tax stamp, you had to commit a crime and incriminate yourself by presenting cannabis without a stamp. But Nixon was quick to act. He signed the

Comprehensive Drug Abuse Prevention and Control Act of 1970, which drastically expanded federal drug laws and police power. It placed cannabis in Schedule I, where it still resides – equally as pernicious as heroin, and even more harmful than cocaine, PCP and crystal meth – at the DEA website:

"Schedule I drugs, substances, or chemicals are defined as drugs with no currently accepted medical use and a high potential for abuse. Schedule I drugs are the most dangerous drugs of all the drug schedules with potentially severe psychological or physical dependence. Some examples of Schedule I drugs are: heroin, lysergic acid diethylamide (LSD), marijuana (cannabis), 3,4-methylenedioxymethamphetamine (ecstasy), methaqualone, and peyote."

All 5,000 years of medical use were trashed. In the UK, a similar study was commissioned, which produced the same results. The report stated, "The long-term consumption of cannabis in moderate doses has no harmful effects … There is no evidence that this activity is causing violent crime or aggression, anti-social behaviour or is producing in otherwise normal people conditions of dependence or psychosis, requiring medical treatment." The study concluded, "The possession of a small amount of cannabis should not normally be regarded as a serious crime to be punished by imprisonment."

Nothing could change Nixon's mind. To promote his War on Drugs, he recruited celebrities, including Elvis as a Special Assistant to the Bureau of Narcotics. As a thank you for his new position, which included an official ID and a gold police badge with an eagle, Elvis gave Nixon a collectors'-item Colt .45. Shortly thereafter, Elvis died after straining to use the toilet. In his blood were high levels of Dilaudid, Percodan, Demerol, codeine and ten other drugs. To whitewash his drug history, his death was ruled a heart attack.

Nixon created the powerful DEA, with a mandate to fight the use of drugs nationwide. Without a warrant, DEA agents could spy on US citizens, break into their homes and arrest people on the basis of suspicion. The DEA was a tool to control all sections of society at odds with the White House such as war protestors, political opponents, blacks and other minorities. The War on Drugs served as a distraction from the bloodbath Nixon was perpetuating in Vietnam. Drug laws were used to round up those shaming Nixon publicly at demonstrations.

Through the UN, he exported his drug policy globally, saddling the world with the hard-line policies that are still mostly in place today. With offices worldwide, the DEA became the most international police force in history. The US rewarded governments who hyped-up drug threats and followed through with heavy-handed responses. By threatening to withdraw aid and commerce, reluctant governments were strong-armed into compliance. Those countries in lockstep with Nixon's crusade sent their police and military to be trained in America to learn how to fight the drug war in the most brutal ways possible. This licensed governments to commit horrific human rights abuses on their citizens. In some countries, drug criminals were hung, shot in the head or beheaded, which still goes on today. Many of the governments were involved in drug trafficking themselves, and they used US military training and aid to torture, kill and wipe out their competitors.

Despite global military-scale operations, cannabis use continued to spread. By the mid-1970s it had encroached on the first strata of American suburbia. Lawyers, bank managers, stockbrokers and even grandparents were getting stoned.

On TV a teenager was asked why she smoked cannabis. "It's really very simple. I smoke it because I enjoy it."

"It doesn't worry you that you're breaking the law?"

"Sure, it worries me. I mean it worries me because I don't wanna get caught. I do not want to go to jail for something that I consider a pleasure and harmless to both society and myself. I'm not hurting anybody. I'm not hurting myself. Why should I be punished for it?"

Don Crowe, a twenty-five-year-old Vietnam vet, received

multiple medals for his military service, including a purple heart. An undercover agent enticed him into selling less than an ounce of cannabis. Even though it was his first offence, he was sentenced to fifty years. On TV, Crowe said, "I had the feeling that I was fighting for my country, and for my fellow man, and it is kind of depressing to know that I should come back [from Vietnam] and be given fifty years for allegedly selling a lid of marijuana."

Only 7 percent of cannabis arrests were for dealing. The hundreds of thousands of arrests for possession and use were mostly of white middle-class American kids, whose criminal records would last for life. Parents started to view the problem not as cannabis, but as cannabis laws. Activists nationwide demanded decriminalisation.

In 1972, the city of Ann Arbor, Michigan passed an ordinance to strike possession from the criminal code. It became a minor offence on par with a parking ticket. In 1973, Oregon decriminalised personal use and ten states followed. Consumed by legal problems of his own, Nixon was distracted from the War on Drugs. He resigned in 1974. In the years following the Oregon decriminalisation, there was no increase in drug use and millions of dollars were saved in law enforcement. President Ford took the War on Drugs to Mexico by ordering US forces to spray a toxic herbicide called paraquat on cannabis fields.

In 1976, President Carter said he was for decriminalisation. "I support a change in law to end federal criminal penalties for possession of up to one ounce of marijuana, leaving the states free to adopt whatever laws they wish concerning marijuana." Carter's Chief Drug Policy Adviser, Dr Bourne, ended up in a cocaine scandal. Due to a media backlash, Carter couldn't appear to be soft on drugs. Congress killed his decriminalisation proposal.

Then came Ronald Reagan: "Leading medical researchers are coming to the conclusion that marijuana, pot, grass, whatever you want to call it is probably the most dangerous drug in the United States, and we haven't begun to find out all of the ill effects, but they are permanent ill effects." He never exhibited any studies by medical researchers. The DEA went on the rampage terrorising potheads. Thousands were arrested daily for possession of a single reefer. Young peoples' futures were ruined forever by criminal records.

At that time, cigarettes were responsible for the most drug deaths in America. It was a product long endorsed by Reagan. Before he became the governor of California, he posed in cigarette ads even though he was a non-smoker. His relationship with the tobacco industry went back to the 1930s when he was a radio sportscaster, but business climbed with the launch of his Hollywood career. He posed for Liggett & Myers Tobacco Company, which lawsuits later revealed to be covering up the adverse effects of smoking through deceptive advertisements.

Reagan oversaw a new wave of demonisation of black drug users. Only 2 percent of Americans believed that drugs should be their nation's top priority and drug crime was declining when Reagan announced, "That brings us to the major and sweeping effort that I'm announcing this morning. We will utilise the FBI, the DEA, the IRS, the ATF, Immigration and Naturalization Service, United States Marshal Services and the Coast Guard. We intend to do what is necessary to end the drug menace and eliminate this dark evil enemy within."

After the Ronald Reagan administration authorised the CIA to facilitate the mass importation of cocaine that contributed to the crack epidemic – exposed by Gary Webb – Reagan went on TV in a dark-blue suit. Sat on a couch holding hands with Nancy Reagan dressed in striking red, Reagan announced, "Today, there's a new epidemic: smokeable cocaine, otherwise known as crack. It is an uncontrolled fire."

The media was flooded with images of black crack smokers, malnourished zombies clutching glass pipes willing to prostitute their wives and children just to get high. Many of the images came from a team of propaganda merchants that the White House had established.

One New York DEA official, Robert Stutman, insisted that

crack will make you kill your own mother, exactly what they said about weed in the 1930s. To a hysterical public, Reagan offered a solution. "The American people want their government to get tough and go on the offensive, and that's exactly what we intend with more ferocity than ever before."

Politicians pushing these programs received contributions from lobbyists representing the pharmaceutical, tobacco and alcohol corporations, all of whom viewed cannabis as their competitor. The This Is Your Brain on Drugs ad, which showed a fried egg, was financed by the Partnership for a Drug-Free America, who, in 1988, received $1.1 million from the same corporations.

Democrats and Republicans teamed up to produce mandatory sentencing laws. They were pushed through Congress at record speed with hardly any hearings held or any experts consulted. Reagan signed in minimum mandatory sentences for drug crimes with crack receiving the biggest sentences, in some cases up to one hundred times the sentence someone would receive if arrested with an equal amount of powder cocaine.

The only difference between the two is that crack is cocaine with baking soda and water heated up. While politicians such as Bill Clinton snorted cocaine at high-class parties, blacks were smoking crack in the ghettos and on the streets. With blacks receiving double-digit sentences up to one hundred years for crack, the prisons filled rapidly. Blacks weren't using crack any more than whites, yet 90 percent of the defendants in crack cases in federal court were black even though blacks were only 13 percent of the US population.

Many judges questioned this discrimination. Some quit in protest. The Sentencing Commission found it to be unjust. Judges and experts presented evidence to Congress of what was happening, but were told, "These people are killing our kids … These people are wrecking our society."

To Rick Ross, it was now clear why so many blacks were incarcerated. But what could he do about it? He was just another drug dealer stuck in prison. Who would listen to him? Who would believe that the government was trafficking drugs through the CIA while incarcerating its citizens for drug crimes?

CHAPTER 6
ALL TRACKS' WITNESSES MURDERED

As Linda Ives pressed on with her quest for justice, strange things started to happen. She would come home to doors open that she was certain she had locked. Men in a pickup truck parked near her house appeared to be watching her movements.

When Sheriff Steed refused to release the funds to investigate the boys' deaths and reneged on his promise to send the boys' clothes to the FBI, Linda went to his office. On the phone, the sheriff hand-gestured her to hush. After five minutes of simmering, she was on the verge of exploding. While he was still talking, she walked up to his desk and disconnected his phone. A startled reporter entered the office.

"I want you to hear this," Linda said to the reporter. Addressing the sheriff, she said, "Why did you send those clothes to the crime lab? You were supposed to send them to the FBI. We never wanted them in the Little Rock crime lab. You knew that! Everyone in this fucking country knew that! James Steed, you are in deep shit," she said, getting in his face.

"Lady, I don't care," he growled, which was later reported by the journalist.

A letter to the editor of the newspaper exemplified the mood of the public:

"We have homicides either directly or indirectly related to the drug trade in Saline County. We have a Drug Enforcement Fund. And we have a sheriff who believes he has a better place to spend the money currently in the fund. Where can this place be? If someone in the drug trade is willing to murder two teenagers, then this person must be awfully deep in the drug trade. Does

Sheriff Steed prefer to chase the minnows of the drug trade rather than hook the big shark that murdered two teenagers?"

At a press conference, Linda chastised the sheriff, and urged the public to vote for his opponent. Having won five previous elections, he lost to an incumbent in an exceptionally heavy voter turnout. The small victory satisfied Linda.

The same night, a re-enactment of the boys' murders was broadcast on *Unsolved Mysteries*, a TV show watched nationwide by millions. Prior to filming, the field producer, Chip Clements, had stated, "There's a lot of different theories, but I don't think the evidence shows that these boys laid themselves down in identical positions and lay motionless until a train ran over them. I think that sounds pretty absurd."

On the broadcast, the host, Robert Stack, asked the deputy prosecutor about the deaths.

"I think that the boys saw something they shouldn't have seen, and it was to do with drugs, either with a crank lab, which manufactures methamphetamine, or certain individuals involved in those matters, and those people felt like the information the boys then had was such that they could not allow them to live. I think there is a distinct possibility that there are other parties involved. The thing is, the case is so complex that the solution could lie in something as simple as a vagrant or a migrant on the railroad track doing it and going away and us never hearing anything from him again, or it could be as complicated as police involvement. Saline County and the central Arkansas area are overrun at this time with drug trafficking, and it's drug trafficking at a high level that extends to other states and other counties."

With Gary away, Linda found it hard to watch the show alone. She was left perplexed as to why the deputy prosecutor had linked the deaths to drug trafficking that extended into other states. The show announced a $15,000 reward for information leading to the murderers, most of which she and her husband had contributed in the hope of getting new information.

Potential witnesses started to come forward. Keith Coney

told his mother he knew too much about the murders and feared for his life. Investigators had been told that Keith was with the boys on the night that they were murdered, and that Keith's cousin was the last person to have seen them alive. Keith had told family members and friends that the murderers worked in law enforcement. Nine months after the murders, he was slashed in the neck. Trying to flee from an assailant on a motorbike, he crashed into the back of a semi-trailer truck and was killed. There was no investigation or autopsy as his death was ruled a highway fatality, even though witnesses stated his throat had been slashed. Reading about his accidental death in the newspaper, Linda attached no importance to it yet.

Keith McKaskle had been assigned to take aerial photos of the tracks where the boys had died. As a big man who managed a nightclub, he had earned a reputation for breaking up knife fights with his bare hands. Linda knew McKaskle had agreed to tell law enforcement any information about the murders that he might pick up from his extensive contacts in the criminal community. Upon hearing that he had been murdered by over 115 stab wounds, Linda grew scared.

On November 11, 1988, the *Arkansas Democrat* published the story, "Informant In 2 Teens' Deaths Slain." A rumour started that McKaskle, two days before his murder and on the night of Sheriff Steed's election, had said, "If Jim Steed loses, my life isn't worth two cents." People assumed that McKaskle, in his role as an informant, had implicated Sheriff Steed in the murders, and Steed had found out. Losing the election had probably made Sheriff Steed feel vulnerable, and eager to eliminate any informants. But investigators dismissed any connection between the murders.

When a neighbour of McKaskle's told the police that his son might have some information about his murder, the police came and interviewed nineteen-year-old Shane Smith, who said he had seen three men in clown masks waiting for McKaskle to come home from work. The police promptly arrested Shane. Many of McKaskle's wounds on his arms were defensive, implying that he had been in a protracted struggle, resisting the onslaught and possibly attempting to grab a knife. Dr Malak ruled the probable cause of death as a knife wound to the heart, and added that approximately thirty wounds had been inflicted to McKaskle's back after his death.

Within forty-eight hours, the police charged Shane Smith, a meek teenager with no criminal history, with the murder. Under arrest, Shane changed his story. His final version of events was that he was at McKaskle's house to purchase a silver tray for his mother, and some porn for himself. After McKaskle arrived, five masked men dressed in black cornered them in the kitchen. He said he had lied about the clown masks because the men had threatened to kill him and his family.

"Two came in immediately," he said. "One came to me and held a gun to me and pushed me down in a chair and told me to stay still. Four of them [were] around Keith, held guns to him, and one told Keith to get out. Keith kept on saying, 'Who are you? What do you want?' and they said, 'Out,' pointing guns for him to go to the carport. And they went out there and shut the door behind them and I heard wrestling going on and Keith yelled out, 'Help me,' about two or three times. After that, about forty-five minutes later, they came in and told the one [holding me] to bring me out there. I went out there and I tripped. I fell on Keith and got blood all over me, and they started laughing and I got up and he handed me a knife and he told me to stick it over Keith and act like I was going to stab him so he could take a picture of it. And he did. After that, he took the knife back and cut my hand [in] two places at the same time, and they told me to leave. I left."

Hardly anyone, including Linda, believed that Shane, who weighed 180 pounds, and had never been hunting nor had a fight in his life, could have killed McKaskle in a one-on-one fight. There was no motive and no murder weapon, yet the police expressed confidence that they had the killer, and it was a crime of passion.

Twenty-six-year-old Greg Collins, a friend of the boys and

Keith Coney, had been called to testify as a grand jury witness, but he hadn't shown up. The authorities had questioned him privately, and rumours circulated that he had been with the boys on the night of the murders. On January 22, 1989, he was killed by three blasts from a shotgun at close range, and dumped in a pine forest.

The number of deaths related to the case were now starting to shock Linda, who suffered sleepless nights. While hoping the investigators would get to the bottom of things, she threw her energy into trying to get Dr Malak removed. She was backed up by numerous people who came forward, describing cases whereby their deceased family members had suffered equally inane rulings about the causes of their deaths.

In 1982, a man's body was found with five bullet wounds which Dr Malak ruled a suicide. In 1985, a North Arkansas man was fatally shot. Dr Malak ruled it a suicide even though the victim had four shotgun wounds to the chest. In 1986, Dr Malak ruled accidental drowning in a case where a victim had been shot in the head. His most far-fetched ruling was that of James Mylam, who Dr Malak claimed had died from ulcer-related natural causes. Mylam's skull was later recovered. He had been decapitated with a sharp knife. Either Dr Malak was incompetent or he specialised in cover-ups.

With so many people having suffered from Dr Malak's rulings, an organisation was formed called VOMIT: Victims of Malak's Incredible Testimony. Supportive local press published pictures of members wearing VOMIT T-shirts. Despite the public outcry, Dr Malak held onto his job due to support from the Governor of Arkansas, Bill Clinton, who had the power to remove him. As long as Dr Malak's rulings supported the governor or the state police, they were left to stand no matter how implausible.

According to Linda, Dr Malak had tampered with evidence in murder cases, and repeatedly committed perjury. "It didn't seem to matter what Malak did," she said, "Clinton protected him, and he [Clinton] made excuses such as he's overworked, he's just stressed out, he's underpaid. They gave him a $14,000 raise, which was an insult to my family as well as a lot of others in the state, who to this day are struggling with asinine rulings in the deaths of children and other loved ones. I was outraged that protecting a political crony of Clinton's was more important than two young boys being murdered."

Linda wrote to Bill Clinton:

"While I would certainly concede that Dr Malak has a communication problem and that he is perhaps stressed out, these are all situations he has brought upon himself. I would also agree with Dr Elders's statement that everyone makes errors. However, it is crucial that a professional person in Dr Malak's position be willing to admit their errors and do everything within their power to rectify them. Dr Malak has historically lied to cover his errors.

"I believe that the lack of credibility in the medical examiner's office has absolutely crippled the justice system of Arkansas. I feel that your statements and the most recent findings by the Medical Examiner's Commission are an absolute insult to the intelligence of the people of Arkansas and certainly raise questions about your own credibility and that of the Medical Examiner's Commission."

Her three requests to meet Bill Clinton were denied, but she did receive a letter from him:

Dear Mrs Ives,

Thank you for your very thoughtful and pointed letter of August 21. Please be assured that I am taking your request and your advice very seriously.

Sincerely, Bill Clinton

In mid-1990, Clinton made an appearance at the Saline County Courthouse. Linda was in the crowd. As he moved along, greeting people, he got closer to her. Realising she would finally be able to address him directly, she felt her heart thump.

Stood in front of her, he said, "Let me shake your hand."

"Yeah," she said, offering her hand. "I'd like to shake the hand of the man who's refused to see me for years." Taken by surprise, he paused. After introducing herself, she said she had been trying to get him to address the problems with Dr Malak ever since the bizarre ruling in the death of her son.

"What if we brought in a panel of out-of-state pathologists to review what he does on a case-by-case basis?" he said.

"Why don't we just fire Malak and get a medical examiner who can do the job right? I think it would save the state money." He nodded and moved on, terminating the conversation.

Later on, a reporter who had overheard the conversation took Clinton to task over it. He stated that he thought Linda had been satisfied by his response. When told that she still had an issue, he acted surprised. She could only wonder what he and other powerful people didn't want uncovered that Kevin and Don had stumbled on.

A friend of the boys, Boonie Bearden, disappeared. His body was never found. In April 1989, Jeff Rhodes was killed before he could testify. Shortly before his death, he called his father in Texas to say that he knew too much about the murders and he needed to get out of the state. His body was found in the city dump, killed by two gunshots to the head. They had also attempted to cut off his head, hands and feet, and set him on fire in the dump. In July 1989, Richard Winters was silenced by a blast from a shotgun, and so was Jordan Ketelson in June 1990.

If powerful people thought that attention to the murders was going to go away, they were mistaken. The scale of the murders was attracting interest nationwide.

On October 3, 1991, Linda left home with a banner that read: Malak's A National Scandal. She arrived at a lawn crowded with people in front of the Old State House. She found a spot to stand with her sign by an iron gate at the entrance to the house. Above her on a balcony, Bill Clinton appeared and announced to massive applause and to the international media that he was running for president.

"I just wanted Bill Clinton to know that," Linda said, "for some of us, nothing had been handled. Nothing was over with. I

66

hoped that he would see me. I wanted him to know that I wasn't going away."

CHAPTER 7
RIGHT WING DEATH SQUADS
FINANCED BY COCAINE

The Montel Williams Show began in 1991. Broadcast to millions, it launched Montel as a famous TV personality. Previously as a Marine, he had risen to the rank of Lieutenant Commander. After leaving the military, he had campaigned for the rights of veterans, young people and people of colour.

Montel took an interest in Rick Ross. After visiting him in prison, he hosted a debate about CIA drug trafficking on his show, which included Gary Webb. The show started with footage of Rick in prison, describing his cocaine business. "[Rick] says he deserves to be a free man," Montel said. "Why? Because he says the CIA used him as a pawn to sell drugs to help fund a secret war in Nicaragua."

The footage resumed. "If it was good for them to sell drugs," Rick said, "then it should have been good for me to sell drugs. The money from the drugs went to buy guns for the Contras."

"Ricky Ross," Montel said, "is right now at the centre of one of this country's biggest controversies when it comes to drugs ... If this controversy continues to escalate the way it has, and it will, I think this country is gonna stop for a second and say, 'It's wake-up call time.'"

The first guest was Mike Levine, a former DEA agent, who had made over 3,000 drug arrests motivated by his brother's death. On February 27, 1977, Mike's brother, David Levine, had shot himself in the head – after battling heroin addiction for nineteen years. His suicide note read: "To my family and friends, I'm sorry. I just can't stand the drugs anymore."

In honour of his brother, Mike made it his mission to arrest traffickers. Working relentlessly undercover, he bought drugs, made arrests and testified in court. By stopping the flow of drugs, he believed he was saving the lives of people like his brother.

"Deep-cover agents are a small group of people who pose as criminals and go into other countries ... to live on our acting ability, where there's no 911 to call. The mission is to reach the top of the drug world ... I lived with Chinese drug dealers in Bangkok, Thailand, during the Vietnam War. I lived with ex-Nazis and Argentine mass murderers ..."

"Wait! At that time you weren't a DEA agent?" Montel said.

"I was in the Hard Narcotics Smuggling Unit of Customs, and the case that I was living with – these Chinese drug dealers – led me right to Chang Mi. It was the first case that was killed by Central Intelligence. It, ironically, was a case that involved the smuggling of heroin into the US in the dead bodies of GIs ..."

"In over twenty-five years, you did this all over the world?"

"... Mexico, Colombia, Panama, Bolivia, Germany, France. You name it. I've been there posing as a criminal ... In every case, including probably the biggest case in our history, I reached the top of the drug world ... [I'd] unwittingly joined the US government mafia, of which part the CIA is the kingpin, the don."

"So you're saying that the CIA is the kingpin of the head of the United States mafia?" Montel asked, smiling incredulously.

"Look ... I've never failed in putting a case before court: conspiracy cases, undercover cases. I've never lost a case ... I have a lot of credibility. I live by my credibility ... I have personal testimony about Central Intelligence killing, murdering cases. One case, the biggest drug case I think in our history, Operation Trifecta, was a case where posing as a mafia don ... we went to Bolivia. We plugged into a pipeline of massive amounts of cocaine, going from Bolivia through Mexico with the protection of the Mexican Army, into California. Both the CIA, and the State Department and the Justice Department, ganged up to kill that case."

"To stop the case! Why?" Montel asked.

"There were several reasons. First, all I can do is testify as I would in federal court to what happened. I'm in Panama. We order fifteen tons of cocaine to go through Mexico, to be paid for in Panama … in a country that was being run by a CIA employee basically, Manuel Noriega. And my government suddenly withdraws logistic support, and I and the other Chicano Mexican undercover agent, we were forced to lie to these people who could kill us in a heartbeat because our government had withdrawn logistic support … My DEA supervisor tells me as an explanation, 'The CIA is in this in four countries. We're not telling you everything.'"

"… Did the CIA know that drugs were coming into the United States of America and help it get here?" Montel asked.

"Absolutely," Mike said.

"Does the CIA do this on a regular basis?"

"Absolutely. I wish I could take them to court."

"And right now, just by virtue of the fact that Montel Williams is doing this show," Montel said, "someone is gonna say, 'You see. It's another black journalist, who is feeding into the conspiracy story.' And most of you who know me, know I'm one of the most conservative people in this country. I spent twenty years in the United States government, working for the military. This show is about finding some truth, and saying to the American people, 'Let us get the answers that we demand because it's our dollars that pay to bring coke into America.'"

After a break, Gary Webb was welcomed and credited for sparking the furore with his story, "Dark Alliance," which he elaborated on. Aware of the key players in "Dark Alliance," Mike Levine corroborated the story. Montel asked Mike why the CIA had not killed him for exposing them in books and on TV.

"The only thing I can say, Montel, I lost my son. I lost my brother because of this phoney CIA-backed drug flow. Somebody once said, 'If you don't have anything in your life to die for, you don't have anything to live for.' After losing my son, that's the story of my life. God bless Gary Webb. I've been trying to tell this, and other DEA agents are now coming out, trying to tell this story."

Montel had interviewed Mike first to back up Rick Ross and Gary Webb. By virtue of his crimes, Rick, the black crack kingpin of LA, lacked credibility to the average American, and Gary was an outsider trying to look into Mike's world.

In 1978, the DEA transferred Mike to Argentina. In Buenos Aires, he posed as Luis Garcia, a Cuban-American Mafia cocaine buyer. Decked out in gold chains, diamonds on his fingers and a fake Rolex, he went to a suite at the Sheraton Hotel to meet Hugo Hurtado, a founding member of the Cocaine Mafia of Bolivia.

Formerly a farmer, Hugo – a boozer with a broad face and chest – was keen to deliver 200 kilos of cocaine to Argentina before traffickers in Bolivia launched a coup there. Hugo warned that a change in government could be started, but you would never know how it would turn out. Mike asked whether change would be a good thing. Hugo disagreed because the change was being done out of anger. He had enough protection by paying $100,000 a year to the head of the narcotics police and $100,000 to the minister.

After knocking on the suite door, a waiter walked in with a bottle of Chivas Regal Scotch Whiskey that no one had ordered. Drunken Hugo failed to see the waiter studying him. Mike was aware, having struck a deal with the Argentine police, whereby Hugo would be allowed to return to Bolivia to fetch 200 kilos, and be arrested. Mike sensed something was wrong.

In a guarded tone, Hugo talked about his niece, Sonia, a powerful trafficker, popular with the military, and how she would be highly connected to the new government. Hearing that Sonia was bigger in cocaine than Hugo piqued Mike's curiosity, but he feared that probing too far would arouse suspicion. Before leaving, Hugo agreed to provide 200 kilos of cocaine at $27,000 per kilo for a payment of $5.4 million.

From the sixth floor, Mike looked out of the window for

Hugo, concerned that the secret police might kidnap, torture and kill his connection for knowing about the Bolivian coup. Around that time, tens of thousands of Argentinians were tortured, using techniques adopted from Nazis who had fled Germany, designed to keep the victims conscious for as long as possible, while enduring maximum pain. After they had extracted the names of people whose views were left on the political spectrum, the police then "disappeared" the victims, many of whom were buried in mass graves or thrown into rivers.

Mike watched Hugo leave the hotel and get into a taxi. Three cars followed it from the parking lot. A fourth screeched to the front of the hotel, picked up the man who had posed as a waiter and took off after the taxi.

Days later, a police contact, Mario – tall, with psychopathic beady eyes, slicked hair and a moustache – entered Mike's hotel room with some secret policemen. He admitted kidnapping and torturing Hugo. Mike feared Hugo was dead. Mario had once boasted to Mike that killing was his number one turn-on and after committing a murder he had to have sex. On the payroll of the DEA and the CIA – a true monster created by the War on Drugs – Mario expressed surprise at Mike's ignorance of the political situation, including the coup in Bolivia. He asked Mike whether he thought that any regime could be changed without their governments being aware of it. Mike wanted to know what the question had to do with Hugo. Mario said that the names given under torture as drug dealers were the same people "we are working with to eliminate leftist Bolivians." Mike asked who he was referring to as "we." Mario replied the Argentines and the CIA.

Mike was waking up to the situation with the CIA – which was launching a coup in Bolivia financed by cocaine proceeds. His undercover work had taken him up the ranks of the Bolivian cocaine traffickers. Six months earlier, he had struck a deal with Roberto Suarez – who *60 Minutes* later described as the biggest drug dealer alive – for 1,000 kilos per month, but his request to set up a sting had been denied. He had been told that Suarez was not in the computer files, and nobody knew who he was. Mike pressed on with the case and two arrests were made of traffickers working for Suarez, who had come to collect $9 million in Miami. Suarez offered $150,000 to anyone who would kill Mike. The DEA made headlines out of the arrests, but after the attention waned, the charges against one of the traffickers were dropped, and he returned to Bolivia. His name was José Gasser, the son of a powerful industrialist and anti-Communist.

Mario said that they had something interesting to reveal about Gasser: he and his father were two of the biggest players behind the coup in Bolivia. Mario urged him to consider why the Americans had released Gasser from jail.

Despite resistance from his superiors, Mike pursued the Bolivian traffickers. He received a call from DEA headquarters from a friend called the Rabbi, who said Mike's timing was off, he had no backup and if he proceeded any further on his own, he would lose. Mike protested that he was just doing the job he had been sent to do. The Rabbi stated that Mike was a solitary man in a tiny corner of the world going against the tide of America's diverse interests. Smarter people than both of them knew things that they didn't. Asked what he should do, Mike was told to take it easy. After objecting, he was reminded of a scary story about a peanut-butter sandwich. The Rabbi insisted that he wasn't kidding and he had only called Mike because he liked him.

Stunned, Mike contemplated the warning. Sante Bario had been a deep-cover DEA agent. Over the course of his work, Bario had learned too much about CIA drug smuggling. He was arrested for smuggling heroin and put in the Bexar County jail in Texas. On the day he was scheduled for trial, he bit a peanut-butter sandwich, went into a coma and died a month later. The medical examiner decided the cause of death was asphyxiation – he had choked upon a sandwich. The prison warden told Bario's wife that his blood had tested positive for strychnine.

On July 17, 1980, the coup began in Bolivia. Pickup trucks

transporting masked men, some wearing swastika armbands, rumbled into Trinidad, firing indiscriminately at anyone on the streets. The gunmen included Argentinians, Spaniards, Germans, French and Italians. They invaded houses and shops, murdering, torturing, raping and robbing.

In La Paz, the gunmen arrived in ambulances, and wiped out men, women, children and even cats and dogs – a strategy formulated by Klaus Barbie, a CIA asset responsible for the deaths of thousands of Jews during World War II, who delighted in chaining up Jews and setting his German Shepherd, Wolf, on their genitals.

Barbie's Fiancés of Death, neo-Nazi mercenaries, stormed the building containing Bolivia's labour union. They shot in the head and captured Marcelo Quiroga Santa Cruz, the deputy leader of the Socialist coalition who had tried to indict a Bolivian military dictator on drug charges. At police headquarters, Quiroga was slowly bleeding to death in the hands of torture experts from Argentina's Mechanic School of the Navy. They castrated him and kept him alive for as long as possible. They tortured to death trade-union leaders, student leaders, priests, political activists and anyone they got their hands on who was in the wrong place at the wrong time – all condoned by the CIA as necessary to protect American interests from the encroachment of Communism. At the headquarters of the Bolivian Joint Chiefs of Staff, female union leaders were gang-raped and tortured. Drug traffickers freed from prisons joined in the orgy of violence.

With the aid of Klaus Barbie's meticulous planning, the coup succeeded. As the blood of humans, cats and dogs mingled in the streets, the traffickers who had financed the coup took over the Bolivian government. They included José Gasser and his co-defendant in the Miami case that Mike had instigated, who was still in jail – but soon to be released.

Klaus Barbie became an honorary colonel in the Bolivian Army, with influence over state security, working under the most powerful of the traffickers, Luis Arce Gómez, the new Minister of

Interior. Playing along with the US War on Drugs, Arce Gómez unleashed the Fiancés of Death on 140 smaller traffickers he had targeted for suppression: incarceration and execution. They rounded up cocaine worth billions of dollars, and deposited it in the vaults of the Bolivian National Bank.

For $150,000 per week, the Bolivian Air Force transported the cocaine. Sonia, the niece Hugo had mentioned to Mike before Hugo was kidnapped and tortured, was put in charge of selling it. She also provided a house to Klaus Barbie's team of torturers. No one came to help those screaming inside.

Argentina was the first to recognise the new Bolivian government. Mike was told that a consortium of ten American banks, headed by Bank of America, had postponed Bolivia's loan repayments, giving the Bolivian government an opportunity to solidify its power through the exportation of cocaine. With Bolivia a dominant cocaine supplier, the Arce Gómez syndicate became the biggest in the world.

Despite receiving the Octavio González Award from the International Narcotic Enforcement Officers Association, Mike was extracted from Argentina and hounded by DEA inspectors out to destroy his career. In the hope of finding some technical violation of DEA procedures, the inspectors interrogated numerous DEA staff Mike had worked with. They inspected hundreds of pages of expense reports in the hope of finding an error that could lead to criminal charges carrying a maximum ten-year sentence.

Longing to return to undercover work, Mike received a break when Sonia, the woman assigned to sell Bolivia's cocaine stored in the National Bank, turned informant. Posing as a Mafia figure, Don Miguel, Mike set up Operation Hun out of a mansion in Tucson. One of the targets was Papo Mejia, a brutal Colombian killer who Sonia owed money. From her extensive contacts book, Sonia enticed over traffickers, including two Colombian murderers.

At a nightclub, one of the murderers was boasting to Mike about how easily he had stabbed someone to death. Suddenly, he extracted a long blade and held it to Mike's ribcage. He said that he loved killing with a knife because it was up close and personal and he could do it while looking someone in the eye. Hoping to diffuse the situation, Mike said that it must be like dancing, which amused the murderer, who tucked away his weapon.

Mike's work was sabotaged. Prospective customers who sampled the cocaine supplied by the DEA found it so impure and discoloured that it put them off doing business – the DEA possessed vast amounts of pure cocaine seized in drug busts, scheduled for destruction. When the busts came down, all of the big players walked, while the authorities made headlines claiming that the little fish were the big players. To ensure that none of the big players were ever busted – which would have revealed CIA involvement – all of the evidence gathered during Operation Hun was destroyed.

Disheartened and fearful, he went to a meeting in a park near the DEA headquarters with the Rabbi, who warned that the world was imperfect and their own missions were secondary to the interests of more important people, which was hard to admit when they were risking their lives. They should have faith in their superiors. Mike said that his faith had been destroyed by them giving the gangsters get-out-of-jail-free cards, while his colleagues were losing their lives busting a few ounces on the street. How could the politicians declare that they were saving kids from drugs when they were protecting the kingpins?

The Rabbi said that those living the American dream were blessed, something its enemies wanted to destroy, from the Nazis to now the Communists. Maintaining strength and defending the American way of life came above everything else, including the drug war. America could not afford to let its southern neighbours fall to Communism, even if that meant working with the traffickers. In countries like Bolivia, drug crops fed the poor. Without that money, they would become resentful and demand changes that are impermissible by America. Bolivia's main export is coca base sent to Colombia. With both countries deeply indebted, the trade must continue otherwise American bankers wouldn't get paid. Asked about supporting mass murderers and torturers, the Rabbi said that even the wisest make mistakes.

Mike protested that he was always held accountable for his mistakes. After risking his life to get enough evidence to convict a murderer, he couldn't understand why his own bosses would turn against him and not protect him when the murderer found out who he really was and attempted to hunt him down. Stating that he had to leave, the Rabbi ended the conversation.

Disillusioned with the War on Drugs, Mike continued to work undercover until 1989, when he fell from the second storey of a building in pursuit of a crack dealer, resulting in three herniated discs, a fractured ankle and knee damage. In 1993, he published *The Big White Lie: The CIA and The Cocaine/Crack Epidemic.*

The dedication reads: "In memory of my son, New York City Police Sergeant Keith Richard Levine, killed on December 28, 1991, while trying to stop an armed robbery by a crack addict with a record of two murder convictions. While the CIA and other covert agencies betrayed us, and while our leaders looked the other way, they left it to law enforcement to clean up the mess they made of America. And we continue to pay with our blood and the blood of our children. To all law enforcement officers who have died trying to take drugs off the street."

Over the years, Mike appeared on various TV talk shows.

"The book is called *The Big White Lie*," said a female presenter. "Its author says that for decades the CIA has protected some of the world's biggest drug dealers, all supposedly in the interest of promoting democracy. Author Michael Levine was an under-cover agent for the Drug Enforcement Agency for twenty-five years. You may also remember his 1990 best-selling book ... Nice to have you back here. I mean, if this is true, the premise is so disturbing. I want to make sure that I understand it correctly: that our government, the US government – particularly the CIA and the Pentagon – have supported and protected international drug barons in the name of fighting Communism."

"That's the pretext. Let me put it very succinctly: what I'm saying is that while working undercover between the years of 1978 and 1982 posing as a mafia drug baron half Hispanic and Italian, I witnessed firsthand the CIA commit high treason. I witnessed the sellout of the War on Drugs in 1978. Let me put it into historic context: in 1978 the demand for cocaine and later crack was skyrocketing. There was the need for a supply, a steady supply of it. The South Americans could not keep up with that demand and what they needed in essence was the General Motors of cocaine. Well, in Bolivia – then supplying up to 90 percent of the world's cocoa base – that General Motors of cocaine began to form. That General Motors of cocaine was comprised of escaped Nazi fugitives, Nazi war criminals like Klaus Barbie, Argentine mass murderers, gangsters from all over Europe and drug dealers. I was assigned to create an undercover sting. I actually created a whole undercover Mafia family and we were assigned to stop that General Motors of cocaine from happening and we were absolutely successful."

"So then what happened?"

"What happened? Enter the CIA. They destroyed the case. They [removed] those elements of the Bolivian government ... that were helping. This was the last vestige in South America of anti-drug bosses. They helped the drug dealers. They helped Klaus Barbie ..."

"Why?"

"Well, the pretext was national security. If you read *The Big White Lie*, I think you'll agree with me. It's just a lie that a lot of rogue CIA agents made a fortune. There were whole others, a whole array. It's an out of control agency. I think they're still out of control right now ..."

"You think the CIA is still out of control?"

"Absolutely. If you read the newspaper events of what's going on in Haiti, it's a repeat of everything that happened. I think it's important to focus on a woman – probably a woman who's unknown until this moment. She was the most powerful figure in the drug world of South America: Sonia Atala. Throughout South America she was known as the queen of cocaine. She was part of the Bolivian government ... This is a Bolivian government that vowed, vowed specifically to invade the United States with cocaine and that was the words of the Prime Minister. The vanguard of that invasion was Sonia Atala. This is a woman who had a detachment of Nazi mercenaries assigned to her beck and call. She was a woman whose house was a veritable torture chamber. That's where those members of the Bolivian government that helped us were tortured to death. She was a woman who was so elusive that of all the figures in the government, her name never appeared in the DEA computer ...

"When the CIA stepped in and destroyed this case, I began to complain ... to the Justice Department. When that didn't work, I complained within the Drug Enforcement Administration. When that didn't work, I went to the media. Suddenly, I was put under investigation by the internal security forces of the DEA and an attempt was made on my life that I described in the book very clearly. I believe the CIA was behind that. I'm then forced to be transferred back to the United States where I'm placed under an intensive investigation. I mean all I wanted to do was win the drug war.

"Now an incredible thing happens: I'm suddenly approached by a DEA agent. He comes in and he sits down in my office and he says, 'We want you to work in the most sensitive undercover case we have. It's called Operation Hun. We want you to work with a woman. She's a woman who sold drugs for the Bolivian government. She's probably the biggest informer we've ever had. We want you to pose as her lover. We want you to pose as her business partner. The catch is that there's a Colombian killer who's after her. She owes him several million dollars and they have people all over the world hunting her. The target of the operation is going to be the same Bolivian government that the CIA put into power.' I'm astounded. I accepted the assignment and they began Operation Hun, which is half the story in *The Big White Lie*."

"With all these allegations that you are making, are you concerned about your own personal safety now?"

"For years, I never thought I'd write this book. You're talking about an agency that's been governed by no laws, so an agency to whom murder means absolutely nothing."

"Did the CIA know that you were in the process of writing this?"

"No, they didn't, and what I do know is that I was, well, my son, New York police sergeant Keith Levine, was murdered by drug addicts, crack addicts. My baby brother, David, was a drug addict for nineteen years. He committed suicide, and at this point I knew that before I died, I wanted history set straight. This isn't an academic book. This is an undercover outcome. This is the way I lived it ..."

CHAPTER 8
NAZI MULTIMILLIONAIRE MASS MURDERER AND TRAFFICKER

Decades before locking one hundred teenagers in a schoolhouse to be dynamited and burnt alive, Klaus Barbie aka the Butcher of Lyon was born in Bad Godesberg, near Bonn, on October 25, 1913. In September 1935, he joined a special branch of the SS, an intelligence gathering arm of the Nazis. In 1940, he was sent to The Hague to arrest Jews and German political refugees, and he was promoted to lieutenant. In 1941 on the Eastern Front, he joined a mobile death squad, instructed to murder every Communist and Jew they could find in Russia and Ukraine, regardless of age or sex. Over a million were killed in less than a year at the hands of SS death squads.

In November 1942, he was sent to Lyon, where he became the head of the local Gestapo, assigned to fight Communists, prevent sabotages and persecute Jews. With a unique zeal for brutality, he devastated the local French Resistance. Those who were lucky enough to have emerged alive later testified about his methods.

In 1944, Lise Lesèvre was arrested carrying mail for the French Resistance. The torture began with spikes inside handcuffs that penetrated her skin. She was hooked up to chains tied to the ceiling. Barbie and his underlings beat her with a riding crop. When she fainted and collapsed, he kicked her in the face. They put her in a bathtub naked and attached her legs to a bar. When he yanked a chain attached to the bar, her head submerged until she almost drowned.

"I thought my lungs were going to explode. They pulled me

up by my hair, then asked the questions again and pulled me back into the water by the chain. If I live to be 100, I will never forget Barbie. That lasted for two hours."

Refusing to provide names, Lise ended up on a rack, an iron rectangular table that pulled her arms and legs until her bones almost broke. Hitting her with a spiked ball, Barbie broke a vertebra. Sentenced to death by him, she was accidentally transported to a labour camp, instead of a concentration camp to be gassed. At the end of World War II, she was freed.

"He was a viper," Lise said. "What struck me was this type of happiness he got when he hurt someone. I wonder where beings like that are made."

Simone Lagrange was only 13 when she arrived with her petrified parents at the Gestapo headquarters in Lyon, where Barbie was cuddling a cat. After her parents refused to reveal the addresses of their two other children, he pulled Simone's hair and hit her in the face. Every day, he extracted her from a cell, and punched her open wounds. He sent her mother to Auschwitz, where she was gassed. While Simone was embracing her father, a German officer shot him in the head.

"He only stopped when you lost consciousness," said Maurice Boudet, a Resistance leader. "Then he woke you up with kicks to the belly, the kidneys, the crotch. If that didn't work, he threw you in a tub of ice water, with cubes floating in it. After the tub, the blackjack: that made your skin swell up. Then he injected acid in your bladder."

Another survivor, Ennat Léger, said Barbie "had the eyes of a monster. He was savage. My God, he was savage! It was unimaginable. He broke my teeth. He pulled back my hair. He put a bottle in my mouth and pushed it until the lips split from the pressure."

Barbie delighted in locking up prisoners with the decomposing corpses of their friends. When his favourite restaurant was bombed, he had five prisoners machine-gunned and their bodies displayed as a warning. When some German airmen were shot, he opened a cell block as if allowing the prisoners to escape. Twenty-four fled, only to be mowed down by bullets. Towards the end of the war, he ordered the machine-gunning of hundreds of prisoners, and the destruction of corpses by using phosphorous grenades and dynamite, which sent body parts flying into the town.

From the winter of 1942 to the summer of 1944, Barbie was involved in 4,342 murders and ordered 7,591 deportations to death camps, making him the third most wanted SS man by the authorities.

On August 18, 1947, with Europe still in chaos, Barbie met two men in a café in Memmingen, a town in Southern Germany. Having worked for the Nazis' military intelligence agency, Kurt Merck had switched sides and was now working for US intelligence. The other man was Lieutenant Robert Taylor, an officer in the US Army's Counter Intelligence Corps (CIC). Merck recommended that Taylor hired his friend, Barbie.

For the next four years, Barbie worked for the CIC. He revealed British techniques of interrogation – which he had experienced – and named the SS men most likely to have been recruited by British intelligence. His main job was to spy on French intelligence. The CIC put Barbie and his family in a hotel and paid him in goods.

Having sentenced Barbie to death, the French almost tracked him down. They requested the CIC give him up, but were rebuffed. Fearing that a captured Barbie would divulge his relationship with the CIC, the Americans facilitated his escape to South America. They paid a war criminal, Father Krunoslav Draganović, to coordinate everything.

After sending several hundred thousand Jews from Yugoslavia to die in concentration camps, Draganović had sought sanctuary in the Vatican. Using his position in the Red Cross, Draganović had established a business charging war criminals $1,400 each to flee from Europe. His customers included the Croatian dictator, Ante Pavolic, who was estimated to have arranged the slaughter of up to two million Serbs. Pavolic delighted in showing his visitors a forty-pound jar of human eyeballs. Many of the war criminals went to Argentina, where they joined the government's military, security and intelligence forces, and formed a neo-Nazi movement.

In April 1951, Barbie and his family arrived in La Paz, Bolivia. A war criminal, Father Osvaldo Toth, helped them settle. Barbie opened a sawmill business, but soon started to advise the government about internal security. The government found him so useful, he was awarded citizenship.

When the Bolivian government refused to use the military against striking tin miners, while maintaining relations with Communist Cuba, the CIA decided to intervene, with Barbie's assistance. The president was told that he could "take a ride either to the cemetery or to the airport." He fled to Argentina, leaving a military dictatorship in power.

Working in the new government's internal security force, Department 4, Barbie gave training in torture and terror techniques, which were enthusiastically carried out on tin miners and indigenous Bolivian tribes. Tin mines had been the main revenue generator for the Bolivian economy, but Barbie's death squads killed so many miners and labour leaders that many of the mines closed.

In exchange for political contributions, the government gave America's Gulf Oil concessions around Santa Cruz. From 1966 to 1967, the CIA invested millions in Bolivia, which helped the regime tighten its grip on labour groups and Indian peasants.

Barbie expanded his business interests to include selling quinine bark, coca paste and assault weapons. He shared the profits from his shipping company with members of the Bolivian government. Initially, he exported flour, cotton, tin and coffee, but eventually he specialised in drugs and weapons, which had the biggest profits. He sold arms to the Bolivian military, which were purchased with money from the US government.

In 1967, he helped the CIA track down the revolutionary

Che Guevara, who was captured by Bolivian soldiers and shot ten times. In 1970, he assisted the CIA in yet another coup against a new Bolivian government that had upset the CIA by confiscating the mineral rights awarded to Gulf Oil and for being overly cordial towards the governments of Chile and Cuba. Thousands of miners and union organisers were tortured and disappeared.

The new government made him an honorary colonel and a consultant to the Ministry of the Interior and Department 7, a counterinsurgency wing of the Bolivian Army, both of which received funds from the CIA. He continued to relay information to the CIA on suspected Communist agents in South America. He taught the Bolivian military how to use medical supervision to keep someone alive while being tortured with electricity. The CIA provided him with the names and addresses of people they wanted tortured and eliminated, including liberationist priests and their friends.

The Bolivian government had established one of the largest drug operations in the world. The fields in Alto Beni generated the raw material for approximately 80 percent of global cocaine supply. Bolivia became the biggest supplier of raw coca and cocaine paste to the Medellín Cartel, headed by Pablo Escobar. These ingredients were transported by planes or on Barbie's ships.

To protect his empire, Barbie used the Fiancés of Death, which included former SS officers and Argentine-trained mercenaries. As well as bodyguarding the government, they wiped out rival traffickers deep in the jungle, and strong-armed the Colombians, who had been messing the Bolivians around by reneging on coca deals, haggling the prices of coca paste down at the last minute and sometimes stealing the paste at gunpoint. The Colombians started to take the Bolivians more seriously after the Fiancés of Death used a bazooka to shoot down a Colombian trafficking plane.

From 1974 to 1980, coca production multiplied so much that the price of cocaine plummeted, generating a surge in US demand, which was supplied by the Colombian cartels. In 1975, cocaine cost $1,500 per gram in America; in 1986, $200.

Throughout the 1970s, Barbie lectured at neo-Nazi candlelight vigils, extolling the virtues of fascism. He travelled to America at least seven times from the late 1960s into the 1970s.

In 1978, the wife, son-in-law, nephew and private secretary of the dictator running Bolivia were arrested for cocaine trafficking in the US and Canada, which led to the dictator's resignation and a general election in 1979. The democratically elected victor was against cocaine, so the right wing devised the cocaine coup described by Mike Levine.

On July 17, 1980, the 6th Army Division announced that Communist extremists were threatening the national security of Bolivia, and the rampage started. Media outlets were bombed. Barbie's mercenaries in ambulances machine-gunned civilians and electroshocked their political enemies. Imprisoned in a soccer stadium, people were shot in groups and disposed of in rivers and canyons.

Barbie became the head of Bolivia's internal security forces and the supervisor of Bolivia's drug suppression campaign – to gesture support for America's War on Drugs. Using money provided by the CIA, he liquidated his rivals in politics and drugs. The following year, the generals running Bolivia made approximately $2 billion from cocaine.

But Barbie's days of being a hero-worshipped multimillionaire Nazi torturer and drug trafficker were ending. On January 25, 1983, he was arrested by a new civilian Bolivian government and handed over to the French who he had dodged for decades. In Lyons, he was incarcerated at Montluc, the site of some of his war crimes. Unrepentant to the end, he told an interviewer, "What is there to regret? I am a convinced Nazi … and if I had to be born a thousand times, I would be a thousand times what I have been."

At trial, he said, "When I stand before the throne of God I shall be judged innocent." On July 4, 1987, he was sentenced to life imprisonment. Four years later, aged 77, he died of leukaemia and cancer of the spine and prostate.

Despite his demise and the constant changes in the Bolivian government, the cocaine empire he had assisted continued to grow. Bolivian cocaine production increased from 35,000 metric tons in 1980 to 60,000 tons per year by the late 1980s, most of it destined for America. The Bolivian police and troops armed and trained by the CIA and the DEA – ostensibly to eradicate coca growers and drug traffickers – continued to terrorise drug rivals and political enemies.

Only after the DEA was kicked out of Bolivia in 2009 did cocaine production fall. According to United Nations data, cocaine production in 2014 declined by 11 percent, the fourth year in a row of steady decrease. Did the Bolivian government launch a blitzkrieg against the coca growers? No. They simply encouraged farmers to make money from alternative crops.

"Bolivia has adopted a policy based on dialogue, where coca cultivation is allowed in traditional areas alongside alternative development [in others]," Antonino de Leo, the United Nations Office on Drugs and Crime's representative in Bolivia, told VICE News. "It's not only about making money off a crop. In the old-fashioned alternative development approach, we substitute one illicit crop for a licit crop. It's about a more comprehensive approach that includes access to essential services like schools, hospitals and roads in areas that traditionally have been hard to reach."

CHAPTER 9
MULTIBILLION DOLLAR WEED
BUST IN MEXICO

In 1983, at a DEA meeting in San Antonio, the boss of the Guadalajara office, Jaime, pinned onto the wall pictures of Kiki Camarena almost indiscernible in the middle of cannabis fields. The officials from Washington and the border didn't react because they didn't care. The DEA and the US Attorney's offices showed no interest in prosecuting the Guadalajara kingpins. There were difficulties in forming conspiracy cases against foreign citizens who rarely came to the US.

In February 1983, Jaime filed a report: "Guadalajara continues to be the home of many major drug traffickers involved in the traffic of every drug of abuse … Corruption within the law enforcement community continues to be the major obstacle to effective investigative activity."

After work, the Guadalajara agents usually drank beer on the veranda of the Camelot Bar and discussed their challenges. As well as being unable to carry guns, they couldn't trust the Mexican police commanders, who would make token arrests, while relaying the activity of the DEA to their cartel paymasters. Even the police they thought they could trust were probably playing both sides. To make an arrest, they had to provide information, which could be used to identify their informants, putting them at risk of being tortured and killed. Recently, a Federale had sold the name of an informant, whose hand had been cut off before his death.

By mid-1983, Kiki knew that Caro Quintero had gigantic plantations in the mountains. Rather than seek permission to do a flyover with the Mexican authorities, he proposed that they hire a plane and do their own independent monitoring. Expecting his idea to be declined, he was overjoyed when Jaime approved Operation Miracle. Jaime believed that the US State Department was purposefully reducing Mexican cannabis growth estimates to maintain cordial relations.

In 1984, Kiki learned of thousands of acres of plants, financed by the Guadalajara Cartel, and that police commanders had even invested in the project. An informant stated that a commander had told him that "he welcomed traffickers to plant in the Zacatecas area and he would provide protection and introduce them to the DFS commander and the military in order to make arrangements with them for protection."

Kiki and Jaime snuck on a plane with a Mexican pilot and confirmed the plantation. In another violation of Mexican law, Kiki went undercover to the plantation and was introduced to Caro Quintero's overseer by an informant. When the Federales announced that they were going to raid the field well before the plants had matured and his own bosses refused to request a delay, Kiki was furious. The media announced that 150 acres had been raided but no kingpins were arrested.

On May 30, 1994, Jaime filed a report: "RAC Kuykendall believes the operation went well despite the low number of plantations located, and he achieved what he set out to do: demonstrate to the government the widespread marijuana cultivation in the state of Zacatecas, the greatly improved agricultural techniques now employed, and the extensive official corruption which has allowed it to occur. The several eradication zone coordinators present during the operation, originally gleeful over a lack of plantation findings, now have little to say in view of the MFJP findings during this long weekend. There truly is evidence of extensive marijuana cultivation and no doubt remains as to malfeasance on the part of GOM [government of Mexico] officials in that area. The MFJP investigation is now winding down, when, if US federal agents were in charge, it should be picking up momentum. The MFJP has done a commendable job. But its investigative interests are considerably different from ours … Prior to kicking off the operation, the suspects were clearly alerted, since they had left for other parts and it was apparent that the Mexican Army in Zacatecas had made a concerted effort to destroy farms during the several days preceding MFJP arrival in the area."

When the arrests at the plantation had been made, the overseer had recognised Kiki with the Federales. Finally, the Guadalajara Cartel knew the identity of the agent who had been harming them.

While Caro Quintero invested in even bigger plantations and bought a mansion surrounded by a seventeen-foot-high wall, the Guadalajara DEA agents investigated banks, hotels, airports, bars and even had an informant infiltrate the MFJP office.

In July 1984, the US Assistant Secretary of State told the House Select Committee on Narcotics Abuse and Control that "current relations between the Drug Enforcement Administration and the MFJP are excellent. DEA informs us that cooperation with MFJP has considerably improved during the past year and that consequently the number of significant bilateral investigations has increased." The rising drug production, he blamed on sneaky traffickers for choosing a "selection of sites which are remote, frequently smaller and more difficult to detect," and he also blamed "improved weather." Following suit, the head of intelligence at the DEA headquarters stated that the traffickers had been "changing the size of their plots, moving to smaller, widely dispersed fields … camouflaging the plants by growing them in between other crops."

On March 28, 1984, an ex-commander of the Federales brought a message to Kiki: it would be better for the DEA to stop investigating Félix Gallardo, who was a businessman with integrity, and the agents should instead focus on Caro Quintero. The warning only increased the agents' determination. In June 1984, information received by the Guadalajara office led to the seizure of $4 million at a hotel in Los Angeles. Paperwork at the scene revealed cartel bank accounts, and another $9 million was confiscated.

In August, information led to the seizure of two planeloads of cocaine in Arizona. (Later in this book is my interview with the American who coordinated those flights for the cartel. He gave me permission to only publish his story after his death.) The loss of the cash and the cocaine incensed Félix Gallardo, who blamed the DEA. In Guadalajara, word spread that retribution was coming to the agents and anyone associated with them.

Although Kiki's wife had become accustomed to living in dangerous environments, by late 1984 she wanted to leave Mexico due to all of the shootings and kidnappings. In Guadalajara, traffickers ambushed rivals and the police. At night, gunshots could be heard.

One of Kiki's contacts had been eating in a restaurant when hit men had charged in. A bullet from a machine gun had severed his spinal cord. Upset by the prevalent drug addiction, theft and prostitution, the contact had documented meetings he had witnessed between Caro Quintero and powerful people in politics and the federal police. Destined to spend the rest of his life in a wheelchair, from his hospital bed the contact told Kiki to be careful as an American would be targeted next.

Kiki ordered his three young sons to never answer the door nor to stray beyond the courtyard walls at the house front. Working almost around the clock meeting informants and Mexican police, Kiki told his wife that the cartel would not be so brazen as to kill a US federal agent.

Within less than two weeks, a hit man fired at a car driven by a DEA agent. The bullets from a thirty-round magazine drew a bullseye on the driver's side. When his vehicle had been hit, veteran agent Roger Knapp had been in bed, while his wife had been just about to take their three children outside to stand by the car, while they waited for the school bus. With the police known for arriving slowly to a crime scene, Roger grew suspicious by the immediate response of senior federal police, as well as DFS and MFJP.

In response to the shooting, the US government warned the Mexican Attorney General and Interior Minister that if anything else happened to a DEA agent "we would consider it an extremely serious matter with very deep and very long-lasting repercussions."

Working on Operation Padrino, Roger felt that he was on the verge of seizing a massive amount of drugs belonging to Félix Gallardo. The shooting meant that he was getting close. After reporting the incident to his superiors, the DEA ordered him to relocate to Texas. After protesting, he was granted extra time. Hearing that the DEA in Los Angeles had seized 372 pounds of cocaine just a few hours after his car had been shot, he grew so worried about his family that he told his wife that it was time to go, leaving only three agents in Guadalajara: Kiki, Jaime and Shaggy.

Ten years older than Kiki, Vince Wallace a.k.a. Shaggy was also a former US Marine from Calexico who had joined the police. After seeing the harm that heroin had caused to some of their friends, he and Kiki had zealously hunted down dealers. In 1974, they had joined the DEA, which was looking for Spanish speakers. With agents reluctant to go to Guadalajara due to the danger, Shaggy had transferred in 1984 to support Kiki. Bracing for something bad, the three agents tried to bolster each other.

On November 6, Jaime wrote a memo to his bosses: "The violence previously reported has increased drastically without any serious consequences for the traffickers. The local government is apparently completely compromised, and unwilling to cope with a deteriorating situation. On some occasions local police officers have been killed in shootouts with traffickers and still no action has been taken. The traffickers commonly travel the streets and highways armed with automatic weapons and usually carry credentials from DFS or some other federal law enforcement agency."

In December 1984, informants reported the existence of a massive cannabis plantation employing thousands in the Chihuahuan Desert. After the DEA reported it to the Mexican government, the Attorney General's Office responded that there was nothing in the desert. Under relentless pressure from the DEA, the Mexicans agreed to raid the plantation with an assault force of soldiers and police. On the day of the raid, the fuel trucks for the helicopters went to the wrong location, and the operation was almost cancelled because of the mistake. Again, the DEA insisted and the aircraft took off.

Near the village of Búfalo, the Americans aboard aircraft spotted barracks and drying sheds bigger than soccer fields. The plantation was so large that it took two days for the raiding party to find it all. Caro Quintero later admitted that he had invested $20 million in the project, and the DEA announced that the street value of the cannabis was $2.5 billion. US media reported it as the bust of the century. Approximately 8,000 workers were rounded up, who had been paid 2,500 pesos per day, which was a pittance. Having drifted into the desert, some had not eaten or drank for three days.

From the workers, the agents learned that the overseers had been forewarned. They had told the workers that they were free to go because of problems that had arisen. The workers were surprised by the aircraft conducting the raid because it was the same aircraft with the blue-and-white markings of the Attorney General's Office eradication fleet that had been transporting important people to and from the plantation.

The raid forced the agents' bosses to finally acknowledge the scale of the problem in Mexico and the extent of the corruption. To protect such a large plantation in the desert, orders must have come down from the top levels of government. In press releases, the US embassy lied as usual:

"The bust is a real credit to the Mexican authorities who coordinated it. It is a statement to the drug syndicates that Mexico is serious about interdiction and there will be no easy transiting of drugs destined for the US through Mexican territory.

"The Mexican Attorney General's Office stepped up their efforts and have publicly gone on record as staunch supporters of the War on Drugs. The recent dramatic sweep actions of the MAGO [Mexican Attorney General's Office] throughout Mexico have clearly indicated Mexico's intention to wipe out heroin poppies and marijuana at their roots ... Since 1974, as the result of their commendable efforts over 24,000 metric tons of marijuana have been destroyed in the field ... a record of which the government of Mexico can be deservedly proud."

On November 26, 1984, another plane load of cocaine was seized in Arizona and the US embassy in Bogotá was bombed by traffickers. The situation in Colombia became the focus of the DEA. Kiki requested a transfer, so Jaime asked for him to be moved to San Diego. Although Mika was pleased, Kiki cautioned her that the transfer could take a few months. She contemplated moving with the boys to California, but Kiki insisted that the traffickers would never shoot an American, so she decided to stay.

After the disappearance of four American Jehovah's Witnesses on December 2, who had been knocking on doors in a Mexican residential neighbourhood, Mika grew more concerned. She pressed Kiki about the transfer; he said that the DEA had not processed the paperwork, but actually he had not requested an expedited transfer because he felt he had more work to finish.

In January 1985, the US House Foreign Affairs Committee sent two investigators to Mexico, raising Kiki's hopes. Although they believed the problems described by the agents, the investigators' best advice was for them to tell the media. The agents refused, and Kiki asked what would have to happen for changes to be made. Would somebody have to die before anything was done?

In January, the cartel ambushed four Mexican police cars. In response, petty criminals were raided and guns confiscated, but the police would not confront the cartel. Mika wanted her entire family to return to America.

Under Mexican law, the DEA agents couldn't even carry guns because if they were detected at roadblocks, they might end up arrested and in jail. Their investigation had brought them into conflict with the DFS, an intelligence agency formed in 1947 with the help of the CIA. With the Cold War beginning, the DFS's objective was "preserving the internal stability of Mexico against all forms of subversion and terrorist threats." Having started out shadowing suspected Russian agents in Mexico, DFS members had evolved into offering protection rackets for the cartel, even selling federal badges to hit men. Stopped by Félix Gallardo's bodyguards displaying badges, Roger Knapp had been questioned as to why he was on a street where the kingpin had an office.

Whenever Kiki had given information to senior Mexican officials, the cartel always knew. One MFJP policeman had revealed that many of its members earning $150 a month delivered cash for the cartel in exchange for up to 300,000 pesos per job. He was also aware that the DFS offered protection and transported drugs. The Guadalajara agents believed that the head of the DEA in Mexico minimised the risks that they were facing and that he accepted that the corruption of the police had to be tolerated to maintain Mexico's special relationship with America.

At 2 PM on February 7, 1985, Kiki placed his badge and gun in a drawer and headed out for lunch with his wife, whom he had promised to spend more time with. On the street, shops were closing for the siesta. He headed for his pickup truck parked at the Camelot Bar. As he unlocked the door, five men surrounded him.

One displayed a DFS badge. "Federal security. The comandante wants to see you."

They grabbed Kiki, threw him into a beige Volkswagen Atlantic and yanked a jacket over his head.

In the restaurant, his wife felt awkwardly alone. With his long hours at work, she had been looking forward to lunch. Keeping her eyes on the entrance, she felt the waiters watching her. After thirty minutes, she called the consulate. "Where is Kiki?"

"He just left."

Thinking that he would arrive at any moment, she waited.

Eventually, she returned home to her sons. At 5:30 AM, she awoke, wondering why Kiki had stayed out all night without telling her that he would be gone. Perhaps he was on an urgent assignment. It was too early to call his colleagues. Expected to be the tough wife of an agent, she endured waiting for another hour, and then called Shaggy, while praying that he didn't answer, which meant they were on a joint assignment.

"Didn't Kiki meet you for lunch?"

Jolted by his response, she knew that something was wrong.

"Maybe he went to Colima with the Federales," Shaggy said, attempting to reassure her but also worried. After hanging up with a sickly feeling, he called Jaime. "Kiki didn't come home."

"I hope to God you're wrong." Immediately, Jaime called informants and contacts. Nobody knew anything. At 8:30 AM, he called the US embassy. "I think we've got a missing man." He sped to the consulate and parked by Kiki's truck. He found the door open when it should have been locked.

In Kiki's house, Shaggy found Mika, who was devastated. After a short conversation, he drove to Kiki's truck.

In the US, the agents could have summoned a small army, but in Guadalajara, they had to convince the MFJP to take action and launch raids. They found only two people working in the MFJP office, an old house, when usually there were two dozen employees.

"Comandante Alberto Arteaga and most of the officers are up in Colima looking for the murderer of our comrades. If you want assistance, you'll have to go to the Jalisco State Judicial Police."

Aware that members of the JSJP worked for the cartel, the DEA agents were annoyed. With no help forthcoming, the American consul general in Guadalajara called the governor of Jalisco, only to be told that he was unavailable.

At 4:30 PM, twenty-six hours after Kiki's disappearance, a bureaucrat informed Jaime that he needed to file a formal complaint. At the state office, a portly police chief saw the agents and disappeared. The state Attorney General refused to see them.

After an hour, they were allowed to provide a statement to a junior assistant prosecutor. Barely holding onto his temper, Jaime filled out a form, and returned to the consulate. Shaggy drove past traffickers' houses and checked hospitals. With no results, he returned to the MFJP office, but it was empty.

Shaggy and his wife moved into Kiki's home. He told her that they all had to stay strong and believe that he was still alive. By cooking and chatting with friends, Mika tried not to think about the worst, but eventually she broke down sobbing and they all cried.

Dozens of DEA agents arrived in Guadalajara from across Mexico and some from America who were fluent in Spanish. In a war room, they formulated strategies and divided the work. The late arrival of Edward Heath, the DEA's regional director for Mexico, upset some of the agents, including Jaime, who scowled at him.

By Saturday, eighty Federales joined the team, but complained that they had no cars. After cars were rented, they said they had no radios. After radios arrived, there were more delays and excuses. Every action by the Mexicans had to be approved by a commander who had arrived from Mexico City, Pavón Reyes, who also had to get approval by telephoning the head of the MFJP in Mexico City.

Acting on information, Pavón Reyes, thirty of his men and three DEA agents headed for the airport. Jaime told the agents not to let the Mexican police out of their sight. At a hangar, they spotted five men with machine guns by a Falcon executive jet. Pavón Reyes told his men to ready their weapons. While they blocked the path of the plane, the men raised their guns. Just when a shootout seemed imminent, Pavón Reyes walked up to the leader of the group, a man with black curly hair, a thick diamond-studded bracelet and countless gold chains and medallions. To the astonishment of the DEA agents, the two men walked behind the plane and hugged. Some of the Mexican police spoke to Pavón Reyes and greeted the gang leader.

"I have to make a telephone call." Pavón Reyes went into a hangar that housed a communications centre for anti-drug aircraft.

"I want you to call the comandante and find out what the hell is going on here," the gang leader told one of his gang.

Pavón Reyes returned, hugged the gang leader and authorised the plane to leave. The engines started and the leader got on board. As it taxied, the leader brandished a bottle of champagne, smiled deviously, drank a large amount, lifted his machine gun and yelled, "My children, bring better weapons next time and not little toys."

Leaving the airport with three Mexican policemen, a DEA agent was told that they all knew that some of their Mexican colleagues were accepting bribes and that it was impossible to detain and question some traffickers because of the risk of retaliation. The root of the problem was that they had allowed the Mafia to get too big. Later, when looking at photos of the Guadalajara Cartel, the agent recognised the gang leader from the airport: Caro Quintero. The drug lord had promised Pavón Reyes approximately $300,000 to allow him to escape.

The DEA administrator, Bud Mullen, was disheartened to learn about the absence of any raids in Mexico and that Caro Quintero had fled. He flew to Mexico City to meet the MFJP director, convinced that he could talk him into taking action. On Sunday morning, the director met him at the airport. He apologised for the inaction and claimed that his men had been in another part of the country, with little means of communication. They had been moved to Guadalajara and he had put his best man in charge: Armando. The conversation buoyed Mullen's spirits.

On the flight to Guadalajara, the head of the DEA's office of foreign operations realised that Mullen's faith in the Mexican police taking action was unrealistic. Having heard all of the promises before, he knew better, so he politely tried to inject some realism. Mullen arrived with a dozen Federale bodyguards, which upset Mika because she felt that those men should have been searching for her husband. Mullen appeared nervous and she disliked Edward Heath for not sending her a message after Kiki had been reported missing. She believed that he didn't care about the men in the field.

"If Kiki returns," Mika said, "he's probably gonna get angry with me, but there's something I've got to say that a lot of wives are afraid to say. Washington doesn't pay attention to Guadalajara, which isn't all that different from Colombia. To the DEA, we're all just numbers. Why hasn't the DEA urged the Mexican government to give our agents diplomatic immunity so they can carry weapons? Why didn't the DEA headquarters send reinforcements to Guadalajara after the shooting of Antonio Vargas and the destruction of Roger Knapp's car?"

She blamed the DEA for leaving Guadalajara short-staffed, which had prevented Kiki from requesting an expedited transfer because he could not leave his colleagues with such a heavy workload. The DEA only seemed to be concerned about agents in Colombia. Kiki had reported that there was extreme danger in Guadalajara. Why hadn't Mullen acted? She didn't know the intricacies of Kiki's business, but she was well aware that any of the agents and their families could be killed at any time. She wanted Mullen to pull out all the stops with the Mexican government, as it would find Kiki if the order came from high. She wanted justice and if he were dead, she wanted her sons to know that he had not died senselessly. She wanted the corpse and his killers punished. "Don't let my husband become a number."

Mullen seemed distant and out of touch. He would later tell the media, "There were orders that were passed onto the field to always run around in pairs, to always be armed, to always account for their movements. In this particular case, it didn't happen. People get lax … I can't supervise the agents' every movement from 300 miles away."

Jaime later denied ever receiving those orders. Carrying a gun would have been illegal in Mexico, so they couldn't order their men to go out armed. Besides, how would Kiki with a gun have fared against a group of traffickers with AK-47s? How can three men travel in pairs? Who would protect their wives and children? "Unless you've got a bus, you all can't be together all the time. Sometimes you have to travel with your family." Plus Kiki hadn't vanished in a dangerous area. He had emerged from the consulate onto a busy street.

No matter what the agents had learned in Guadalajara, the US government insisted to the public that Mexico's participation in the War on Drugs was a "model program." Everything was under control because the relationship between the Mexican police and the DEA was "excellent." In the media, US officials championed Mexico's permanent campaign against drug trafficking. The State Department sent $10 million a year for the campaign, which was supposedly based on the eradication of cannabis and opium fields by dropping poisonous chemicals such as paraquat from aircraft. Officials from all over the world were invited to Mexico to witness the spray helicopters. In 1980, the Mexican government had announced that it had virtually wiped out the cannabis and heroin business. The Narcotics Assistant Unit attached to the US embassy was in charge of monitoring eradication, but it lacked the staff and organisation to fulfil its duty, so it relied on figures provided by Mexico.

From an informant, Kiki had learned that when a helicopter landed, the field manager would come out and hand over cartel cash. Whenever the agents had filed reports about such fields, the US embassy would inform the Mexican Attorney General's Office, which governed the eradication aircraft provided by the US State Department at the taxpayers' expense. Reports came back from the Mexicans that no drug crops had been seen or that the fields had been sprayed. For verification, Kiki would send an informant who would invariably return with a freshly plucked section of a cannabis plant. If the plant was submitted as evidence, the response was always that the informant or the agent was wrong.

Kiki had learned that officials in the Attorney General's Office were obstructing the spraying by taking bribery, while pocketing the money from the US taxpayers. The officials responsible for distributing the funds accused the agents of being cynical and poorly informed. The agents responded that the State Department had to say that the programme was successful to keep the cash coming. If they told the truth, Congress would reduce their budget or abolish the programme. One agent stormed into the embassy and argued with State Department officials, who insisted that some fields had been sprayed. The agent waved some of the cannabis at the officials and yelled, "If you can show me any paraquat on this pot, I'll eat the son of a bitch."

When Ronald Reagan was asked by a *Newsweek* reporter about America's cooperation with Mexico, the president replied, "You have to recognise that some of these countries are limited in their means and their ability and their personnel in handling a problem as big as this. And it wouldn't do any good to punish them for not being able to do more. It would be up to us to find ways where there could be better cooperation and where we can all be helpful to each other." This told the agents in Guadalajara that the US wasn't interested in exposing the corruption in Mexico that promoted the drug trade. When it came to the Reagan–Bush administration, the drug issue only mattered for propaganda purposes if the countries involved were pro-Communist.

With no demands from the top of the US administration, the Mexican government responded, "Someone's simply gone missing. He could be sunbathing in Guadalajara. It's not a priority."

On February 10, with Kiki missing for three days, DEA boss Mullen put enough pressure on the Mexican police for them to start raiding the traffickers' houses, but they were empty. A witness came forward who said he had seen the kidnapping, but had not reported it because he thought it was the police making an arrest. A businessman had witnessed Kiki in the back of a car getting beat with what looked like pipes. An informant reported that Caro Quintero had paid a fortune to the police commander who had allowed him to fly away and a former MFJP and DFS agent had delivered the cash.

With Kiki missing, the CIA contacted the DEA. As well as offering assistance, the CIA wanted to know whether any of their counterparts in the DFS had been arrested and if they talking.

On February 25, a Tijuana MFJP commander announced that they had arrested the mastermind of the kidnapping and two accomplices, all from the DFS. The Mexican media described them as sacrificial lambs.

In an interview with *Newsweek* magazine, DEA boss Mullen said, "People talk of sending the FBI down or sending in more DEA agents, but there is only one government in the world that can clean up Mexico, and that's the Mexican government and the Mexican Federal Judicial Police, and they've got to do it. We can go on forever making a seizure here and there, but until the Mexicans themselves root out corruption, I don't think we'll ever stop the flow of drugs from Mexico. Everybody seems to know it's there and it's happening, but nobody wants to talk about it publicly. I think it's time to ignore the sensibilities of some individuals and face the fact that we have a problem down there. People here say, 'Well, there's a different mentality down there and we should accept it. This is the way it is.' I just don't agree. It is not acceptable. Not when it's affecting our country the way it is, and their country. I think it's just a blight on Mexico that this could happen. People disappear, and that's it. They don't even have an investigation. I just can't believe that people still go down there."

Pressure from the DEA forced the US government to impose border searches, which slowed commerce with Mexico and frightened US banks that had invested in Mexico's debt. An assistant to the Mexican administration stated, "How can the United States make such a scandal over one of its agents' abduction? You should not find it surprising that anybody fighting drug trafficking is abducted or killed."

CHAPTER 10
GARY WEBB SHINES ON TV

By appearing on *The Montel Williams Show*, Gary Webb hoped to wake up the American public. With the host so sympathetic, everything seemed to be going well.

"What we can call rumours," Montel said, "the rumour that the CIA was involved in making sure that cocaine made it to the streets of South Central LA back in the early '80s and then helped to develop and turn it into crack, which was then spread across America, and is the reason why most of our inner cities are in the plight that they are in. A lot of this has been out there for years, but it wasn't until recently that the story broke again, and my next guest is a reporter ... from the *San Jose Mercury News*, and he wrote a story called 'Dark Alliance.' Please welcome Mr Gary Webb to the show. Gary ... I think that the current fervour over this issue is because of you. A lot of people may not be familiar with what the 'Dark Alliance' meant and stands for. Why don't you tell America what the story is about first and then we'll talk about the issues."

"This was about a cocaine ring," Gary said, "that operated along the West Coast in the United States throughout most of the '80s and they were funnelling, they were selling cocaine in South Central. They were also selling it in Oakland. They were selling it in San Francisco. They were selling in San Jose and some of the money they were making was going to support an army that the men who ran the cocaine ring worked for called the FDM. This was an army that the CIA started in 1981 and supported."

"Better known to us," Montel said, "[as] the Contras [in] Nicaragua. So, go ahead."

"The men that were running the cocaine ring were top officials of this Contra army and what we found was that they were selling this stuff in South Central, which is you know a predominantly black section of Los Angeles. Immediately, before the outbreak of the crack-cocaine epidemic, they started selling powder. Tons and tons and tons of powder cocaine was going into this one small area of the city and from there they sold to Freeway Rick, and Freeway Rick took the powder and turned it into crack, and starting in 1983–1984, [he] began distributing it to predominantly the gangs, the Crips and the Bloods in Los Angeles and they spread it from there."

"Since this has happened, have you butted heads with anybody in Washington, DC?"

"Yeah, we worked on this for a year and it was only because some people at national archives believe freedom of information means freedom of information, we got some documents that showed that pretty strongly there was some CIA connection to the story."

"Let's talk a little bit about those documents for a second," Montel said. "There's a gentleman that we talked about yesterday on the show; his name is Danilo Blandón, who was a person who was a member of the aristocracy of Nicaragua … and then he fled and comes to the United States and decides while he's in the United States, so you can all understand this, he wants to raise money for their revolutionaries who were trying to overthrow the government that just overthrew them …

"So, here in the United States they try to do fundraisers and that doesn't work and then Blandón gets to scheme: well, I can get some cocaine cheaply with some help from some of my friends and get it into the United States of America; all I need to find is somebody who can sell it. So, they find a gentleman by the name of Rick Ross who is Freeway Rick. Rick Ross comes in and starts selling cocaine in the beginning one or two grams and within weeks, two, three, four kilos a week. Within months – what was it? – ten to fifteen kilos a day.

"Ricky Ross was selling cocaine to the point of making $3 to $4 million a day. He sold so much cocaine it hurt his fingers to count the money, not only in Los Angeles but in Cincinnati in St Louis, and all the way across America. So, some can say, and this is the reason why people are so angry at you and your article is that Ricky Ross, the dope dealer, was supplied by the CIA because Blandón was an operative for the CIA, correct?"

"Blandón and Meneses were working for an army," Gary said, "that was a wholly owned subsidiary of the CIA. They were meeting with CIA agents and this came out in court. I mean Danilo Blandón is now a government witness. He works with the Drug Enforcement Administration and we've paid him $166,000 over the last eighteen months because he's such a good informant. So, they put him on the witness stand in Ricky Ross's case and he testified that in 1981, he went to Honduras. He met with the military commander of the CIA's army and he was instructed to go raise money in California for this Contra army and he was told that the ends justified the means."

"And those ends mean sell cocaine if he had to?"

"Well look, he was in the room with the Nicaraguan representative of the Cali Cartel, Mr Meneses, and he was in the room with a government marketing expert named Danilo Blandón. Now, if they weren't talking about selling cocaine, I don't know what they were talking about."

"And this was all information they could find on the website, on the Internet. So, we'll put that up, so you can go and research."

"You can look at these documents yourselves."

"So you can look at the documents yourself and judge it." Montel turned to Mike Levine. "But Michael now, I mean, there's a stretch here. Here's a guy who is obviously a CIA operative, Mr Blandón, who is working with this government-backed army that we've kind of created in Nicaragua, but how the heck does this guy get to bring in tons of cocaine? I'm talking tons: three, four, five, six, seven, eight tons of cocaine weekly in the United States of America for seven years and no one can ever catch him."

"Well, number one: Mr Meneses was actually indicted in 1984," Mike said. "He was known within – my own sources in the DEA told me he was known as El Rey De Las Drogas: The King of Drugs. He was in more than forty files and indicted mysteriously and people within the DEA say that it was CIA intervention that kept this sealed indictment from ever being opened. So, he was well known. The connection between him, Blandón and Calero, who was the head of the Nicaraguan government in exile, is clear. There's a clear evidentiary trail. Now, if you want to follow that trail up, you have to first understand how the CIA and DEA work. I was a country attaché assigned to Argentina; now, during those years there were people who I inherited on the payroll who were murderers. They were also on the CIA payroll."

"Murderers on the CIA payroll?" Montel said.

"Not only murders, I'm talking about mass murderers and I wrote about it in books that I thought would have Americans marching on Washington, but nothing ever happened … God bless Gary Webb. I've been trying to tell this and other DEA agents are now coming out trying to tell their story."

"Let me take a break," Montel said. "When we come back, we've got a lot of people who disagree with all of this. They're here today. We'll have a good argument. We'll be back right after this." After the break, he said, "My next guest is the director of media analysis for Accuracy in Media and says that what Mr Webb wrote is incorrect. Please welcome Mr Joe Goulden to the show and also welcome the host of his own radio talk show on WWRC in Washington, DC. Please welcome Mr Joe Madison to the show. Mr Madison has dedicated the last three weeks of your broadcast …"

"Oh no," said Joe Madison, a black man in a dark suit wearing gold-rimmed glasses, his fingers steepled below his chin. "It's been seven weeks, three hours a day, five days a week to this issue. They will not allow me to talk about anything else. When I say they, I mean the people in this 50,000-watt station from Philadelphia to the hills of West Virginia; black, white, Hispanic, every colour you can imagine, every nationality, every economic social group. People want to know; America wants to know."

"Mr Goulden, you say that this is really out to lunch, right?"

"Montel, this is journalistic malpractice of the grossest sort," said Joe Goulden, a bulky grey-haired man with a hillbilly twang. "We need an investigation of this – not whether the CIA was in the drug business – that has been investigated *ad infinitum*, but why a supposedly respectable newspaper group such as the Knight River newspapers would publish ill-sourced contradictory stories that rely more upon innuendo and disinformation than fact."

"OK, well, when we talk about misinformation and innuendo," Montel said, "here's something Michael has right there. Michael, you have a document that I saw on a recent show."

"Yeah."

"This document is a transcript of Oliver North's diary, right?"

"I can go on for the next two hours," Mike said, "of incidents with the CIA and I put thousands of people away in jail, Mr Goulden, a lot less than you see here. This is Oliver North's diary."

"Mike, listen to me," Joe Goulden said. "Mike, that's great. That came out in the 1980s when they had three congressional committees …"

"The only trouble with that was this was not given to [John] Kerry," Mike said. "This was held back from Kerry."

"Nobody's ever denied that people in the Contra movement were involved in drugs." Joe Goulden pointed at Gary. "This man has claimed that this was a CIA plot …"

"People have to understand about the CIA," Mike said, "whose chief of counterintelligence for eight years sold America's top secrets as if it was a New Jersey garage sale and nobody stopped him. The FBI had to fight the CIA to arrest him … This is an agency that was experimenting with mind-control drugs, putting LSD in the food of patients. Let's talk about reality …"

"If I could just say something," Joe Madison said. "One of the things I've always noticed – and I hope I can do it without interruption – is that as soon as facts are being made, you'll notice as soon as he pulled out that document, interruption. Now, let me tell you what we're asking for is a congressional Records Act. In other words, let's take all of the records classified and otherwise, put them out before the people and let's see who knew what and when they knew it. Here is the accusation: the accusation isn't that agents were on the street corner selling drugs; the accusation is that drugs are being sold by the Contras and that the CIA knew about it and didn't do anything. That's the accusation. So, what we need is a Records Act … Now, he says he knows what the CIA knows. He's saying more than the CIA is saying."

Joe Goulden admitted that there was testimony to the Kerry Committee about people in the Contra movement who were involved with drugs … "We have Ricky Ross here who started in the drug business in 1979 when Blandón was still in Managua …"

"And then the CIA operatives," Gary said.

"So, what?" Joe Goulden said.

"We've got pictures of them meeting with the drug dealers," Gary said.

"Let's stop this for a second," Montel said. "What all the people of this country are asking for is let's investigate this and the reason why is because for things like what Mike's been trying to show. Mike, if I can do this real quick, this is just an excerpt from Oliver North's diary where he says particularly about talking to the same person that Mike just said and Mr Goulden said he talked to last week, Mr Claro, the same person you talked to last week. It says in Oliver North's diary, contact him so that we can get 1,500 kilos."

"We have to investigate this," Mike said. "It's never been investigated. Quickly, this is just one piece of several hundred pages of Ollie North's diary reflecting drugs. It is a phone call from Dewey Claridge. Who is Dewey Claridge? He is a top CIA official who was convicted of lying to Congress and pardoned by President Bush. During this conversation, they speak of a phone call to Calero. Calero, there's a direct evidentiary chain from

Calero right to Ricky Ross. It's there to be investigated. So, in this, and mind you there were two attempts at classifying this. In this they reflect, 'Want aircraft to pick up 1,500 kilos.' Now, I promise every one of you if you as a DEA agent got this in your diary, you would have a hundred DEA agents around you around the clock and this is one page of several hundred. They've never been investigated."

"Mike, kilos of what?" Joe Goulden said.

"Let me tell you," Gary said.

"You tell me what!" Mike said.

"Let me take a break," Montel said. "When we come back, we'll be joined by Congressman Charles Rangel who says that, 'You know what: all we want to know is the facts. Let's look at the facts and give us all an opportunity as citizens in this country to evaluate the facts, that's all everybody wants to do, every American wants to know the truth.' We'll be back right after this." After the break, he said, "Ladies and gentlemen; please welcome Congressman Charles Rangel to the show and before we take even one more step, I'd like to be able to set this up for our viewers at home so they understand what we're talking about.

"What we're talking about here is that there is at least information that alludes to the fact that over a period of time from 1982 until about 1988, there is a person who is a known paid informant for the CIA, who is funnelling drugs to a crack dealer, dope dealer in Los Angeles.

"This is the part that's a known fact for most information. This person was known to be a CIA operative. He is the person providing cocaine, tons of cocaine that's coming into the United States under protection. No one ever busts him. His partner is the biggest drug dealer in Central America: a guy by the name of Meneses who obviously is supplying for him. Everybody completely looks the wrong way.

"For eight years, this gentleman Ricky Ross is able to sell his drugs with the assistance of this guy Blandón, selling drugs all over the place, he never gets busted. He goes to jail. A month away from getting out of jail, the CIA or the DEA sets up an elaborate sting to bust him as soon as he walks out of jail. He's in jail not selling any drugs. Ricky Ross is now back in jail awaiting sentencing for another bust that took place after he got out of jail the first time.

"So, the question is: was the CIA – did they just turn their backs and allow drugs to come into America? If they did that, are they then not responsible for the epidemic of crack in America? That's the next conclusion for some people. Some other people could say, 'No. The end justifies the means. If this was the only way we could pay for an army to fight overseas, that's the way we do it.' But do we do that at the cost of American citizens? Congressman Rangel, what do you think?"

"I think that Congresswoman Maxine Waters," Rangel said, "and commentator Joe Madison and of course, my old buddy Mike and Webb here will be able to say as a legacy that they're leaving to their children, that at long last someone pulled the reins in on the CIA. We are not just talking about whether or not they devastated communities throughout the United States. We are just saying that the CIA has been and is now completely out of control and I don't understand, Montel, as to why all of America isn't completely outraged.

"You cannot target a black community with cocaine, with crack cocaine any more than you could with poison gas without it destroying America and as far as I'm concerned, the CIA is being charged with mass murder and it's time for this allegation to be exposed and it should not take sixty days to do it."

"Mr Goulden, what do you say to this?" Montel said.

"I think Charlie's jumping to conclusions here. We had three congressional committees look at this in depth in the 1980s – a special council – but they found that there was some stuff on the fringes of it. This is the germ of truth in Webb's fantasy organisation …"

"Can I ask you a question, Mr Goulden?" Montel said. "Did we not just have two congressional committees look into the Persian

Gulf War syndrome and come back and say, 'We had nothing to do with the fact that our soldiers and sailors are sick'? Now, last week they just came back and said, 'Oh, by the way, we did give them a pill and oh, by the way, when we did bomb the thing they probably got some nerve gas and oh, by the way, we might be responsible for the injuries of thousands of Americans.'"

"What Charlie Rangel is doing," Goulden said, "and Joe Madison here, are taking allegations, very flimsy allegations. If anybody sits down and looks at the analysis we've done and wants to impose himself, which is not a CIA defender, and tear this thing apart on evolutionary grounds, Ricky was already in the dope business when Blandón was still in Managua."

"How do you explain Blandón's testimony," Gary said, "under oath as a government witness that he was selling cocaine for the Contras and that the CIA was in charge of it? How do you explain that?"

"That's not him," Goulden said. "His testimony; that's unfortunate. It's what you have under your whip."

"It is," Gary said. "It's in the grand jury transcript."

"I've read it."

"It's posted on the Internet," Gary said, "so everybody in the world can read it."

"I chaired one of these investigative committees," Rangel said, "when I was chairman of the select narcotic committee of crime. Let us all agree on one thing. Let's get to the point where there is no challenge. One, that the CIA hired people to commit illegal acts. Two, with smuggling guns illegally to Nicaragua; no challenge, right? Alright, and the second thing is that these same people were involved in narcotic tracking."

"Some of the same people who were kicked off the payroll when it was discovered," Goulden said, falling back on the default excuse whenever the CIA's drug trafficking was uncovered: the Agency would always blame rogue operatives.

"Listen, now we're getting closer to agreement," Rangel said. "Some of the people that were legally taking guns over there were involved in narcotics. That's agreed to. Let's say something else. Colonel North knew that some of these people were involved in drug smuggling. Would you say that?"

"And they have made money," Gary said.

"You see," Rangel said, "once you start agreeing to all of these things, then comes the question … They said prove that the CIA knew it."

"Wait," Madison said, "I've got to make another point that keeps getting mistaken here. You see, the committees did not investigate whether the CIA condoned drug trafficking. So, that's what we need to get clear."

"We'll take a break and I'll let you in," Montel said. "So, when we come back, I'll put you right in, but the other point they're making is: back two and a half years ago, I did a show about the Persian Gulf War syndrome and everybody said, 'Montel, you're out to lunch. You're crazy. Why are you telling people in America that we have to be worried about some disease? These sailors are all stupid. They're all crazy. All the army guys are crazy. It's all made up.' Now, two weeks ago, Congress investigates and all of a sudden we did some stuff wrong and now we've lost our pants! So, we'll find out about this. We'll take a break and when we come back, we have an attorney who said the CIA needs new guidelines. That's what this is all about."

"I just have a comment, more so than a question," said a female audience member when they returned. "This is something that we've been talking about for a long time. What is the surprise now? The black race has always said, 'We don't have the money nor the means,' and it's always been, 'I've heard it since I was a child,' and now all of a sudden it's a big surprise. We've always felt that way."

"It's not a surprise," Madison said. "We don't grow cocaine in the ghettos of America. It's got to come from somewhere and the only thing that I will ask is that my good friend Charlie Rangel here, if he will go back and help get legislation started that will create a Records Act. Once we create a Records Act, then we can all see what's there classified or otherwise and make up our own minds black or white."

"I was hired by the government as a tactician," Mike said. "Right now, what we're succumbing to is what Central Intelligence wants: we're making it a black issue and it's not. My brother died, my son died, millions of Americans suffered. The important thing that we've got to remember is that it is not a black issue and the proof that they're waiting for it to go away is that both presidential candidates are not saying a word about it."

"I can tell you, Montel, that my audience," Madison said, "much like your audience, is across the board. I mean, I read and this ain't accuracy in media where they claim that this is a get-whitey campaign. Well, let me tell you something: there are black, white, Hispanic dealers; black, white, Hispanic distributors; black, white, Hispanic users and the CIA, I assume, is not all white. So, you know, this is an American tragedy. It's not a get-whitey tragedy. It's to get who's responsible and hold them accountable."

"Please welcome my next guest," Montel said, "who was the former-serving special counsel to the Senate Committee on Foreign Relations in 1989. Please welcome Mr Jack Blum into the show. Jack, what do you think about all of this?"

"We've been there and we've done that," Blum said. "We did this investigation; we did it ten years ago. We had witnesses under oath. We can say for a fact that Contras dealt cocaine; that the secret war in Nicaragua created conditions that opened the door to a flood of cocaine in America and we know that the CIA and Oliver North and people in the White House knew about that. We say that in the public report."

"I had a call last week from an agent who said, 'Montel, I will give you the location of the airfield they flew into, one of them is in Texas at a US Army Air Force Base.' So, why can't we go after these guys because that means that it wasn't just Reagan and Ollie, but it may have been Bush and somebody?"

"They didn't just know about it," Mike said. "They actively destroyed cases. They actively put DEA agents' lives on the line to protect the drug flow. I was one of those agents."

After the next break, Blum said, "We have been engaged in a holy war against Communism for fifty years. This didn't start in Central America with this problem and it didn't end there. We started with Khun Sa in Burma, helping the Kuomintang against the Communist Chinese; he became a major heroin dealer. In the Vietnam War, we worked with Hill tribesmen who were in the heroin business. You may have seen the movie: *Air America*. The problem here is it's going on again and again and again. We just recently worked with people in Afghanistan who were great heroes against the Russians and against Communism, but we trained people who came back and planted a bomb at the World Trade Center and are dealing heroin. As we speak, Afghanistan and Pakistan are one of the world's great heroin centres. It ain't new. The problem is control …"

"[By] 1993, the Cold War was over," Mike said. "Central Intelligence is caught red-handed smuggling a ton of cocaine from Venezuela, that bastion of Communism to the United States – red-handed. The head of the DEA on *60 Minutes* said there's no other way to describe drug smuggling, felony drug smuggling. I went to California and spoke to the DEA agent directly involved who told me that Central Intelligence came to her in Venezuela with what she described as a wacky suspicious idea to smuggle a ton of cocaine and she told them, 'Don't do it.' They did it anyway and were caught by Customs, specific people and no Cold War, no investigation."

"Let me ask Jack," Gary said, "what happened when you did this report which I've read, which was extensive? How did the press react when you put that out?"

"We were assaulted on all sides by the administration," Blum said. "Every time we had a day of hearings, every time we had a witness, the Reagan people came down on us like a ton of bricks. They said, 'The witnesses were lying. They were drug dealers who were trying to get off. We were in it for politics,' and in a way, it's a wonderful thing to have this resurfaced in a context where we don't have the official establishment weighing in on it. So, maybe now, somebody will go back and read what we did."

"But I think Mike is right," Montel said. "What will happen tomorrow is – since I'm the only show that's doing this – it'll be put off as being a black person feeding into the conspiracy. Now, one more point. The bottom line in this whole thing is Blandón, the gentleman that we are all talking about, who was just paid $166,000 by the CIA and DEA, is in Nicaragua hanging out at a ranch and we all for nine years tried to track this guy down for being one of the biggest cocaine dealers. He's got a ranch in Nicaragua, a free man walking free and Ricky Ross is sitting in jail and Blandón was his supplier. How does that happen in America, tell me?"

"Mike, I know a few congressmen," Goulden said. "Let's do this. I'd love to take you down to Washington, let you get under oath and sit at a table … What do you say to that? Would you do this under oath?"

"I want to tell you something," Mike said. "I don't have any faith in Congress. Senator Frank Church is a waste of time. A friend of mine who was flying drugs … says I'm invited down to testify to the Senate. What do you advise he says? He actually flew the drugs?"

"You don't trust Rangel here?" Goulden said.

"I don't trust them," Mike said. "I don't believe the Congress of the United States has been able to control the Central Intelligence for twenty years. They've been working as apologists for them …"

"Mike, one thing that's coming out of this," Rangel said, "is that there should be outrage in the United States that any federal agency can plan to murder American citizens whether they're black or white. The delay has been that they said that they targeted it for black communities. What we're saying is let the CIA get on the line, let's open the records, let the president, let [Bob] Dole and everyone see what's going on."

"If you're at home," Montel said, "watching this television show, I'd like you to get on your phone … Get on your phone this minute. Call your local congressman and you tell your congressman that Montel asked you to call and we want hearings within a week. You can call us, so I can track how many people call, and we'll get called by a hundred thousand people."

"I trust the American people," Madison said. "I trust Montel Williams and God bless you and Gary Webb for doing this show because you've done something *The New York Times* won't do. *The Washington Post* does a little job to try to make black people look like they're paranoid and the reality is, the more informed we are, the freer we are and that's the most important thing."

"We're almost out of time," Montel said, "so I would advise you to go out and read *Triangle of Death* by Mr Michael Levine … if you want to know any more information about what goes on deep inside the CIA. Let's stop hoodwinking the public. Let's just get the truth out there. Mr Blum, you wanted to make a final comment."

"Well, we've had all the investigations we need. We know what happened. The time has come to debate serious reform. There was a debate over intelligence reform. It wound up with an addition of people and an addition of money. The time has come to take a look at what we're doing. The Cold War is over. Let's find some new solutions, maybe even a whole new agency. We don't have to dig through this anymore. We know what happened."

"The only reason," Montel said, "why I would advise to dig through this is to make sure we find out who was culpable."

"The CIA should be proud," Rangel said, "to open up their records and let it all hang out. The President of the United States should be in a position to say, 'Not on my watch should Americans break the law and sell poison to kill other Americans.'"

CHAPTER 11
DRUG DEALING ARKANSAS
PROSECUTOR

So far Linda Ives had pinned her hopes for justice on Dan Harmon, the prosecutor in charge of the grand jury. Shortly after the deaths of the boys on the tracks, Harmon had volunteered to help her. Impressed by his passion, down-to-earth style and quick-wits, she had welcomed his assistance. He had persuaded a judge to name him the special prosecutor to supervise the investigation. In the first year or so, spending lots of time together, working on the case, Linda had grown close to Harmon, whom she trusted completely. But three years later, she realised that all he had done was use her tragedy to generate publicity and political support for himself. No one had been indicted for the murders nor had he discovered any solid leads. She felt duped.

Unknown to her, while Harmon had been supervising the grand jury, the federal authorities had been investigating him for drug crimes. Before the deaths of the boys in 1987, informants had reported him for buying and selling drugs and providing dealers with protection. In the middle of the night, Harmon and officers from the Benton Police Department kicked down doors to find the informants. He summoned the informants to testify at the grand jury he was supposed to be helping Linda with. He used the court process to find out the extent of their knowledge and to taint them as murder suspects in case they were ever subpoenaed to testify against him.

He also went after Jean Duffey, the head of a federally funded drug task force assigned to eliminate drugs in Arkansas. "That bitch is crazy," he told Linda. He swore that he would get her fired. As Jean learned more about his drug enterprise, he stepped up his campaign against her, culminating with a warrant being issued for her arrest. Fearing for her life and the lives of her informants, Duffey went into hiding, and eventually fled to Texas.

"I had no idea just how dangerous certain elected officials thought me to be," Jean said, "until a brutal media campaign launched against me. For months, there were daily allegations of everything from misspending funds to ordering illegal arrests. Every attempt was made to keep me from running the drug task force. We were even shut down completely for several weeks during a bogus state-police investigation. In spite of crippling disruptions, the task force was making significant discoveries about drug trafficking in central Arkansas, some of which led to the very people who were conducting the massive media campaign against me. We discovered that drug trafficking in central Arkansas was linked to public officials in frightening proportions. A great number of people came to me with testimony about astonishing criminal activity of very high-level public officials. Many were willing to testify before the federal grand jury. Although there was an abundance of evidence, and word kept reaching me from the grand jury that they were ready to indict, no indictments came … I can provide information that has tentacles to Governor Clinton's administration."

Jean and Linda were both filmed for a documentary called *The Clinton Chronicles*. When Jean watched Linda in the video, she realised that Linda had lost her faith in Harmon. Linda watched the video in a state of shock and bewilderment, as claims were made that Mena, Arkansas was a hub for international drug trafficking sponsored by the CIA and run with the approval and protection of the State of Arkansas under its governor, Bill Clinton. Could such grandiose claims be true, and if so, how did they factor into the death of her son? Jean and Linda met. They hit it off and shared their files. They decided to team up and work with the FBI to try to get the murders solved.

Some of the claims in the documentary did not seem so grandiose to Don Henry's father, who had his own theory about his son's murder, which was documented in the notes of Scott Llewelyn, a former drug task force member who had interviewed Curtis Henry. Llewelyn was convinced that Saline County was corrupt to the core and the deaths of the boys were being covered up. Curtis told Llewelyn, "... the boys were in the field when a cocaine drop was made from an airplane." He added that he had spent "night after night" at the crime scene, and had noticed a small airplane making landings every week between 2 AM and 3 AM on a grass airstrip by the tracks. Curtis had given this information to the Arkansas State Police, who never followed up on it.

Llewelyn wrote:

Curtis knows that there would have had to be someone present that Don felt comfortable around or he would have run off into the woods. Curtis is positive that no one would have been able to "get the drop" on Don out there because Don had hunted in that area for all his life and he was too good an outdoorsman to be caught if he didn't want to be. There is also the possibility that the boys had been put up to meeting the shipment and stealing some of it by someone who knew about the cocaine operation and was offering them money to do so and therefore the boys may have been a little too brazen in their attempt to get some of the shipment.

Either way, once the boys were apprehended, they were walked to the part of the tracks where they were laid, since it was close by. Curtis feels at this point the men who had the boys began to beat them and interrogate them as to who had sent them out there, who knew they were out there, or who the third boy was, if there indeed was a third person who managed to get away. Then Kevin was smashed in the head with Don's rifle and he fell to the ground, possibly dead at that point. Don took off running and was chased for about a hundred yards before being caught again. He was then stabbed from behind while maybe being held, when he did his "corkscrew" maneuver and came out of his shirt, turning it inside out. The stabbing either was that severe or he was knocked to the ground where his head was smashed open by one or several blows from his rifle.

Linda's hopes were further raised by a new officer, Deputy Brown, being assigned to investigate the boys' deaths. In May 1993, Brown interviewed Sharlene Wilson, one of Jean's confidential informants. Sharlene had "dated" Harmon – while he was married – who she described as "a big cocaine user." "He was good to me. He bought me clothes. He called me his little country bumpkin, but evidently I had an air of something he liked … He took care of me."

Her information led to Brown announcing to Linda that he had solved the case. Sharlene had been transporting bulk cocaine from Arkansas to the Cowboys Stadium in Texas, all without any interference from the authorities. Sometimes she had delivered it to Dan Harmon. Other times, Roger Clinton had picked up the heavy big bundles. She admitted being at the tracks on the night of the murders, with the prosecutor, Dan Harmon, the now deceased Keith McKaskle and two other men. The men were agitated because in the summer of 1987, one of their drug shipments had disappeared. On the night in question, Harmon had stationed his men to protect the area. In a car, Sharlene was high on drugs. She had been instructed to await the men's return. Hearing loud screams added to her terror. "There had been a small band of kids that had tried to already rip off the drop. There was supposed to be a drop of three to four pounds of coke and five pounds of weed. Several of the boys had got away, but they had caught two – Kevin Ives and Don Henry – one being deceased at that point." She claimed McKaskle had killed the other. When Harmon got in the car, there was blood all over his legs.

In 1991, Sharlene filled out a questionnaire:

Q. Tell us about your drug dealings with Dan Harmon.

A. He kept me high a lot. On occasion I would make specific drops to different areas for him. I got high with him a lot.

Q. If you were going to conduct an investigation on Dan Harmon, how would you do it?

A. I would go to his ex-wife Rebecca. Then I would check his money background with a fine-tooth comb. Then I would go through drug task force records to see who all they let go of on pay-offs, drugs, etc.

Q. List the five most important causes that would have led to Dan Harmon selling drugs and using drugs.

A. (1) His family history. (2) Letting people go that had enough money to buy him off. (3) Drugs confiscated but not actually being reported. (4) Letting big-time dealers off free. (5) Common knowledge of his use for years.

Q. Write in detail one drug deal you conducted with Dan Harmon.

A. Le Bistro Club, with Dan Harmon, Roger Clinton, and myself, known as the "Lady with the Snow," in 1978–79. One Saturday night we met in the parking lot and made an eight-ball exchange.

Q. Do you know who else deals drugs with Dan Harmon?

A. [Wilson listed four men.]

Q. While filling out this form, what were your emotions?

A. Scared but ready to come clean.

On the same day, Wilson filled out a second questionnaire:

Q. Tell us what you know about the circumstances that might have led to the deaths of Don Henry and Kevin Ives.

A. I feel that Dan Harmon has more knowledge of the two boys' deaths than he has ever told. In late summer, in August, I drove Harmon to Alexander to meet with, I assume, Keith McKaskle to make a pick-up. A couple of days later they have on TV the two boys' deaths, supposedly ran over by a train.

Q. Write in detail what happened on August 22, 1987, from when you got up till you went to bed that evening.

A. I got up, did some coke and crystal mixed called high-balling, cleaned up the house, left, and went to find some more. Later on that afternoon Dan wanted to show me a house and we went in his car and looked at a house in Alexander. We came back to my house and I ate a sandwich and put on more makeup. Dan asked me to take a ride back out to Alexander with him and asked me to pull down, I think, the old quarry road and wait. I got high while waiting on him to come back and when he came back he said, "Let's go!" We left and went back to my house. He told me to take a shower. I asked him if anything was wrong and he said NO. I took my shower, went and laid down, and we made love, and he showered and left. I went to sleep.

Q. What would you say if it was later determined that you lied on this form?

A. No way.

Q. While filling out this form, what were your emotions?

A. Pissed off.

Q. Were you afraid while completing this form?

A. Yes, because Harmon doesn't like me.

Things didn't end well for Sharlene. She had been promised that her name and those of the other witnesses would never be revealed, but someone in the US Attorney's office had given Harmon the list. After that, the witnesses started to die.

Without knocking, state police entered Sharlene's home. Arresting her, Harmon said, "Bitch, I told you if you ever brought my name up or brought anything up about the past dealings that we've had that I'd take you down. You're going to prison. I'm gonna put you in prison." She was arrested for possession of cannabis and methamphetamine that they had allegedly found inside, and was sentenced as a first-time offender to thirty-one years.

The drug allegations against Harmon were correct. In 1997, he was convicted of one count of racketeering, three counts of conspiring to commit extortion and one count of conspiring to possess and distribute cannabis. He had been using his position as a prosecutor to run a drug operation involved in distributing cocaine and methamphetamine, extorting protection money from dealers and reselling drugs seized by the police. He was never charged with any involvement in the murders of the boys on the tracks.

Disgruntled at the lack of progress, Linda demanded a meeting with the FBI. With her husband, she met two FBI agents and a lawyer in Little Rock.

"I think I know why you're here," an agent said in a cold tone, "but why don't you go ahead and tell me anyway."

"We want to know the status of the case." She read a comment made by an agent in February 1994: if she would just sit back and let the FBI do its job, the case would be solved by the end of the year. "Well, it's the end of 1995."

The agent responded that the FBI had found no evidence of murder. The two-year FBI investigation was closing – just like all of the other investigations. She almost fell out of her chair. "It might be time for you to consider that a crime was not committed."

Linda was shaking and crying and having difficulty breathing. She threw down her pencil and snatched her purse. "I don't have to listen to this bullshit." She stormed out of the room and took a tranquilliser.

CHAPTER 12
DEA AGENT TORTURED TO DEATH

On March 6, 1985, Mexican TV announced that Kiki's decaying body had been found buried at a ranch. Before the discovery, the MJFP had slaughtered everyone at the ranch, including women who appeared to have been shot in the back.

Years later in the Witness Protection Program in America, a Mexican ex-cop detailed some of what had happened. Raul had been a state policeman in the house on Lope de Vega Street on February 7, 1985 during the torture. Before the kidnapping, approximately forty people were present at the property owned by Don Neto, including Caro Quintero, Félix Gallardo, bodyguards, DFS agents and state police. At 12:30 PM, a worker from the American consulate arrived and everybody focused on the kidnapping. The consulate worker told one of Don Neto's top hit men that everything was ready according to the schedule "I gave you earlier." He said that Camarena would take the south-door exit on Calle Libertad.

Four vehicles headed to the consulate: one as a getaway, the others for surveillance. Raul was in the vehicle with the consulate worker until after 2 PM.

"Look, there he is," the worker said in Spanish.

Raul and two others approached Kiki.

"The comandante wants to see you," said Don Neto's hit man, flashing a DFS badge.

"When we are summoned," Kiki objected, "and our services are needed it is done through …" With a gun shoved into his ribs, he was thrown into the back of a car. Raul pulled Kiki's jacket over his head for the ride back to Don Neto's house.

On a radio, the lead hit man announced, "The doctor has seen the patient." In the house, he brought Kiki to a patio, where Caro Quintero, Don Neto and a Mexican Army colonel were sitting. "You said it could not be done, but here he is." Blindfolded, Kiki must have realised that he hadn't been taken to a police station to meet the commander.

Caro Quintero stood. "I told you, you son-of-a-bitch, that you were going to fall into my hands."

"I'm of more use to you alive than dead."

Their familiarity puzzled Raul.

"Why did you betray me?" asked Caro Quintero's half-brother.

"What are you talking about?" Kiki asked.

"You got a lot of money."

"I never got any money." Investigators working for Operation Leyenda would later learn that Caro Quintero had dispatched $4 million to Kiki, which had been pocketed by the delivery men who were Mexican federal agents. Kiki was oblivious.

"Let me talk to Caro. We understand each other."

"How do you know you are talking to Caro Quintero?"

"Who else would have me detained like this?"

With an arm around Kiki, Caro Quintero escorted him into a room, accompanied by a DFS commander with a tape recorder. (From an informant, the CIA learned that Kiki's interrogation had been taped. The Mexican police had not acknowledged that any tape existed. When pushed by the DEA, they admitted it had been found in the home of one of Caro Quintero's business partners, whom they had arrested, but they couldn't release it because it was too sensitive and in the custody of the head of the Camarena investigation. Under more pressure, the police agreed to play the tape at the Attorney General's office. The DEA could listen and formally request a copy provided its existence was never disclosed.)

In and out of the room, Raul claimed to have seen a man who went by the name Max Gomez a.k.a. Félix Rodríguez of the CIA, a close friend of George HW Bush. In *American Made*, I wrote about the role of Félix Rodríguez in the importation of cocaine to Mena, Arkansas. Money from the cocaine operation was used by the Reagan–Bush administration to finance an illegal war in Nicaragua. In his book *Compromised*, Terry Reed described his work with Rodríguez and Barry Seal, who flew cocaine in and weapons out for the CIA. Terry Reed quit working for the CIA after he had been assigned to Mexico, where he discovered that the Agency was involved in shipping cocaine into America.

Three different interrogators asked Kiki about the DEA's mission. They demanded to know who the Americans were investigating and they wanted names and addresses. The torture began with slaps and punches to Kiki's neck and face. He remained blindfolded, with his hands tied behind his back. They broke his nose and the bone above his eyes. When he was unconscious, a doctor arrived. They washed off some blood, threw cold water onto his face and he revived. They wanted names and to know how the DEA obtained information. Electrical wires tied to his testicles delivered shocks, while he screamed and flailed. A screw was positioned on his skull which turned and bore into the bone.

"Leave my family alone," he repeated. "Please don't hurt my family."

While they asked for names and addresses, there were more slaps, punches, electric shocks and teeth removed. Men jumped off a bed onto his back, breaking his ribs, which pierced his lungs. A red-hot iron rod inserted into his anus created a new level of screams. Judges and police who eventually listened to the tape recording of the torture reported that it had provoked vomiting and sleepless nights.

Don Neto entered the room, only to be told that the torture had gone too far, and that Kiki was on the verge of death. "This was not the plan," he said angrily at Caro Quintero. He stormed out and headed for another property, where in his own entryway, he fired an AK-47 out of frustration.

A doctor arrived, examined Kiki and told Caro Quintero that Kiki would die unless he went to a hospital. "I don't care," Caro

Quintero said. "He will pay for double-crossing me. Keep him alive so that he can answer more questions."

According to Raul, nearby in the living room were Cabinet Secretary Bartlett Díaz, Defence Secretary General Juan Arévalo Gardoqui, Interpol Head Miguel Aldana Ibarra, Félix Rodríguez of the CIA, DFS Head Sergio Espino Verdin and Juan Ramón Matta-Ballesteros, a Honduran trafficker and airline company owner who provided flight services to the CIA.

Stepping out to the kitchen, Raul heard someone say, "As we found out through our own means, I wanted you to hear the same words from his own mouth. That they were going to put a stop to drug trafficking in the state of Jalisco."

"The bodies of Camarena and Zavala must be well hidden," the Defence Secretary said.

"Things are going well and in the right direction," the Cabinet Secretary said.

"Don't worry," Caro Quintero said. "We're going to kill all of them anyway. You [the Cabinet Secretary] are going to make it all the way to the top. We need you at the top."

On February 9 at 10 AM, Don Neto returned to the house to find Kiki dead. His argument with Caro Quintero grew so hostile that bodyguards for both sides drew guns. After everybody calmed down, Kiki was buried in a park on the edge of the city. His pilot friend was buried alive. After the Mexican authorities reported the US backlash to the cartel, the bodies were moved to another state for the Americans to find them, which would take two months.

In Guadalajara, DEA staff converged from all over the world. The US Customs Commissioner had every vehicle entering America from Mexico stopped and searched, which caused traffic to back up for miles, halted commerce and drew the focus of senior politicians on both sides of the border.

According to the journalist Charles Bouden, a tall white man called Lawrence Harrison had been working for Don Neto and the CIA, who had embedded him into the DFS. Raul corroborated that he had seen Harrison lots of times in Don Neto's house. After attending the University of California at Berkeley, Harrison had been recruited by the CIA in 1968. Teaching English at the University of Guadalajara, he had befriended and done legal work for leftist students. Every time he had reported about a radical that student would disappear. Working for the DFS in Guadalajara, he had guarded drug shipments and was hired by the cartel as a communications expert. Eventually, he moved into Don Neto's house.

In 1990 in LA, Harrison testified at one of the trials concerning Kiki's murder. He said he had listened to thousands of cartel communications and had attended the parties. Asked about the DFS badges owned by Don Neto and his men, Harrison said, "I saw it first … in the last part of 1983. They used it to sniff cocaine in their office."

In 1989, during a DEA briefing, Harrison said, "By that time, I'd figured it out that it was a very strict cooperation between the government and the traffickers. By that time, it would have been very difficult to get out. I mean real difficult."

Harrison had asked Don Neto, "Why don't you just get out of this business? You have enough money. Why don't you just take it all and leave?" The drug lord had replied that there wouldn't be any trouble with the Americans. They could do anything they wanted with the Americans and the Cubans, who they were trying to get to cooperate with refuelling stops.

The DEA man hunting for those responsible, Hector Berrellez, believed Harrison. Working in Mazatlán, Berrellez had received information about large planes landing in the night – just like the locals had reported in Mena, Arkansas – and after informing the Agency, he was told by the DEA to ignore them. During Operation Leyenda, he had received numerous reports of flights and airfields, including that CIA-leased planes were flying cocaine into and weapons out of air force bases in places including Homestead, Florida and Tucson's Marana airfield. To double-check Harrison's credibility, he sent him for a polygraph.

Over three days at the DEA in Washington, Harrison passed every test.

In a DEA-6 report, Berrellez documented the connections between the cartel, the DFS, the Mexican government and the CIA. The response warned him to stick to investigating Kiki's murder, which was his job, and that he was never again to investigate a sister agency. While the DEA fully understood the gravity of what he had reported, such information must never be filed in any DEA-6s, which would be legally accessible to the defence in court cases. The information could be included in secret internal DEA memos, and a task force would be created to investigate the claims. On the assumption that the information about the CIA would be investigated, Berrellez filed secret internal memos.

Harrison stated that Don Neto believed that Kiki would only be interrogated and not killed. That death had happened because Caro Quintero had been unable to stick to the plan. The Guadalajara Cartel lacked information on the DEA. The drug lords would have never figured out Kiki's role, unless someone had informed on him.

"I'll tell you what," Harrison said, "other authorities were there during the Camarena interrogation. They had to have said to them, look this is the guy that screwed you … This is the one that wants to put you away." Throughout his career he had never seen the DFS or the drug lords tape record anything. He doubted that they could even use a recorder. He emphasised that they had to be taping it for somebody else.

"I don't think the CIA would've gone directly. They would've sent the Mexicans. The CIA are not so stupid, [that] they were gonna go in there themselves. They are gonna send some of their own minions in there."

DEA Administrator Jack Lawn ordered Berrellez to get the doctor present at Kiki's torture into America, so that he could be arrested. The Mexicans refused to deliver Dr Humberto Álvarez Macháin from Guadalajara. In April 1990, the doctor was thrown onto the tarmac from a plane in El Paso, and arrested by Berrellez.

In 1993, President Clinton told the president of Mexico how upset he was over the DEA's role in the kidnapping of the doctor. The new administration wanted to extradite him back to Mexico, where he would now face certain death.

With the information compiled by Berrellez having established all of the senior players in Kiki's murder, including three witnesses who put the Mexican Cabinet Secretary in Don Neto's house, Berrellez found himself ridiculed by his superiors for claiming that Mexico's political leaders were mixing with the traffickers. Berrellez was put under investigation for coaching witnesses to commit perjury, and threatened with extradition to Mexico for kidnapping the doctor. With his world destroyed, he turned to alcohol. At home, he repeatedly listened to the Kiki tapes.

In 1984, Berrellez had testified on behalf of a wealthy individual who coordinated business between the Mexican president and the Gulf Cartel. They had bonded during a gunfight in Sinaloa. Guillermo González Calderoni had fled to America with $400 million, and Mexico wanted him back. Testimony from Berrellez prevented his extradition, so as a return favour, Calderoni explained the real motivation behind the death of Kiki.

One goal of Kiki's Operation Padrino was to seize the drug money, but the beneficiaries of the cash extended way beyond the traffickers. As well as the senior politicians, police and army, money was being used for weapons and support to fund the illegal war in Nicaragua, a cause cherished by the Reagan administration. Calderoni advised Berrellez to drop the matter: "My son, the CIA killed Camarena. Hector, listen, the CIA was working with the drug guys to get money for the Contras. Félix Rodríguez [Max Gomez] was working with Juan Ramón Matta-Ballesteros. Kiki was to be picked up, but they went too far and they killed him."

After his career had been destroyed, Berrellez read a story in the *San Jose Mercury News* about cocaine, the Contras and the CIA. Incredulous that it had been published, he met Gary Webb at a steakhouse in LA in 1998. "I want you to know that everything you wrote was true. I have a CIA operative who will tell you it was true." He introduced Webb to Lawrence Harrison. Over drinks, they talked for hours. After getting hugged goodbye, Gary cried.

In October 2013 on Fox News, Berrellez used the story about Caro Quintero getting released from Mexican prison to describe what he had learned during Operation Leyenda. Although it became big news in Mexico, no one in America followed up. His former boss and head of the DEA provided a quote: "As a youth I read Aesop's Fables. This is another fable not worthy of individuals who would serve in the DEA."

CHAPTER 13
CIA COCAINE PILOTS

The CIA-facilitated trafficking was boosting the supply of cocaine across America, from Rick Ross in LA to the drug drops in Arkansas, at the time of the death of the boys on the tracks. While visiting a Nicaraguan prison, Gary Webb had been told that US pilots were transporting the cocaine. One was Beau Abbott.

As a successful businessman, Beau sold Olivetti equipment and used machines in Europe. During the Cold War, he was approached by the CIA, who gave him equipment to sell to Russians to track where it went. When the CIA warned him that his cover was blown, he shut down his operation. Having moved back to the US in 1971, he continued to work for Olivetti. In 1972, he set up a business importing motorbikes and parts. After his business was robbed, the Houston police told him to contact the DEA because they suspected the involvement of a drug gang. To help catch the culprits, he agreed to work for the DEA.

Over time, Beau met various officials at the Houston DEA office. At that time, the heroin-smuggling operation of Aristotle Onassis was a big case. Beau noticed that the DEA office was only interested in the smaller players. When it came to the top echelon, the DEA dropped the cases.

"Me being a young man believing in my country," Beau said, "believing that I was doing the right thing, believing that I was helping the people of America stay away from illegal drugs, this really confused and confounded me." He was told that the CIA was involved and there were national security interests, which he accepted and he continued his work. The DEA sent him to Mexico, West Texas and across the US. In Mexico, as a paid undercover agent, he helped to break up heroin-smuggling operations.

The DEA asked him to become a pilot to help infiltrate drug gangs. In 1978, he was sent to the FAA Academy in Oklahoma City, where he was trained in DEA aircraft, how to make soft-field and short-field landings and ocean survival and jungle survival in case he crashed. His undercover assignments extended worldwide.

In 1979 in Bolivia, it dawned that the policy of the DEA was only to bust the small players. He discovered that the world's biggest cocaine supplier was not only shipping to the Cali and Medellín Cartels, but also the CIA. "My job was to notify all the large-scale Bolivian smugglers that were working for the CIA on impending arrests and drug busts in Bolivia, so the higher echelons would not be arrested. In particular the Roberto Suárez organisation was a protected organisation ... The CIA eventually started shipping ... tons of cocaine into Panama into Tocumen Airport ... They were flying LAB-marked 727s and 707s, and they would pull into a warehouse district on the backside of Tocumen Airport, where they'd be protected by the Panamanian Defence Forces, where they used forklifts to unload pallets of cocaine. This cocaine was flown into Nicaragua and Belize. The planes were refuelled there and then it was flown into the United States ... Arms were also put in these warehouses ... and flown to the Contras in Nicaragua."

What Beau had learned made sense in the context of Gary Webb's discovery that the money Rick Ross had used to purchase cocaine was flowing back to the Contras by way of arms. Beau knew several of the pilots flying drugs and arms for the CIA.

Eventually, Beau was assigned to fly planes into Arkansas. "I had flown money out of Arkansas and Eastern Arkansas, just west of Memphis, near a little town called Marianna ... Also, I had flown arms and money out of this area into Belize and Nicaragua and Panama. And, at one instance, I picked up a load of cocaine out of this warehouse in Panama and flew it on a plane that was provided to me by the DEA out of Panama, and I flew it into this airstrip. A DEA agent out of Memphis met me. The airport was protected by Arkansas State Police ..." He started to believe that transporting drugs was the true reason why the DEA had trained him for short-field and soft-field landings.

Flying cocaine into Arkansas and weapons out, he worried that he knew too much about CIA–DEA drug smuggling, and that he might be viewed as a liability and end up dead. He began gathering information: locations for flying arms, drugs and money throughout Central America and Arkansas, Texas and Louisiana, the names of banks ... He gave the information to his Swedish fiancée in Stockholm, who put it in a safety deposit box in Germany. He even had tape recordings of General Noriega talking to CIA officials about drugs and arms smuggling. If the CIA ever made a move against him, he hoped to use the information to secure his freedom.

"I began to wonder what the real agenda of the United States government was. At first, I believed there was a War on Drugs. That they were trying to stop drugs and protect the people ... Over a period of time, I began to question what I was doing and I wanted out. My Swedish girlfriend convinced me to stop working for the DEA and the CIA, to take up Swedish citizenship, and to completely cease and desist from all US activity and never come back into the US again."

After he stated that he wanted to quit, his CIA contacts in Panama said that he couldn't leave because he knew too much, he was too valuable and had made too many connections. Insisting until they gave in, he stopped his undercover work and married his Swedish fiancée.

Three weeks later, he learned from the Aspen police that people with high-powered rifles had been spotted on his land, watching his house, and they weren't hunters. Realising there was a hit on him, he flew to Houston in one of his private planes. He told his ex-wife he was moving to Sweden and said goodbye to his daughter. When he stepped from the house and walked down the street, he was surrounded by plainclothes agents. While a helicopter chased him, he ran for his life and hid in an empty building under construction. When he saw the helicopter lights at the end of the building, he bolted from the other side. He heard one of his pursuers say, "Don't shoot him in the back." He ran through a bayou and escaped.

Later that night, men claiming to be DEA agents came to his ex-wife's house with an arrest warrant for him. They searched the premises and left. His parents reported that an agent had come by the house, but they had denied knowing where Beau was.

A week later, he contacted an attorney in Dallas, who called the DEA three times in a week, offering to surrender him. They said they didn't want him. The attorney called the DPS, who also didn't want him. "It was clear to me that whoever wanted me was going to kill me."

Eventually, they caught up with him in Cancun, Mexico. "I was accosted, beaten, wrapped in chains by thugs that the US government had hired. I was brought back to the United States on an airplane in chains. I think that's called kidnapping." He learned that other DEA officials had been arrested. They were the lucky ones. Other CIA contacts who he had flown drugs, arms and money with had been murdered. One former colleague had his throat slit and his tongue extracted – a Colombian necktie – and another was fed poison in a peanut-butter sandwich in a US jail (as described in Chapter 7).

While Beau awaited trial in San Antonio, the prison chaplain summoned him to the chapel to receive bad news. His Swedish wife, the mother of his child, had been found on a railroad track in Germany. Just like with the murders of Kevin Ives and Don Henry, the official verdict was that she had committed suicide. He knew that his wife's death was a message that if he went to trial, he would end up dead, so he pled guilty for smuggling cocaine from Panama. The press attempted to find him, but he was moved from jail to jail. When they finally tracked him down at Federal

Correctional Institution, Bastrop in 1983–84, the warden told Beau that there was a murder contract out on him, and that he had to go to solitary confinement for his own protection.

After ninety days in lockdown, he was offered a new trial. His previous judge had quit the profession and his lawyer had suffered a nervous breakdown. Due to threats to his family, he pled guilty again. "When your life's on the line, you don't put up a very good fight in court."

After serving three years, he was released in 1986. Due to his criminal record, he could only get a job washing planes. He was going to testify at the General Noriega trial about the drug flights, but before that could happen, he was taken to jail with two other men without any of them being arrested. The authorities searched the plane he had been washing and several cars and homes. Unable to find any evidence of illegal activity, the police had to release all of the men.

As Beau was walking out of the jail, a DPS officer said, "No. Hold this guy because we're gonna get his parole violated for being in Austin without permission from his parole officer."

"That's not your job," Beau said, wanting to go back to Dallas to talk to his parole officer himself. Again, he was jailed without being arrested. The next day, they got an arrest warrant.

Ninety days later, he was taken into a back room at Federal Correctional Institution, Bastrop near Austin, and charged with being out of bounds. He pled guilty and accepted a penalty of sixty days. Leaving the room, he felt that the parole-commission members were up to something. He was brought back and told that he had an additional charge of smuggling drugs and conspiracy utilising his flying ability, and that he was facing a twenty-month sentence. Specifically, he was charged with transporting an unknown drug through an unknown country with unknown co-conspirators.

He protested that it was a ruse to keep him from testifying at the Noriega trial and embarrassing the US government. Later, he appealed the conviction. He asked for the specific drug he was smuggling, the countries he was smuggling it through, the names of the co-conspirators, the specific airplane and when he had done it. The parole commission said that his conviction was affirmed because he had failed to convince them in his appeal that he was not doing what he was accused of. "This seemed like an Orwellian thought crime."

He wrote down information about drugs and arms flights, and the CIA's involvement. An inmate worker smuggled it out of prison and mailed it from a post office box on a golf course where he was a cleaner. Beau confirmed over the monitored prison phone line that the letter had arrived at the designated address. He wanted the information turned over to General Noriega's lawyer and the press. But the DEA raided the recipient's home, and confiscated Beau's notes. Even though no drugs or any evidence of criminal activity were found at the house, the recipient of the letter was charged with conspiracy to smuggle drugs. A high-profile lawyer got the case against the recipient dismissed, and filed pre-trial motions to get the letter back, but it was never returned.

The authorities moved Beau to the United States Medical Center for Federal Prisoners in Springfield, Missouri, where he was housed with the mentally ill. Under protest, he was given a forensic evaluation. It was discovered that he had caught TB in one of the jails. He was given medicine to prevent the further onset of TB. While at a prison transportation stopover on the way to Alabama for a competency hearing, he was given TB medicine in a small county jail. When the elderly nurse turned her back, he stole his medical file, which stated, "No psychosis found." He mailed the file to author Rodney Stich, who documented Beau's story in his book, *Defrauding America*. A second psychiatric exam-ination was ordered. He protested, but ultimately participated in the examination, which was less than two hours.

In court, he distrusted his government-appointed attorney, who he told to sit down and shut up. Beau thought he did an excellent job interrogating the psychiatrist who had declared him insane. The judge agreed with the psychiatrist that Beau was insane, and sent him back to the prison in Springfield for a 120-day mental observation. Beau said that fraud was being committed in the court because he had a copy of the original diagnosis, stating no psychosis was found. The judge responded by committing Beau to a second 120-day observation. The psychiatrist said that he was hopelessly insane, incurable and unable to go to trial. They obviously didn't want him to say anything in court about the DEA and CIA drug trafficking.

Told that all of his future court hearings would be handled by mail, he was assigned a dangerousness hearing. A committee at the prison in Springfield was designated to determine if he was a danger to society and whether he might injure himself or someone or property if he were ever released. The committee found that he was no danger. So that he would never be able to state anything for the public record, his case was dismissed by the judge in the interest of justice and he was freed.

After his release, he discovered that the DPS officer behind his latest conspiracy charge to smuggle drugs had been arrested for involvement in a conspiracy to smuggle twenty-five tons of cocaine. The pilot in the conspiracy was alleging it was a CIA operation. In an appeal demanding a new hearing, Beau notified the US parole commission, pointing out that the DPS officer was charged with committing perjury in court. The parole commission refused to grant him a new hearing.

He called his mother-in-law in Sweden to try to get information to see his child. Angry at him, she said that he had caused her daughter's death. In a roundabout way, he knew that she was right. The mother-in-law said that her daughter had extracted the information about CIA drug trafficking from his safety deposit box in Berlin. With the intention of flying back to Stockholm that night, she was on her way to give the contents of the box to the press in East Berlin. She told her mother not to feed the baby because her breasts hurt. She wanted the baby to be hungry when she got home. She never made it to the media conference.

Beau had come to believe that the attitude of the DEA and

CIA people he had worked with was that drugs equals money equals power, and that if anyone was going to make money off drugs it should be the US government.

Chip Tatum's story is similar to Beau's. Formerly a CIA deep-cover agent for twenty-five years, Chip flew cocaine into Arkansas. Realising he was expendable, he stored documents and conversations he had recorded that incriminated the CIA and top officials such as George HW Bush and Bill Clinton. When he refused to surrender the documents to the CIA, he was imprisoned for embezzlement and so was his wife. In jail, he broke the leg of a Mexican Mafia debt collector, who subsequently put a hit on him. Realising that if he died, the documents would be released, the CIA had him released from the prison.

In an interview with Ted Gunderson, former head of the FBI in LA, Chip was asked, "Do you have any direct knowledge that Clinton was aware of the drug operation coming into Arkansas?"

"When I was at Fort Campbell, Kentucky," Chip said, "I actually flew several missions carrying medical coolers again with money and drugs in it to Arkansas. It was delivered to us by the 3/24th Med Battalion out of South America. It was flown by C-130 to Fort Campbell, marked medical supplies. Donor organs this particular one was marked. And we were advised to give it to Dr Lasater at Little Rock Air Force Base … We found a large sum of money and kilos of cocaine in one cooler. In the other cooler, we found all cocaine. Those two coolers were picked up by Dr Lasater, who actually ended up being, as we found out in later years, a man called Dan Lasater, who was convicted for trafficking cocaine in Arkansas, however he was pardoned by Bill Clinton."

"Did you have any information that Clinton had direct knowledge of that?" Ted asked.

"We had to wait over an hour and a half for Dr Lasater … He showed up in an entourage of vehicles. There was a van. There was a stretch limo and an unmarked police car. Coming out of the stretch limo, Dr Lasater came forward. He had two people with him. One stayed in the car. One came over. He introduced the one that walked over to the aircraft to pick up the coolers as the Governor of Arkansas, and the Governor of Arkansas extended his hand. That's the first time I shook the hand of William Jefferson Clinton. He wanted to let me know that the people of Arkansas appreciated me bringing those donor organs."

"He didn't know you'd looked into them [the coolers]?"

"He didn't know I'd looked into them."

CHAPTER 14
CARTEL PILOT'S DEATHBED CONFESSION

Shortly before he died in Arizona, I chatted on the phone with a former American pilot, who flew loads for the cartel, but switched sides and ended up saving the life of an agent who had been kidnapped in Mexico like Kiki Camarena. Speaking to the pilot was how I first learned of Kiki's story. As a privacy measure, I shall refer to him as Dan. He requested that I not publish any of the information he provided until after his death.

"Guess what?" Dan said in August 2013.

"What?" I said.

"There's a guy named Caro Quintero, who was the one that helped kidnap the DEA agent, Kiki Camarena, who was tortured to death and they recorded it. He got out on a technicality. Arrested in Costa Rica, he ended up in Mexico, where he corrupted them. They've got a warrant out for him again here. He's got to be sixty to sixty-five. Yes, it was just a few days ago that they let him go."

"He sounds like a slippery character."

"He's a cold-blooded murderer. I'm surprised he stayed in for as long as he did. But I don't think he thought this through: he's a liability to his buddies now. His own friends are probably going to kill him. Look at all the heat he brought on them by doing something like that, when he wasn't supposed to. You don't torture a DEA agent to death and then be stupid enough to record it and let the tape be found. By far, that's not the first person he had killed. I think we had him tagged for seventeen murders of US citizens. And that was just US citizens. Some were just tourists at the wrong spot. These two tourists walked into a bar. He owned quite a bit of property. He'd been up all night getting high and when he's high, he's crazy."

"Was he coming after you at one point?"

"Kind of the other way around. We're not the best of friends. But, like I said, I don't think he thought this through. At a certain point, you become a liability. Because of his actions, he brought the wrath of God down on a few people."

"In Mexico?"

"And here."

"I'm surprised he's still walking around."

"He may not be. The article was only a few days old. If he lasts long, I'd be surprised. At some point, if they can't get him over on this side [the USA], we'll kill him because you are not going to do that to a US police officer and ever live it down. The message has always been very clear about that. He thinks he's the king of the world, which is probably going to cause him to pop his head up somewhere, and when it comes up, it's likely to get lopped off."

"So how come you were on his case?"

"I don't like murderers any more than anyone else. I don't like innocent Americans getting killed. Some were Jehovah's Witnesses who just happened to be in the wrong neighbourhood after he had been up all night, and without a word, he killed them."

"Did you get close to him?"

"Well, yeah. I went after him at that point and helped to bring him back."

"How long did he serve?"

"Over twenty years, but he's not done yet. He's either going to go to jail here because they already have a warrant for him or he is simply just going to get killed. By the way, none of what I just told you is something that I would tell anybody but you."

"I understand."

"It's a sensitive issue. This guy's too crazy. I got enough problems without adding to it."

On the next call, Dan said that he had relocated to Mesa.

"Mesa is where my friends ... Well, they're not my friends anymore. It's where they got caught with 1,100 pounds of cocaine."

"What kind of sentences did they get?"

"I don't know that they were ever even charged with it. The drivers and people like that were. These are the same people that killed Kiki Camarena."

"The guy you mentioned on the last call, Caro Quintero?"

"Yes, he's still out and breathing."

"How are you keeping abreast of this?"

"Oh, I have my ways. His release was headlines in the newspapers here because that is a pretty sore spot with people. You don't take a US cop and torture them to death, and I don't care where in the world you are, and expect to ever live it down. The United States will chase you until the day you die and even help speed that day along. The cocaine was lost in the 1980s and another 1,100 pounds was lost in Kingman, Arizona. Same people. When I talked to the cartel about that, I said, 'Look, there are only two people in the United States that knew where that plane was going to land, and I'm one of them.' They knew the other guy, too. They said, 'No. No. The problem is down here, and we're going to find the problem and solve it.' The next thing I know is that I read in the newspaper that they have kidnapped Kiki Camarena, a block from the US consulate in downtown Guadalajara. You know, a consulate is one step down from an embassy. As it turns out, the co-pilot on those loads was playing both sides of the fence. He was giving information, while still flying and being paid for it. So the cartel snatched him up first, and he gave up the DEA agent who was working with him, then they snatched up Kiki Camarena."

"Is that because they were holding him responsible for the drug seizures?"

"Well, yeah, but you've got to understand that we [the cartel] had already got away with it eleven times on that runway, so it was bound to happen, sooner or later. We actually believed at first what they'd printed in the paper on the first load by Globe [in Arizona] that somebody had just seen a plane land on a remote airstrip that ranchers use, and called the sheriff. But when it happened again in Kingman, the story became a little unbelievable. They said a DEA agent was on vacation trapping fur. I don't know if you've ever been to Kingman, Arizona but there's no fur to be trapped up there. But I had no idea they were going to do it. I read about it in the newspaper just like everybody else. There's a whole lot of interest in Caro Quintero. The technicality they released him on doesn't make any sense, even by Mexican standards. They were paid off. He's got five brothers. They are all called Caro Quintero, too, so you have to identify him by his first name, which is Rafael."

"How were you instrumental in his arrest?"

After a long pause, Dan said, "I helped him get on the plane. He was a little reluctant. I told him, 'Don't worry, you won't need any luggage. Your bags will follow you.' The murder of Kiki Camarena was more of a financial decision in a way, but also ego on Caro Quintero's part. It was a total of 5,000 pounds of coke. That's quite a bit of money, especially back then. It was $35,000 a kilo."

"What was the total street value of the loss?"

"The government put some kind of crazy number on it: hundreds of millions. It wasn't that, but it was still, I'd say realistically, at least $100 million. If they had stuck to killing Mexican citizens, they would have got away with it. If they'd have stopped at the co-pilot, who was a Mexican citizen, they would have been all right, but once they killed the DEA agent, tortured him to death and recorded it, they'd gone too far. I don't know how we got our hands on that recording, but we got it. It's not a pleasant thing to hear. In the end, he's begging them to kill him. He knew he was going to die and he just wanted to get it over with. That's how bad they hurt him."

"Why would they record it?"

"I don't know."

"Maybe as a warning to other DEA agents not to mess with them?"

"It could be, but it's hard to say what goes through Caro Quintero's mind because he's crazy. I'm sure in his mind, he had some justifiable reason for doing it or something made sense to him, but I can't fathom what it would be. Talk about evidence! What better evidence?"

"How come he never got killed in prison?"

"He has more money than God even though he's not the leader of that organisation. He carried power with him into the prison system. The head of this organisation was Miguel Félix Gallardo. His nephew is the one that killed those seventeen people in Tijuana. It was a war with mostly dead bad guys, but they got pretty crazy by leaving dead bodies on the streets and cutting people's heads off after they were dead. It all took place down there, but Tijuana is pretty damn close to the United States. We talked about those Jehovah's Witnesses. They were just minding their own business and he killed them. With Félix's nephew, it was a power-play of some kind, but all it did was draw attention to them. The United States put a $5-million bounty on him."

"Look at all of the people getting killed over the black market in drugs."

"It's like a war zone down there. I wouldn't recommend anyone to go to Mexico right now. Drug trade or not, it's just not a safe place to be. They seem to move around. For a while, Colombia was the kidnapping capital of the world. Every once in a while, one country becomes a lot more dangerous than the other ones and right now it's Mexico."

"Are the Mexican cartels the most dangerous Mafia in the world?"

"They are. Everybody hates them because they go after people's families, too, which you just don't do. Shit, they went into a drug-rehab place and tried to recruit people to bring drugs into the states, and when they wouldn't do it, they killed all of the people in the drug rehab. They made a big deal about, 'Oh, we have a new president coming!' and blah blah blah. 'Things are going to be better. He's not going to put up with this.' Well, a week before the actual election, we had a film of him accepting a $6 million bribe in cash from a cartel."

"Which president was that?"

"The one before this one. We are giving money to them as well to fight drugs and for other reasons, so they're getting money from us on one side and the cartel's giving them money on the other side. Most of the time you see these busts down there now. It's staged just to keep the United States happy. Everybody contributes a little dope, and they make a big deal out of the bust. Once in a while they make a legitimate big bust. I think they got seventeen tons of cocaine from one spot not long ago. That's a chunk of change there."

"But then don't they just turn around and sell it through other avenues?"

"Correct."

"It's like a theatre game."

"It's pretty sick. There is no reason to sell poison."

"The US consumes more than any other country."

"We need to recognise it for what it is," Dan said. "Most of these guys who are hooked on drugs are not real criminals. I mean they'd be perfectly content to stay at home and watch TV. It's the need for money that drives them out to commit these crimes because of the price of the drugs."

"If they decriminalised it, would that go away?"

"The crime aspect would get its legs knocked out from underneath it. And eventually, a lot of the problems would go away because if the people can get something better quality for next to nothing, they are going to go there. All you're doing is changing who the dealer is and the dealer would be the United States. You'd know who the people were every day, and you could make it real clear to them that if they even got arrested for shoplifting or jay-walking, you'd cut them off, and you'd soon see some crime-free people."

"Is there a vested interest in keeping the crime going?"

"Yes, and not just from the cartels. Keep in mind how many

people the United States is employing in this supposed War on Drugs. Thousands upon thousands would have to find something else to do. There's a lot of things they could be doing that would be more useful. They could reallocate all of those resources. It's a war they are never going to win, so why not just control the market."

"With 9/11, one of the reasons the feds gave for not listening to potential terrorists was that they were all listening to drug dealers. That was using up all of their resources."

"Right. Since 9/11 happened, they backed off and got real crazy about the terrorists."

On the next phone call, Dan said, "The big thing here now is these damn pills: OxyContin and prescription pills."

"From Mexico?"

"A lot of them come from here. You can doctor swap. You go to one doctor and get a script for thirty of them and then you go and fake the same symptoms to another doctor. There's enough doctors around that don't have any scruples that let that happen, so it's not all coming from Mexico now. They'll probably find a way to get into it. Making pills isn't that hard at all if you've ever seen a machine. It's getting the precursor chemicals. You pour them into the machine, which automatically mixes it and pills start pouring out of the other side."

"Did you never think about getting into that line of work?"

"No. The only reason I know about it is because a real-estate guy in Scottsdale owed me money, and he wanted to pay it back with a machine in this building that they owned. I didn't do it. He had twenty sacks of Quaaludes that this machine had made. There must have been 100,000 Quaaludes in those bags. That's one drug you can't get anymore. Did you ever hear the story of how that came about?"

"No."

"One of the basic chemicals in Quaaludes, like a lot of drugs, comes from a plant. This plant only grows in India. There was a company there that was supplying chemicals to American companies to make legitimate Quaaludes. The DEA went to them and said, 'Look, you guys aren't making that much money from this.' And they weren't. They were a big corporation and this was just a little something they were doing to keep the United States happy for a little extra money. The DEA told them, 'Why don't you just quit selling the chemical to anyone?' And they did because they weren't making that much money from them because there wasn't a big legitimate use for them. Most doctors didn't prescribe them. I know one psychiatrist who gave this friend of mine a prescription for Quaaludes to cure his cocaine addiction. Talk about out of the frying pan into the fire."

"Did the DEA pay the Indian company to stop making the precursor?"

"I don't know if money changed hands or not. Probably some form of money or favours did. But when they tried to do that with the precursor that made speed, Sudafed, the companies making that type of drug were making millions of dollars every year, and they weren't about to quit making it. One of the ingredients you start out with comes from a bark from some plant that doesn't grow over here. That would make legitimate speed. I don't know all of the steps, but what you see mostly over here is the equivalent of bathtub gin. These guys go into drugstores and buy a shitload of Sudafed, which are allergy pills for stuffy noses or something. The ingredient for speed in Sudafed needs to be separated chemically from the other ingredients, and you don't get a high quality."

"Is that how they make cheap crystal meth?"

"Yes, but it's one of the drugs you can't get anymore. I had a friend who was in the business and he knew some people who had a warehouse in Utah of all places. They were buying it directly, the plant stuff, and companies were shipping it through there. I saw an interesting thing here on TV. As it turns out, there have been spikes in the use of methamphetamine here. For a while, it's widely popular, then it slowly wanes. A reporter got interested in it and discovered that when it started to wane, it was the quality of the speed. There are people addicted big time who will probably never kick it and ones who got involved with it when the quality was high. The ones who got involved when it was the local chemist making it in his bathroom, it's much easier for them to quit because they never had the pure methamphetamine feeling. You could see it on the chart that he had. The crime went up and down. Usually, it was related to when one cartel had forced another cartel out of business, and the quality went up again for a few years and then slowly waned. It never occurred to me that you are going to identify with that drug or any drug based on what your first experiences with it were."

"If you feel strong about it from the get-go," I said, "it keeps you coming back. But the feeling is never as good as the first time. You're always chasing those early highs. I'm surprised that meth has only just trickled into the UK. A lot of people in this country didn't even know what meth was until *Breaking Bad.*"

"It'll be there. As law enforcement makes it harder to cross the Mexican border down here, I'm sure the cartels are already looking for new markets and Europe is going to be high on that list. The cartels are like worldwide corporations. Crystal meth is a nasty drug. I've never tried it myself, but the stories I've seen and know to be true are pretty gruesome. There was one guy who was hooked on it pretty bad who was driving in his family van with his two kids. He pulled over to the side of the highway, killed one of his kids cut the head off and left it alongside the highway. Then he just got back in the van, and drove the rest of the way with the other kid. People think that it gives you more energy. It does keep you awake, but not in a good way. You need that sleep. A lot of problems are caused by sleep deprivation. Some of these guys will brag about it: 'Hell yeah, man. I haven't slept in five days.' What's wrong with them? I like to sleep!"

"I did use meth. In the beginning, it gave me energy, but the downside is dark."

"I wouldn't put anyone down for trying it. You seldom learn about anything like that from other people's advice. You've got to do it yourself and make your own decisions."

On the next call, Dan had heard from a contact in the federal government.

"Have you had any new news about Caro Quintero since his release?" I said.

"I got a phone call, and I looked into it a little bit. If the United States or Mexico is unable to catch him, they'll whisper in somebody's ear who is already his enemy down there, 'This is where he's at.' I'm pretty sure they know where he's at even though they didn't come right out and tell me that. I know how they work. They're not going to send any law enforcement from the United States to go down and assassinate him. They prefer to let things take their own course. They are pissed off because he killed a DEA agent and now he's walking around again. Believe me, that doesn't sit well with anyone who was involved with that case. Even me, I don't like the idea of this nutcase out there. His karma will take care of him either now or later on. I don't have to lift a finger and I don't intend to. I've done my part in that whole thing. I don't have the strength anymore to go down there and bring him back. That's a young man's game."

"How did you get involved with him in the first place?"

"I was in prison with some of Caro Quintero's cartel guys. I ended up doing various jobs for them. After we lost the cocaine load in Globe, Arizona, I found the cartel a place by Kingman. A remote airstrip that nobody was really using. We went to do it there. The very first time: *bam!* It happened again: busted. They snatched that co-pilot first and tortured him to death. He gave up Camarena ...

"You know, the United States wasn't exactly a saint in all this either. They should have got him out of that country. There's a certain point where you just cut your losses and get the fuck out of there. There's some things you can't control and a nutcase like Quintero is one of them. The cartel, on the other hand, should have done the same thing. They should have said to him, 'Look, we know it's you. You've got a day or two to get out of this country or else bad things are going to happen to you.' And he would have left, but he wasn't being properly supervised in my opinion. We dropped the ball there. It was more financial to the cartel than anything to be honest with you. Those loads were worth a lot of money. Even at wholesale prices: 5,000 pounds of pure coke is getting up there."

"Throughout your life, how many situations like this have you been in?"

"Too many. Way too many. None of this is for publication while I'm alive. I'm not proud of it, believe me. Some of the worst things I ever did was when I worked for the government. In my normal course of events, I didn't shoot people. I did when I worked for the government. To me, you don't kill people, and I don't care whether you work for the government or not. It's just wrong. I mean, they tried to kill me first. It was a matter of self-defence, but I'm the one who put myself in a situation where they had a shot at me and they certainly took it."

"Was that in Mexico?"

"Yes, I've got a nice chunk missing out of my forehead. I took a 9mm slug to my head. They started shooting before they even knew who I was, before I could even get out of the truck I was driving."

"Who were the guys you were going after?"

"I was there to negotiate something else. They had set up a pretty big sting operation with a Scottsdale detective and his informant who was a pilot. They were both down in Mexico, and at the very last minute they told the cop, 'We want you to stay until he lands and we know the load is safe.' So, the pilot took off and left. Never heard from again. Believe me, they moved heaven and earth to find that guy. The cops came to me because they knew I knew those people. Not the ones who were guarding the cop, but I knew the bosses. They wanted me to intervene. My response was: 'You guys screwed this up. You fix it.' I, at first, told them no because I wasn't involved in it up to that point at all. I didn't know the pilot or what was going on.

"That's one of the dangers of working in a foreign country.

First of all, half the people in the government there that you think are pro-American are really corrupt. They are taking money from the US and the cartels. Depending on the situation, their loyalty might be more towards the cartels or it might be more towards the United States. The US gives them billions of dollars yearly to fight drug traffickers, and they don't want to lose that money because they are not spending it to fight traffickers. They are buying houses in Spain and stuff like that. They don't want to lose that and the cartels will flat out tell them, 'You've got a choice: silver or lead.' In other words, 'Take our money or we're going to shoot you.' You couldn't pay me to be a higher-up in the Mexican government right now. All of the people who run for president down there in the high offices say stuff like, 'I'm going to crack down on the cartels.' One guy had made many such public statements. He didn't know they were looking at him pretty carefully and they caught him on film taking something like $3 or $6 million from the cartel just a week before the election."

"So what happened to him?"

"He got elected. It's a crazy game, and that's one of the reasons I'd like to see it legalised. You'd take a lot of the crime out of it. They are not doing it to enlighten people's minds. They are doing it to make money. If you take the money out, they'll have to go and find something else to do or retire. Most of these guys have so much money, it's not even funny.

"The cops let me listen to the tape of Kiki being tortured. Then they introduced me to the cop's wife and seven kids. They would have killed him. I knew how those people were and I just couldn't see not doing anything. They gave me some cash to negotiate with. I went to Mexico. Caro Quintero didn't want the money. He had more money than God anyway. He wanted the pilot who had disappeared during the sting operation. He said no. I listened to Caro Quintero make some phone calls. Because I knew a lot about the cartel's operations, by listening to him on the phone, I started to suspect where the cop was being held.

"I took off in my truck and arrived at a barn. A Mexican

emerged, and opened fire, shooting at me through the truck window, and a bullet hit my head. There was blood, but I didn't have time to contemplate the injury. I rolled out of the truck. Using my door as a shield, I returned fire, killing the Mexican. Another Mexican emerged from the building. Immediately, I shot and killed him. Cautiously, I entered the building with my gun drawn. I found the agent inside, handcuffed to an old-time milk container, a big one filled with cement. His body was covered with cigarette burns. I freed him and helped him back to the truck. I wanted to race away as fast as possible before more people arrived, but the engine had been shot, and I had to keep pulling over, getting out and adding water to the engine. Eventually, I got him to the border and the US authorities hospitalised both of us.

"Having took a 9mm slug to my skull, a chunk of my forehead was missing. As the adrenaline filtered out of my system, I started to contemplate the day. In my normal course of events, I didn't shoot people. I justified it by telling myself, *They tried to kill me first. It was self-defence. They started shooting before they even knew who I was, before I could even get out of the truck that I was driving.* But then I thought, *I'm the one who put myself in the situation where they had a shot at me, and they certainly took it.* I found it ironic that the worst thing I'd ever done in my life, killing two people, I'd done while working for the US government. Working for the cartel, I'd never killed anybody."

"How did you go from being a young person smuggling weed to getting in so deep with all of these characters?"

"It happened slowly. I started this when I was in high school. Me and my friends would go down to Mexico with our backpacks. Because I'd gone deep-sea fishing with my dad, I knew people my age in Mexico. It was easy to get the pot, put it in the backpacks and bring it back."

Dan emailed the story of how he entered the drug business:

This is a brief story about how I got started smuggling marijuana into the USA from Mexico. I was just seventeen years old and a senior at Westwood High School in Mesa, Arizona. I would not want the reader to think I am proud of this. I am not. Everything is true with the exception of the names of a few of my old friends who are still among the living. All the places I've named exist to this day.

The full moon rose like a big brilliant orb over huge saguaro cactuses, some of which were nearly 200 years old. These giant sentries stood with their arms upraised towards the heavens as the marijuana was passed over a three-foot barbed-wire fence, which in those days was the only barrier which separated the USA from Mexico. The place was Organ Pipe Cactus National Monument in Southern Arizona.

Organ Pipe had been designated a National Monument in about 1937. It was, and still is, a true national treasure. Hunting has always been prohibited in all national monuments and this meant the park was teeming with all types of wildlife. There was a large contingency of coyotes and more rattlesnakes than I have ever seen in my life. Most of these animals were nocturnal and Organ Pipe came to life each night. The State of Arizona lawmakers originally deeded the land to the federal government during prohibition. Prohibition banned all sales of alcohol in the United States. As strange as it might seem, the legislative record from that time frame clearly shows legislators wanted a paved highway to facilitate the movement of illegal alcohol through Arizona. Go figure. All I can say about this is: only in Arizona.

On that night, I waited until the full moon began to rise and took myself and five friends to an isolated spot along the border that separates the USA from Mexico. It was not by accident that I chose a night when I knew it would be a full moon. Out there in the middle of the deserted desert, under a full moon, it was like daylight. Nor was it by accident that I had chosen this spot to cross the border that night. I had earlier that night climbed a hill in Mexico as it began to get dark. I could easily see the headlights of the Customs and Border Control trucks as they headed out for the night to set up shop. They tended to pick a spot each night and most often stayed at that spot until morning. They always stayed close together; safety in numbers was, and still is, a rule of thumb out there in the "Pipe." Even back then, it could be a dangerous place to be alone.

I had taken five good friends on this adventure. Most of them I had known since childhood. I knew they were all trustworthy, honest and in great shape physically. Some were high-school athletes. More importantly they trusted me and were willing to do as I asked. I told them I would give each of them three kilos of pot, about seven pounds, for their efforts that night. I had purchased expensive backpacks, one for each of them, and made sure they all had good boots to wear. The desert in Organ Pipe is hard on regular shoes and can destroy a new pair of tennis shoes in one night.

I had already placed the kilos in large bags and secured them to backpacks and had only to remove them from the vehicle once we reached the border fence. I did so, placing the loaded backpacks on the ground and had all but one guy grab a backpack and cross over the fence. I told them each to grab one backpack and follow me. I took them to a spot about thirty yards from the border, loaded the packs and told them to wait for me to return.

I quickly went back to where I had left my best friend Tommy. I went a few yards back into the desert on the Mexican side of the fence and cut off a small branch from a bush, which had many small leaves attached to it. I told Tommy to take the one remaining backpack, cross the border fence and watch me. I then proceeded to use the branch from the bush and used it to erase all of the footprints on both sides of the border that might give away our location to any law-enforcement officers who might drive along the dirt road on the American side of the fence. I felt that seeing a bunch of footprints would be a dead giveaway that something was going on in the "Pipe" that night. I then followed Tommy back to the others erasing our footprints. I explained to Tommy that I wanted him to follow all of us, making sure no one got lost and to erase our footprints whenever we crossed a sandy wash. He simply nodded his head. He was, and still is, a man of few words.

By the time Tommy and I made it back to where I'd left my other friends, they had put on the backpacks, which had the pot tied and taped shut in them. One for each and Tommy had one already on his back. I carried nothing but two gallons of spare water. Each of my friends had also been given one gallon of their own to carry. Each backpack held about fifteen kilos, about thirty pounds. It added up to about 150 pounds, far more than I'd ever had at one time in my life.

By the time I returned with Tommy to where my other friends were hidden, the young coyote pups had just begun to cry out for their parents who were no doubt out hunting for food for their children. Despite what many people think, adult coyotes are extremely family orientated. Both parents take part in raising their young pups. Because no hunting of any kind had been allowed in Organ Pipe Cactus National Monument for over forty years, the coyote population had thrived and there were great numbers of them. For anyone hearing these pups yelp, it is like no sound you have ever heard. It's otherworldly and actually a little scary. At least that had been my experience the first time I heard it. It usually starts with just one or two pups and rapidly increases to many hundreds of them. When the yelping reaches its full crescendo, it's quite loud, which under the circumstances suited me just fine. It's easily loud enough to cover the sound of a few men walking through the desert at night. I explained to my friends what all the noise was and they seemed to relax a bit.

One of my friends asked, "Dan, how the hell do you know where we are going?" I pointed to the lights of the parking area of the visitor center, which were clearly visible, and told all of them that's where we are going. One commented that it seemed only a few hundred yards away and I explained that in the pristine desert things often seem closer than they are. I also told them for the first time that I had already done this by myself just to make sure it was safe. I also told them that it would take between one and one and a half hours of steady walking to reach our destination that night. Actually, I had already done this twice. The first time I carried nothing but water and the second time I carried fifteen kilos myself. I had used the money I made from those fifteen kilos to finance this trip. So off we went on our first great adventure together.

Something else I did not tell them was that I had recruited another of my best friends to drive the pot from the rest area back to Phoenix. As planned, he had taken a room in an old landmark motel named The Space Age Lodge in Gila Bend, Arizona. As far as I know it's still there. I knew my friend was already at the motel because I had instructed him to leave the car we were going to use to transport the pot in plain sight. I had seen the car as we drove through Gila Bend earlier in the day.

The Space Age Lodge sits on the main drag going through Gila Bend and you can miss it as you drive through the town. To get to Organ Pipe you leave Phoenix, drive through Gila Bend, then on to a small town called Ajo. From Ajo, you drive a few miles from town and come to a small hamlet called Why. At Why, you have two choices: drive through and go to Tucson, or turn right and head to Mexico. The entrance to Organ Pipe Visitor Center is on the right side of the highway about six or seven miles from the actual border separating the USA from Mexico.

A few hundred yards beyond the entrance to Organ Pipe Visitor Center there is highway road sign telling you that the border crossing closes each day from midnight until 6 AM the next day. I felt I could use this to my advantage. I had instructed my friend who was going to drive the pot to not leave Ajo until it would be too late to cross the border that night. I told him rather than drive right into the visitor center to instead drive right past the entrance until he saw the sign, pause long enough to read the sign and turn around and go to the visitor center. I did this on the off chance that someone – Border Patrol or custom officials – might be watching the entrance to the visitor center at that time of night. It would simply appear to them that arriving too late to cross the border that night, the person driving the car had simply decided to spend the night at the visitor center. I had told my friend to park as close to the edge of the parking area on the side nearest to Mexico. He had already done this once with me when I brought the fifteen kilos across myself so he knew exactly what to do and why. The only difference was that we were in a different car this time. I told my friend to simply park the car and set up the little two-man tent he had next to the car and crawl into it. I also told him to take the key to the trunk of the car and leave it in the trunk lock.

My friends who were carrying the pot and I arrived about one and a half hours after we started. We had, at my insistence, taken about a fifteen-minute stop to rest a little and drink some water. Upon our arrival just below the parking area, I had everyone stop. I told them to take off the backpacks and wait for me to return. I went up the steep incline to the rest area to make sure the car had arrived safely and was in the proper place. It was. I then returned to the others and had Tommy help me to take the backpacks to the rest area and place them into the large trunk of the car. My friend Tommy had never met my friend in the tent and never even saw his face that night because I told him to stay in the tent while the pot was being loaded into the trunk of the car. When we were done, I took the key to the trunk with me when I left. I did this not out of fear my friend would try and steal anything from me, but rather on the off chance if he was to be pulled over on the way back to Phoenix he could honestly tell anyone who wanted to look in the trunk that he did not have a key.

All went well that night and the next day. It was the beginning of what would turn into my worst nightmare in just a few short years. I fully realise that I have given anyone who reads this a blueprint for smuggling small amounts of pot into this country. I beg you to please pay close attention to what I'm about to tell you. All of this took place in the early 1970s. If you tried to do this today you will get busted the very first time. Times – and border security – have changed. Aside from being illegal, it is morally wrong. It set me on a path in which heartache and death became commonplace. As I said, I am not proud of all this. Truth be told, I am ashamed.

But pretty soon, backpacking we couldn't bring enough, so we started using horses and mules. When that wasn't enough, it eventually evolved into airplanes. This was before cocaine was popular. Cocaine was $35,000 a kilo back then. The only people who could afford it were rock stars and drug dealers. Then it was pure economics. A planeload of coke is worth a hell of a lot more than a planeload of weed. That's how it all started, plus my greed.

On the next call, Dan said, "Starting out, I never saw the damage being done by this drug. Back then, we thought cocaine was just like marijuana: non-addictive. I learned my lesson about that. A lot of the times I'd take my profit in coke because I could double that money. Rather than take ten grand in cash, I'd take ten grand in coke, and end up with twenty to twenty-five grand.

"I was selling a lot of coke to a guy I'd known for years, an old weed customer. He never snorted anything in front of me. He'd buy four or five ounces at a time, twice a week. I thought everything was cool. Right around Christmas one year, there's a knock at my door and it was his wife. She tells me, 'You have got to stop selling that cocaine.' He had second-mortgaged their house. Rather than go home, he was staying in hotels. He had kids and stuff and here I was feeding into that habit. These people were my friends. I used to eat dinner over there. I knew his sons. So that was an eye-opener for me. It made me start looking around. Up till then, I never saw the bad effects of it because I was never around those type of people. A lot of times the people I sold to never did use it. I never sold to street people. It's an evil drug."

"So, you never used it?"

"I've snorted it a few times, somewhere between five and ten times, all back in the '70s, just to be chic. I used to keep a mayonnaise-size jar at home just for people who would come over. It was good bait for the women, and as embarrassing as it is to admit it, a lot of it was ego on my part. I liked the idea, even in high school, of being the guy that you had to go to. I was pretty ruthless. God forbid if I found out that you liked cocaine because you would think that I was your best friend and that I was so cool giving you coke, but before you knew it, I had people doing things, sometimes illegal things. I basically turned them into my own personal slaves. They'd be washing my car. I took advantage of their addiction. I'll always regret that."

"What was your first arrest?"

"Mexico. This is a very real story. It happened in Mexico in the mid-1970s and still, at times, haunts me. There is no need for me to use made-up names since all the principals, with the exception of myself, are long dead. I do not want or need sympathy. I fully realise that I brought all this into my life because in my younger days I was a very greedy, manipulative and selfish person. It is a story of an out-of-control ego, mine, which ran amok."

Dan emailed the story:

I woke one morning handcuffed to a dead man. His name was Jaquine Reyes. I had nicknamed him Jack. He simply called me Gringo. Jack was a dear friend, a good man, a simple man, a farmer, who I had talked into growing marijuana for me and my partners in crime. I was determined to control my pot business from actually growing it all the way through the retail sales of my product. This was before the big Mexican drug cartels took over.

I found myself locked-up in a small cell belonging to the federal police in Uruapan, Mexico. Uruapan is a relatively small town nestled in the Tierra Caliente Valley in the Mexican State of Michoacán, Mexico. I was under no illusions. The federal police had known about me for some time and had tried more than once to find me, but while I did maintain a home in Mexico, I was seldom there.

Before waking up handcuffed to the deceased Jack, I had been pulled over for a simple traffic violation and the whole situation escalated from there. I had absolutely no marijuana with me at the time I was pulled over, not even a seed. This did not seem to matter to the federal police. They saw this as an opportunity to finally nail me to the wall and were not about to let this chance slip through their hands. You see, I had been performing all my nefarious deeds in Mexico without paying bribe money to anyone. This more than anything seemed to upset my captors.

When the Mexican federal police captured me and my American partner in my pot-growing venture, we were taken to Uruapan. Over the course of the next few days, they began to round up and arrest Mexican citizens who they thought were involved in my nefarious deeds. They put them with us in a police compound. All told, including my friend Jack, they brought in nine people. Five of whom I had never met in my life. They didn't even know my name nor I theirs.

During the day we were free to roam the compound and at night we were locked into two small rooms. After a few days, two of the Mexican nationals they brought in escaped at night by simply getting out of their room and climbing over the compound wall. Needless to say, my captors were none too thrilled about this and from that day forward they handcuffed us together at night while we were locked in these two rooms. I was always handcuffed to my friend, Jack.

The compound itself was a strange place. Under a two-story covered part was stacked up at least ten tons of marijuana. We felt free to pilfer small amounts for our personal use. The police knew we were doing this but did not seem to mind in the least. When we grew hungry, we were allowed to send out for food from a local restaurant provided I paid for it.

The police who had us were a strange lot, friendly one minute, brutal the next, often times apologising for the brutality saying it was only their job, nothing personal. I did not know about the others, but I did take being tortured personally. Although for the most part they were far more violent with the Mexican citizens than with Americans, I nonetheless got a pretty good taste of some of their "questioning" skills. The very first day they had me my right elbow was broken with a rifle butt. It still at times bothers me to this day.

I was also subjected several times to the Mexican version of waterboarding. What they did was this: A popular mineral water was given several good shakes while still sealed in the glass bottle. A towel was stuffed into my mouth, so I could only breathe through my nose. I was tilted backwards in a chair. They poked a small hole in the bottle cap and shot the bubbly water up my nose. The sensation was akin to drowning and burning at the same time – a tad uncomfortable to say the least.

After about eight or nine days of this, Jack was brought back to our cell about dusk. They had been very hard on Jack that day and he was clearly in a great deal of pain. He had seemed hurt, but not too badly. His last words on this earth were, roughly translated into English, "Son of the one who got fucked. These Federales are real pieces of work, but don't worry, Gringo, in the morning all will be better." Didn't happen. Jack died in his sleep.

In the morning, I awoke to his dead eyes, wide open and staring at the ceiling of their small adobe cell. I knew instantly that he was dead, but at first refused to believe it. As usual, I was still handcuffed to him. I went crazy. Absolutely barking mad. I began screaming at the guards that I would kill all of them. They were afraid to even come near me and as such I remained handcuffed to Jack's dead body for the next day or so. Being handcuffed to a dead man creates many logistical problems. Going to the bathroom for instance. I began to talk to Jack, hoping somehow it would bring him back to life. I was so crazy that I thought he was answering back. It was the closest I have come to pure insanity in my entire life. Dead people can, at times, have quite a lot to say. During the next two days, we had many conversations. The dead, under the right circumstances, can be quite talkative.

About two days after the handcuffs were removed, which had connected me to my dead friend, the federal police who had questioned me flew me back to Guadalajara in a private twin-engine aircraft and placed me in a local jail. A few days after that I was transferred to a Mexican prison, where I spent the next two years trying to escape. The federal police's last words to me were, "Gringo, the next time you come to our mountains, you need to work with us. If you buy one ton of marijuana from us we will give you another ton for free." Believe me, they were quite serious. I know because I later took them up on their offer.

On the next call, I asked Dan, "Before you were arrested and handcuffed to Jack, why were you in Mexico in the first place?"

"I'd just come back from Indonesia, and we'd talked the people in Mexico into growing nothing other than sensimilla, which means with no seeds. This was long before people knew that much about it. But I started getting loads of marijuana that were full of seeds, so I was just going down there to tell them to get it together and not to send that stuff anymore. To begin with, I just got pulled over for a traffic ticket as I knew better than to have any dope on me. They had their way of questioning you. After they broke my elbow with a rifle butt, it took me a few days of holding out. If I had to do it over again, I would have told them the first day. That's how I ended up being handcuffed to Jack."

"So, the Federales knew what you were up to, but they had no evidence?"

"Right. They made it pretty plain that evidence wasn't a problem. They'd come up with evidence. The one thing that really pissed me off was that there was a day or two when they were really beating me up bad, basically torturing me, and they had me blindfolded. Now they had never done that before. It was clear to me that there were American law enforcement in the room because of the questions they were asking. They were being prompted by the Americans, who were sitting there watching an American being tortured."

"How old were you at this point?"

"Twenty-one to twenty-two."

"Did the situation with the dead man make you want to exit the business?"

"Oh, yeah. But you have to understand: I'm an adrenaline junkie and that's every bit as addictive as gambling, drugs … My mom used to tell me: 'You're happiest if you go to the Grand Canyon and you're leaning out over a cliff and it's a mile straight down and you just bend over further and further in the front until you're going to fall and at that last millisecond, you pull yourself back.' I started thinking about it and it's true. In that millisecond that you make the decision and pull back, that's when I always felt most alive. An adrenaline rush is not like drugs. An adrenaline addiction ruled my life in all aspects. It played a role in about every decision that I made.

"I did everything that an addict would do: I got out and promised my family that I wouldn't get involved in the drug business anymore and blah blah blah I went and got a regular job, but within a month or two, I started up again with marijuana. It was so easy for me to get. All I had to do was make a phone call and Mexicans would show up on my driveway with a truck full of weed. Part of the problem was that I made too much money when I was too young and I never really recovered from that. I'm not good around money simply because most of my life I never had to worry about it. At a certain point, it just becomes monopoly money. I mean when you have to weigh it rather than count it because there is so much. We'd put it on a triple beam and weigh it. Different bills weigh different, like ten grand in twenties weighs more or less – I can't remember which – than ten grand in fives. We knew all the weights. The cartel has all these machines which will do it, but I was always afraid to purchase the machines because what business did I have that needed a machine that only casinos need?"

"Were you in Indonesia smuggling Thai sticks?" Thai sticks were grown by the hill tribes in north-east Thailand. They generally used silk line to hold "Thai buds" together around bamboo sticks or hemp stalks.

"Yeah. In those days Thai sticks were the most expensive weed you could find. Really good Mexican marijuana could be had for

$100 a pound easily, but Thai sticks sold for $2,000, which was good money in the '70s. I got into a Volkswagen Porsche repair business with a Dutch Indonesian, who was twenty years older than me. When I told him about the price discrepancy, he didn't believe me. He said that they used to make their houses out of Thai sticks, little huts and stuff. So I had him come over after we got off work one day. I had arranged for some people to buy some Thai sticks from me that I had bought out of California for $1,500 a pound and was selling for $2,000 to $2,200. I was making decent money, but being a greedy bastard, I thought, *Why should I let those people in California make all the money when I can do this myself?*

"He sat there and watched while I sold these people Thai sticks and saw how much money they were worth. Within a week or two I had him on a plane over there. He had pretty good connections with the government over there. In those days, the Indonesian government trained all of their fighter pilots at an airbase, just right outside of Mesa, Arizona here where I'm at called Williams Air Force Base, so he was already in that crowd to begin with. The Indonesians all stuck close together, especially when they first got here because they didn't know anybody. He befriended a lot of them, which came in handy.

"Over there, you don't do drug business unless you are hooked up with the government – not unless you have some kind of death wish. It's the death penalty for weed. Now if you're an American, they won't kill you. You'll get life in prison, which, over there, you'd be better off being dead. I did see an Indonesian prison outside of a town. It was just a chain-link fence with barbed wire around the top and no permanent building at all. The prisoners had made little huts out of cardboard. The townspeople, one of their favourite things to do when they were bored, they would go down there with rotten vegetables and throw them at the prisoners. That was considered a good sport."

"How long did you spend in Indonesia?"

"The longest I was ever there without coming home was close

to a year. Off and on, I spent close to two years there. I loved it. Even if I hadn't been in that business, I still would have loved it because every day you wake up and see new stuff that you have never seen before. Just even the fruit. I stayed at the Intercontinental Hotel when President Ford was visiting Indonesia. He stayed in the presidential palace, but Kissinger stayed in my hotel with all of the Secret Service guys he lugged around with him. That's where I learned to play backgammon. Some of the guys guarding Kissinger worked all night and then would sleep during the day, but a lot of times they would come down to the pool and play a couple of games of backgammon. The day they were all leaving, one of them came up to me. He was a nice guy and he said, 'Look, you need to be careful because you may think you are operating under the radar here but you're not. We've got nothing against you. You're not a threat to any politician or anything.' He made it pretty plain that I wasn't as incognito as I thought. He was just being friendly, trying to give me good advice. I should have taken it.

"The first time I was in US prison was because I came back from Mexico on a prisoner exchange. They transferred the conviction up here, and I was in the federal prison in San Diego for a month or two, until they arranged to put me on federal parole. If you look at my criminal record, it's very misleading. If you look at the record, it shows that I was in prison doing this and that, when I wasn't even in prison. A federal judge is a powerful guy. He can sign an order, and it appears to anyone trying to find you that you are in prison. There were quite a few times in my life when that wasn't the case. Everything is not always as it seems. Definitely when it comes to the government and its supposed War on Drugs. We've been fighting for forty years and gone backwards.

"Both sides have a vested interest in not seeing drugs legalised. Of course, the cartels don't want to lose their profits. On the other hand, there are hundreds of thousands of people who work for the government employed to handle the War on Drugs. They don't want it legal either. What would they do? That's their jobs. So, there are some powerful lobby interests involved even though most people in the DEA and people who I met in that line, including US attorneys and federal prosecutors, will tell you that they wish it was legal, too. They'd much prefer to concentrate on getting people like murderers off the streets."

"The private prison lobby is huge."

"Say you are the director of prisons in Arizona like Terry Stewart, when you quit your job, Corrections Corp of America hires you. Meanwhile, before you quit, they are supporting you and getting you to pass more and more laws that create the need for private prisons. Then they fill that need and make pretty good money. That's where most of the past directors of prisons in Arizona who are still alive ended up working. Terry Stewart did, and he had been instrumental in getting laws passed: let's be tough on drugs and crime, mandatory sentencing and all that crap. There just wasn't room to lock all of those people up, so they created the need for the private prisons. It's all about money."

"I just read that with the crime rate going down, they are tightening laws to keep the prison bunks filled, and even if the bunks aren't filled that it's written into the contract that they still have to be paid."

"That's right. They got real sweetheart deals with most of the states, but like anything else, those chickens will come home to roost. If you lock somebody up for twenty years for a relatively minor crime, when he gets out, you've got one angry person who probably doesn't give a damn anymore. The system has probably created a murderer."

"Then multiply that by hundreds of thousands of people," I said. "I just read that there are seven million people in the system, including probation and parole."

"It's number two or three in the budget now in Arizona. In most states, the Department of Transportation is the number one money eater, and the Department of Corrections is number ten to fifteen on the list, but in Arizona it's number three and it's getting ready to be number two and, in not too long, it will be the biggest ticket item on the budget. We're spending so much money warehousing people who really don't need to be in prison and we are ignoring that there are kids in Arizona who go to bed hungry every night and that just makes me sick to my stomach."

"What number is education on that list?"

"It's way down there. Arizona is number forty-eight out of fifty states in education and has been for years. We lose a lot of the really good talent, which goes out of state to be employed. Most of the really good teachers, the ones we need, they don't want to teach in Arizona."

"So are young people in Arizona groomed to be in the prison system?"

"Especially the poor ones. That's why whenever I see someone who has just had a little brush with the law, I'll bend over backwards to prevent them from getting in the system. In Arizona, once you get into that system, it's very difficult to get out. You're an exception, and there are a few, but not that many. Recidivism is 60 to 70 percent. That tells you right there that they are doing something wrong. It's called the Department of Corrections. Well, what are they correcting? They should change the name to what it really is."

"Here in the UK, our politicians are bringing over the US privatised prisons model."

"A lot of times, they use the United States like a test dummy. It's like cigarettes. For quite some time now, it's been against the law to advertise cigarettes on TV or billboards that would attract young people e.g. Joe Camel. The cigarette companies know that if you haven't started smoking by the age of eighteen, then you're probably never going to smoke, so they've got to get you while you're young. So, what do they do now? They follow the law here, but in all of the foreign countries where markets are opening up such as China, they do exactly what they used to do here. All the ads in China and Japan are geared towards young people, making it look glamorous to smoke or you'll get all these women if you smoke and stuff like that. To me that is so ruthless and devious.

They know they are selling a product that is killing people, but they don't care. It's just money."

"Is it still the drug that kills the most people?"

"Nicotine is the number one drug problem in this country. Then alcohol."

"Right now in the UK, alcohol is the biggest killer of men under fifty."

"A lot of people die from it here, too, or from offshoots of it. The death certificate might not say died from drinking but that heart condition they have or whatever it was that actually killed them was brought on by the excessive use of alcohol. They make it all sound so glamorous, but let me tell you something: if you're watching someone you care about slowly die from smoking, it's not glamorous. All of the executives from the cigarette companies got called on the carpet here to testify before Congress. Every single one of them stood up, raised their right hand and said, 'I do not believe that cigarettes are addictive.' It was almost laughable if it wasn't for the fact that people are dying."

"Here in the UK, alcohol is the biggest killer of young people. Each week, three young people die from alcohol poisoning from binge drinking. Then even more die due to the violence around alcohol. It is the number one drug in murder, violent crime – about 50 percent of violent crime – sex crime, date rape, paedophilia, incest and pretty much everything. It really bothers me that people who drink alcohol and smoke cigarettes can lock young people up for possessing weed, which doesn't cause as many problems. It's moral relativism."

"The word has got out here that alcohol can kill you if you are young because your body is not used to taking in that much alcohol that quickly. A lot of crime including violent crime is tied to alcohol. There are people who are pretty reasonable, good people, but get some alcohol in them and there is a personality change that's hard to believe sometimes. They say some people are happy drunks, but the opposite is also true. They get so mean and obnoxious when they drink."

On the next call, Dan said, "I thought the cartel bosses should face justice for killing and torturing people, and I knew damn well that they would never face justice in Mexico. Last I heard, Caro Quintero is still walking around, but we know where he is. That's not a business where you can really make a comeback after twenty years in prison. He still has money, but most of it he can't get to. That's how they tracked him down. He's going to be in prison, dead or on the run for the rest of his life. The Kiki recording is gruesome. It's one of the reasons I agreed to go get him."

"Were you scared going after him?"

"A little bit. Not enough to stop me though. Back then, I liked living on the edge. I knew Caro Quintero from way back. He had more reasons to be scared of me than I had of him as it turned out. I actually thought that I would end up shooting him, but I didn't. I'd like to say that the world would be a better place without Caro Quintero, but the people that replaced him are worse than he was in some ways. The cartel guys think nothing now of killing you, your family, and cutting off some heads and leaving them on fence posts outside of town. You get up in the mountains of Mexico and there is no law per se. It's just on paper. The majority of the police work for the cartels.

"The ones that killed my friend that I was handcuffed to, his brothers went and killed the cops who had done that. I was already in prison down there. They came to me. They were going to arrest me for it. I said, 'Fuck! I'm in prison! How the hell could I have done it?' They knew that I'd been getting out at night, but it had happened so far away, I could not have escaped and done it and come back. They knew I didn't do it, but they were threatening to charge me with murder. I think they wanted me to give up the names of the people who actually did it, but I didn't know their names. They weren't happy that their brother had been treated like that. They tracked them down. They got two of the cops one day and one the next.

"I know that it is far worse now than it was back then. They really have taken over down there. And guess who their biggest customer is? The US. Although they are spreading their wings in Europe now, too, particularly Spain, and they are starting to put heroin in England. They are taking over the meth business as well. Crystal meth used to be manufactured in the States, but they made some of the precursor chemicals hard to get here. You can buy them readily in Mexico in huge quantities and nobody says anything. They just use the same routes into America that they use for marijuana and coke."

CHAPTER 15
EX-COP EXPOSES CIA DIRECTOR

In November 1996, with the black community of Los Angeles enraged by Gary Webb's exposure of the government's role in trafficking cocaine, Representative Maxine Waters invited the CIA director, John Deutch, to offer an explanation at a town hall meeting at a high school in Watts. The former MIT professor showed up to a crowd of 1,000 angry people. All of the major newspapers and network news teams were present, including Ted Koppel's *Nightline*.

A Congresswoman who used to be a teacher approached the microphone. "It's not up to us to prove the CIA was involved in drug trafficking in South Central Los Angeles. Rather, it's up to them to prove they were not."

As Deutch got up to speak, the crowd booed and jeered. "I'm going to be brief. I want to make four points, and only four points. First, the people of the CIA and I understand the tremendous horror that drugs have been to Americans, what drugs do to families and communities, and the way drugs kill babies. We understand how ravaging drugs are in this country. CIA employees and I share your anger at the injustice and lack of compassion that drug victims encounter."

"He sounds just like Clinton!" someone yelled.

"During the past two years," Deutch said, "while I have been director of Central Intelligence, our case officers' intelligence operations have directly worked to capture all of the Cali Cartel drug lords. We have seriously disrupted the flow of coca paste between the growing areas of Peru and Bolivia to the cocaine processing facilities in Colombia. We have seized huge amounts of heroin grown in the poppy fields of Southwest Asia. Our purpose is to stop drugs from coming into the US. So my second point is that the CIA is fighting against drugs."

The audience grumbled.

"Our activities are secret. Accordingly, there's not a lot of public understanding of what we do. I understand that people are suspicious of the CIA, and in the course of recruiting agents to break up those groups that bring drugs into the US, our case officers, our men and women deal with bad people, very bad people, sometimes at great risk to their lives. These are criminals with which we must deal if we are going to stop drugs from coming to the country. They frequently lie about their relationships with us for their own purpose. So it is hard for members of the public to know what is true and what is not true …

"Now we all know that the US government and the CIA supported the Contras in their efforts to overthrow the Sandinista government in Nicaragua in the mid-'80s. It is alleged that the CIA also help the Contras raise money for arms by introducing crack cocaine into California. It is an appalling charge that goes to the heart of this country. It is a charge that cannot go unanswered," Deutch said, pounding on a table. "It says that the CIA, an agency of the United States government founded to protect Americans, helped introduce drugs and poison into our children and helped kill their future. Now, one who heads a government agency – not myself or anyone else – can let such an allegation stand. I will get to the bottom of it and I will let you know the results of what I have found.

"I've ordered an independent investigation of these charges. The third point I want to make to you is to explain the nature of the investigation. I've ordered the CIA Inspector General to undertake a full investigation." The crowd yelled its discontent so loud that Deutch had to wait a minute before continuing. "Let me tell you why he's the right official to do the job. First, the IG is established by law of Congress to be independent, to carry out activities, to look for fraud and crimes within the CIA.

Secondly, the Inspector General has access to all CIA records and documents, no matter how secret. Third, the IG has the authority to interview the right people. Fourth, he is able to cooperate with other government departments. For example, the Department of Justice, the DEA, the Department of Defence, all of which had operations ongoing in Nicaragua at the time. Finally, the IG has a good track record of being a whistle-blower on past misdeeds of the CIA. For example, just last month he uncovered that some CIA employees were misusing credit cards and they are now in jail."

"What about Guatemala? What about those murders?" a man yelled, referring to CIA-sponsored military regimes in Guatemala murdering thousands of civilians.

"Most importantly, when this investigation is complete, I intend to make the results public so that any person can judge the adequacy of the investigation. Anyone in the public who has a wish to look at the report will be able to do so. I want to stress that I am not the only person in the CIA who wants any American to believe that the CIA was responsible for this kind of disgusting charge. Finally, I want to say to you that as of today, we have no evidence of conspiracy by the CIA to engage in encouraging drug traffickers in Nicaragua or elsewhere in Latin America during this or any other period."

"I'd like to know how this incident differs from what happened at my school, where, for forty years, the government denied inflicting syphilis on African-American men," said a graduate student of the Tuskegee Institute in Alabama.

Deutch conceded that what had happened at Tuskegee was terrible. "Let me say something else. There was no one who came forward forty years ago and said they were going to investigate."

"Where I live there are no jobs for the children and our kids are just seen as commodities," a woman said. "They are being cycled through the prisons. They come back to the street and are marked and scarred for the rest of their lives. You, the president and everybody else should be highly upset. You should be saying, how did this cancer get here?"

A man stood up. "And now we are supposed to trust the CIA to investigate itself?"

Deutch tried to quell the malcontents by emphasising the Inspector General's independence, which only incensed the crowd.

"Why don't you turn it over to an independent counsel? Someone who has the power to issue subpoenas. It would have more credibility."

Deutch responded that no independent counsel was possible because no criminal complaint had been filed.

"I am a former Los Angeles Police narcotics detective," Michael Ruppert said, balding, bespectacled and speaking with authority. "I worked South Central Los Angeles and I can tell you, Director Deutch, emphatically and without equivocation, that the Agency has dealt drugs in this country for a long time." The host asked him to repeat his statement. "I will tell you, Director Deutch, as a former LAPD narcotics detective, that your Agency has dealt drugs throughout this country for a long time." There was an explosion of applause. While the host tried to maintain order, Deutch remained seated, nervously wringing his hands.

"Director Deutch, I shall refer you to three specific Agency investigations known as Amadeus, Pegasus and Watchtower. I have Watchtower documents heavily redacted by the Agency. I was personally exposed to CIA operations and recruited by CIA personnel, who attempted to recruit me in the late '70s to become involved in protecting Agency drug operations in this country. I've been trying to get this out for eighteen years. My question for you is very specific, sir. If in the course of the Inspector General's investigation, you came across evidence of severely criminal activity, and it is classified, will you use that classification to hide the criminal activity or will you tell the American people the truth?"

With the audience in uproar, the host attempted to maintain control, while the director played with his hands and shuffled in his seat.

"If you have information about CIA," Deutch said, his hands

clasped and elbows on the table, "[and] illegal activity and drugs, you should immediately bring that information to wherever you want. But let me suggest three places: the Los Angeles Police Department ..."

The crowd laughed. "No! No!" people chanted.

"It is your choice. The Los Angeles Police Department, the Inspector General or the office of your Congressperson ..." Hecklers halted his response. "Let me say something else. If this information turns up wrongdoing, we'll bring the people to justice and make them accountable," Deutch said, tapping the table for emphasis.

After a congressman requested that Michael Ruppert get in touch later on, the ex-cop got back on the microphone. "For the record, my name is Mike Ruppert, R-U-P-P-E-R-T. I did bring this information out eighteen years ago and I got shot at and forced out of LAPD because of it." There was cheering and applause. "I've been on the record for eighteen years non-stop, and I would be happy to give you, Congressman, anything that I have."

"My question to you is," a man said to Deutch, "if you know all this stuff that the Agency has done historically, then why should we believe you today, when you say certainly this could never happen in Los Angeles, when the CIA's done this stuff all over the world?"

"I didn't come here thinking everyone was going to believe me," Deutch said. "I came here for a much simpler task. I came here to stand up on my legs and tell you I was going to investigate these horrible allegations. All you can do is listen to what I have to say and wait to see the results."

"But how can we know how many viable documents have been shredded and how can we be certain that more documents won't be shredded?"

"I don't know that anybody has found any lost documents in the operational files," Deutch said. "I know of nobody who has found any gaps in sequences, any missing files, any missing papers for any period of that time. That may come up."

"Hey, do you know Walter Pincus?" a man asked, referring to a journalist who spied on American students abroad for the CIA.

"Yes," Deutch said. "Why?"

"Is he an asset of the CIA?"

Dutch clasped his head and shook it.

The crowd directed its anger at the lady who had invited Deutch to the meeting. "I don't know why this lady is saluting Deutch's courage for coming here today, when everybody knows this building has got hundreds of pigs in it. There's pigs behind those curtains. There's pigs on the roof. We're not going to get no ghetto justice today."

The crowd murmured its approval.

A man stood and pointed at Deutch. "To see you coming in this community today in this way is nothing more than a public-relations move for the white people of this country. So you are going to come into this community today and insult us, and tell us you're going to investigate yourself. You've got to be crazy."

Refusing to take any more questions, Deutch finished with, "You know, I've learned how important it is for our government and our Agency to get on top of this problem and stop it. I came today to try and describe the approach and have left with a better appreciation of what is on your mind."

Immediately, the media tried to spin the meeting in a way favourable to the CIA. Via satellite, Ted Koppel of *Nightline* interviewed members of the audience, trying to extract a positive testimony, only to get rebuffed by questions such as, "You come down here and talk about solutions. We have kids that are dying. We have hospitals for babies born drug addicted. When are you guys going to come down and bring cameras to our neighbourhood?"

"I'm not sure that anybody even thought that was why Director Deutch came there today," Koppel said. "He's here because a lot of you are in anguish. A lot of you are angry. A lot of you are frustrated by what you believe to be the CIA's involvement in bringing drugs to South Central LA. Now, I want to hear from someone who thought it did some good."

"Well, I am glad Mr Deutch was here today," said Marcine Shaw, the mayor pro tem of Compton. "I'm glad Congresswoman MacDonald had him here because that's what it took to get your cameras here, Mr Koppel."

Koppel shook his head. "Yes, but that's not the question." Koppel finished his broadcast with, "If any suspicions were put to rest or minds changed, there was no evidence of it in South Central this evening."

In 2019, searching for answers about CIA drug trafficking, I interviewed the famous conspiracy researcher, David Icke, author of numerous books, including *The Trigger* about 9/11. The three-hour podcast is available on YouTube: <u>Conspiracy Crimes Of The Illuminati: David Icke | True Crime Podcast 33.</u>

Shaun: What do you think about the War on Drugs?

David: The War on Drugs, overwhelmingly, is an Orwellian inversion. If you're going to run drugs, the best way to do it unsuspected is to do it from an anti-drug agency. This is what the Clintons and the Bushes were doing. So, father George Bush was one of the major drug runners in America. He was having Wars on Drugs when he was president and of course, the War on Drugs from the Bushes' point of view is a War on the Competition, right? Bush was exposed by the *San Jose Mercury News* – a very proper journalist reporter [Gary Webb] – for putting crack cocaine on the streets of Los Angeles. And by the way, who attacked the reporter more than the rest of the bloody media in America for actually exposing this story?

Drugs are used one, to create enormous amounts of money to spend on this agenda outside of government traceable funds and also to absolutely destroy human society. Look at the opioid epidemic in America now. It's destroying vast numbers of people and so they talk about a War on Drugs, but what they are doing is making them circulate.

Say what you like about the Taliban and a lot should be

said about the Taliban. When they got control of Afghanistan, the poppy fields disappeared. When the American military sent the boys in, they suddenly went to record levels of poppy production because – I go into this in *The Trigger* – the ISI, the Pakistani military intelligence, which is very close to the CIA, they were running an operation through Afghanistan to get the source of the drugs to make the drugs and get the drugs into America. Mohamed Atta was almost certainly flying drugs out of the Venice airport where he was supposed to be learning to fly. According to *The Times* of India, he was wired $100,000 on the behest of the head of the Pakistan ISI just before 9/11. So, of course, the media says he was wired that money because it was for 9/11. Two questions: why then aren't you arresting the head of the ISI who wired the money if the money was involved in 9/11? Why was the head of that ISI in Washington, DC on September the 11th meeting with CIA representatives and why has nothing ever happened to him? That money wired was to do with drugs that Atta was involved in. Atta was just put in the wrong place at the wrong time. He wasn't even on the plane, but he was in the right place to be blamed for it.

Shaun: You mentioned these presidents through the CIA's black ops coordinating drugs coming into the country, while ramping up the War on Drugs themselves. The cost of this was mass incarceration, hundreds of thousands of non-violent drug possessors going to prison. At the peak of the War on Drugs, you had over half a million arrests a year for weed possession. When I was in the jail in Arizona before I got arrested, I thought prisoners were paedophiles, murderers and rapists. When I got in there, the average arrest was a black kid or a Mexican kid with a little bit of weed, getting a two- to five-year sentence.

David: Yeah, and what they're doing now, they're pushing the legalisation of it. Why? Because corporations are taking it over. Corporations are going to take this whole marijuana thing and make an industry of it.

Shaun: Because it was made illegal in the first place out of

California. The pharmaceutical societies there didn't want people growing free medicine in their own backyards, so now you still can't grow in your own backyard, but you can buy it from a corporation.

David: Yeah and of course they will produce a form which will not be – I mean, even the stuff today as I understand it from listening to people who've researched this, it's not the marijuana of the '60s that people are having now, and so the corporations have hijacked it. That is what they do. That's why they've hijacked the food supplement industry and synthesised it and if it's synthetic, it's freaking useless, but they sell it in their stores at high prices. "I take this good stuff. I only have natural." "No! You're having synthetic." It's not natural. With natural, it will be good. So why would a psychopathic empathy-free zone like Big Pharma be interested in the well-being of the population? Whether it's synthetic food supplements and vitamins or marijuana, they wouldn't.

Shaun: I read a story about a biochemist in the medical profession and he got prostate cancer, so he went to his doctor and basically he said, "Your chances of survival after this treatment are very low." He had a friend, a hippie, out of San Francisco and she said, "Get on the cannabis oil." He got on the cannabis oil and he went back for an X-ray and the cancer was completely gone. (The story of biochemist Dennis Hill is available online and in the next chapter. Diagnosed with Stage 4 prostate cancer, he cancelled his upcoming chemotherapy and used illegally sourced cannabis oil with THC to defeat the cancer.)

David: I know a story just like that. A friend of mine in Canada, quite a well-known guy, I spoke to him and he was basically in terrible pain with cancer in bed. And he went on the cannabis oil and I spoke in Toronto and I knew he was still alive. I invited him to the event and I invited him to come and have a chat beforehand, and I was kind of expecting this frail guy to walk into the hotel bar [but] this guy was absolutely healthy as hell [on] cannabis oil from late-line cancer, and there's so many people who die, so many people who suffer who don't have to if only we were allowed to have all information and possibility, instead of only that which we are allowed to see and allowed to access.

Shaun: It breaks my heart that hundreds of thousands of people must have died, maybe even millions, because they couldn't get this free medicine and all these little kids now that have the seizures, they have multiple seizures, they can go into a coma and die. All the people who have died in the past because of them getting denied access to the oil, but now these evil psychopathic politicians who care mostly about votes, they can't go up against these little sick dying babies.

CHAPTER 16
MEDICINAL CANNABIS

"Now is not the time to send a message to our young people that marijuana is medicine. It is not. It is a dangerous illegal drug." Barbara Bush.

Sir William Osler, a Canadian physician, has been described as the "Father of Modern Medicine." He wrote the first textbook of internal medicine, which described cannabis as the most effective medication for the treatment of migraine headaches. Experiments in 1949 demonstrated its use in treating epilepsy. People with Crohn's disease were able to stop using steroids and other medication when treated with cannabis. They had less abdominal pain and diarrhoea. It reduces anxiety for people with Alzheimer's disease, and muscle spasms with Parkinson's disease. With PTSD, it's useful for reducing fearful memories. The Israeli and Croatian governments give troops cannabis to treat PTSD. With arthritis, a topical application reduces pain. Some people have claimed that cannabis oil has cured their cancer.

The National Institute on Drug Abuse, a research institution run by the federal government, has grudgingly admitted that cannabis is capable of killing certain cancer cells. A publication from the NIDA, revised as of April 2015, stated that "recent animal studies have shown that marijuana can kill certain cancer cells and reduce the size of others. Evidence from one animal study suggests that extracts from whole-plant marijuana can shrink one of the most serious types of brain tumors. Research in mice showed that these extracts, when used with radiation, increased the cancer-killing effects of the radiation."

In a remote Canadian town called Maccan in Nova Scotia, Rick Simpson stumbled upon the medicinal use of cannabis and became a leading advocate. He was born in 1949, when cancer was rare. In 1969, his twenty-two-year-old cousin was diagnosed with it. Having never heard of anyone so young getting cancer, he wondered if it were a misdiagnosis, but after an agonising three years, his cousin died. It was the first person he knew whom cancer had killed. Three years later, he heard a radio broadcast about an active ingredient in cannabis called THC killing cancer cells, but he didn't think much about it.

He worked in the hospital system, from the 1970s until 1997, when he suffered a work-related head injury and post-concussion syndrome, which caused a noise in his head that prevented sleep. Prescription medication aggravated the condition and fogged his mind. During those twenty-five years, he became increasingly perplexed by the exponential growth in cancer and other diseases that had been rare. He hadn't yet concluded that cancer rates were due to the increased toxicity of the environment.

In 1998, he saw a TV show, *The Nature of Things*, with Dr David Suzuki, which featured people smoking pot to address medical conditions. Rick obtained some, smoked it and felt a relief in his head that enabled him to rest. He tried to get medicinal cannabis prescribed under Canada's Marihuana Medical Access Program, but the medical staff warned that it would be bad for his lungs and that the possible medical benefits were still under study. By 1999, his suffering drove him to contemplate suicide.

In desperation, he told his doctor, "What would you think if I was to get a cannabis plant and take the essential oil from it, and ingest it instead of smoking it?"

With a cautious expression, the doctor said, "It would be a more medicinal way to use it." The doctor refused to give him a prescription.

In 2001, Rick's brain was in such a poor condition that he could hardly remember his name. He was told there was nothing more that the medical system could do for him. Again, he was denied a prescription for cannabis, so he started to ingest small doses of cannabis oil that he had manufactured himself. Right away his blood pressure regulated and he lost some weight as his body detoxified. Finally, he was able to sleep for over eight hours a night. His eyesight improved. His arthritis disappeared.

Since the '90s, he had been noticing three discoloured patches on his body that wouldn't heal: one by his eye, one by his cheek and one by his chest. In 2002, suspecting skin cancer, he approached his doctor, who couldn't confirm the diagnosis until he received a pathology report. After the patch by his eye was operated on, it became infected. Examining it at home, he remembered the radio broadcast about THC curing cancer. He couldn't understand why he had skin cancer if he was ingesting cannabis oil. It occurred to him to apply the oil topically. He almost didn't do it, but thought, *What the heck. I'll give it a try.* He applied the oil to bandages and stuck them to the areas with the skin cancer. The puffiness and feeling of splinters in the carcinoma immediately stopped. For four days, it felt as if nothing was happening under the bandages. Upon removing them, he was in shock. The patches were gone and only pink skin remained.

He enthusiastically told everyone he knew. Thinking he was crazy, most people laughed at him. After six weeks of abuse, he believed that he had gone mad. Then the cancer by his eye returned. Watching it develop, he suffered the splinter feeling again. He applied the oil and a bandage. Four days later, it was gone. Eleven years later, it was still gone. All instances of his skin cancer were cured.

Wondering how that was possible, he visited his doctor's office for the pathology report. He wanted to be certain that he had actually been diagnosed with cancer. The receptionist that day was the doctor's wife. About six people were waiting. The report stated he had basal cell carcinoma.

"I'd like to come back in the evening and talk to the doctor about something I've been working on," he said.

"What's this about?" she asked.

"The cancer that was removed came right back, so I cured it and the other two using hemp oil."

Her face soured. "The doctor will not go there!" she yelled. "The doctor will not provide this!"

In the truck on the way home, he thought, *If I were a doctor and one of my patients had cured cancer with something natural, I'd want to know about it.*

Perplexed, he contacted TV shows, politicians, cancer societies and the United Nations. Nobody wanted to hear about his experience. He concluded that vested interests didn't want people growing cheap and effective medicine in their own backyards.

In 2003, he started sharing his hemp oil with others suffering from skin conditions such as psoriasis, warts and moles. After positive results, he contacted more people and organisations, including two federal ministers of health in Canada. Most never replied.

In April 2003, he was advised that the Pain Management Clinic in Halifax might grant him a licence to grow hemp, but a recorded message stated that there was a twenty-one-month waiting period and all applicants had to be referred by their physicians. In 2004, desperate to be heard, he contacted newspapers, who published lengthy articles, detailing his activity and results. The attention resulted in the police confiscating 1,600 cannabis plants from his backyard.

Rick Dwyer, the president of the Maccan Royal Canadian Legion, started hearing about the healing powers of Rick Simpson's oil. Sick people were taking small drops orally or applying it topically. At first, he doubted the claims of serious illnesses such as cancer being cured. In late 2005, with his dad suffering from lung cancer and diabetes – a difficult combination for doctors to treat – Dwyer was running out of time. His dad had been given forty-eight hours to live. Funeral preparations were being made. Chemotherapy had swollen his dad's entire body from head to feet. With nothing to lose, Dwyer requested a meeting with Rick.

At the Legion, Rick explained how he had used the oil to cure skin cancer and diabetic ulcers. Dwyer felt that Rick was sincere. The two bonded because their parents were war veterans. Dwyer asked to see the people Rick had helped. They all confirmed that they were cured and provided medical documents.

Dwyer took some oil to his dad, who thought it was a scam because of Rick's lack of medical background. His nurses refused to break the law by administering it. It took plenty of persuasion to convince Dwyer's dad to take a dose. The dying man slept soundly that night and woke up smiling. Within a few days, he left hospital for home. It took the fluid off his lungs, repaired his prostate and got his diabetes under control, so he didn't have to take insulin.

Dwyer joined Rick's crusade. He held a meeting and it was decided to send a letter to the editor of a local newspaper: "We the executive and membership of Royal Canadian Legion Branch 134 in Maccan wish to inform the Canadian people that we support Rick Simpson and the use of hemp oil as medicine. We request from our system an honest review concerning what Mr Simpson has proven with hemp medicine." The president and treasurer signed it.

Dwyer spoke three times to the provincial command of the Legion, urging him to come and direct the next step. The provincial command refused to address the issue. As members of the Legion were sick and suffering horribly with cancer, Dwyer decided to take the issue to Parliament by petitioning to enact legislation in support of the clinical testing of cannabis oil. He contacted politicians, health professionals, law enforcement officials and anyone else relevant to the issue. He asked them all to come to a meeting where he would present all of the scientific, human and medical evidence.

Before the meeting could happen, Dwyer went to the Legion and found that the doors were locked. Two Royal Canadian Mounted Police told him that he wasn't allowed on the property. The Maccan branch had been shut down. The charter had been pulled and the executive suspended. The Nova Scotia Legion

Command issued a statement that they would not allow the Legion to be used as a soapbox for political messages, especially one involving illegal drugs. They feared it would damage the Legion's reputation and integrity. The Legion informed Dwyer that he wasn't even allowed to tell anyone why his branch had been shut down. He felt as if he were under martial law.

"If they shut us down over a cure for cancer, who's doing the right thing, us or them?" he said. "What greater integrity or honour for the Royal Canadian Legion to speak up on behalf of all the men, women and children who are suffering." In response to the illegality, he said, "I don't care if this medicine comes from a tomato plant, a potato plant or a hemp plant. If the medicine's safe and helps and works, why not use it?"

When interviewed on TV, his dad stated that he had been given twenty-four hours to live before taking the oil, which he credited for him still being alive. Finally, TV stations were running the story:

"There is a big-time controversy brewing in a small town over [hemp oil]. Is it a cure-all or contraband?"

"In a small Nova Scotia town, one man is trying to get the word out about what he says are the healing properties of hemp oil ... Where he's spreading the word has created a major headache with no cure in sight."

Rick gave the oil away for free, which incensed the authorities, who ordered so many raids on his home that he relocated to Europe.

On YouTube, Dennis Hill is slim, silver-haired and softly spoken. Behind thin-rimmed glasses, his eyes gleam with serenity, perhaps a credit to decades of meditation practice. Born in Texas, he graduated with a degree in biochemistry from the University of Houston. He researched cancer for ten years at the University of Texas MD Anderson Cancer Center, a preeminent cancer hospital. At Baylor College of Medicine, he studied advanced work in medical and human physiology. After ten years of research, he obtained an MBA. He went to work in hospital administration, clinic management and research management.

By 2011, Dennis was working as a software engineer and teaching meditation. Having swam competitively for eleven years as a scholarship athlete in college, he was used to being in excellent physical condition. When his prostate started to swell, he considered it a benign enlargement. He requested treatment and his urologist insisted on a biopsy. When his Gleason scores came back at 7 and 8, he was in shock. Gleason scores above 7 are associated with cancer that is unlikely to be cured. Even worse, his prostate cancer had metastasised to the bladder and other tissues. Due to his extensive knowledge, he knew he was likely to die. Immediately, the urologist scheduled him for radiation, chemo-therapy and surgery. He was told that his chance of survival was 3 percent. In preparation for the treatment, he was shaved and marked.

In anguish, he complained about his terminal cancer to a female friend.

"Have you heard that marijuana cures cancer?" she replied.

"No way! Are you serious? What are you talking about?" His only experience with cannabis had been smoking it in the '60s and '70s. Initially, he had enjoyed its meditative quality, but he had eventually quit so that he could meditate more peacefully. He credited cannabis for starting his thirty-year meditation journey.

"Yeah. Research it."

"Well, how do you know?"

"My nephew was just here in San Francisco at a medical-marijuana conference, and he told me all about it."

"Are you sure about this? Marijuana cures cancer!"

"Well, you look it up. It's on the Internet."

During decades in the field, he had never come across any information about cannabis and cancer or heard of anyone using it medicinally. Due to his previous experience of smoking it, he was receptive to his friend's suggestion, even though it was coun-terintuitive to his conditioned beliefs. Surely cannabis oil wouldn't be as harmful as chemotherapy. He knew he could tolerate the effects of THC, the component in cannabis that creates the high.

Googling the subject, a Rick Simpson video came up. Watching *Run from the Cure*, Dennis was impressed by Rick's groundbreaking work, sincerity and the testimonies of the people who had beaten cancer. To postpone his radiation treatment, he told his doctor that he wanted to pursue an alternative therapy.

Reading led him to discover that the endocannabinoid system had started to reveal itself to researchers in the 1940s. Yet, he had been working in the field after that, and had never heard of it, not even in medical school. By the late 1960s, the basic structure and functionality of the endocannabinoid system had been laid out. The endocannabinoid system has been in every chordate creature for the last 500 million years. It is a fully mature biochemical technology that has maintained health and metabolic balance for most of life's history. It's a comprehensive system of biochemical modulators that maintain homoeostasis in all body systems, including the central and peripheral nervous systems, all organ systems, all somatic tissues and all metabolic biochemical systems, including the immune system.

The mechanism by which cannabis oil battles cancer involves a partnership between the immune system and the endocannabinoid system. A function of the immune system is to get rid of dead and dying cells. But the immune system on its own is only moderately effective in fighting cancer because cancer cells are essentially modified "self" cells, which the immune system usually doesn't recognise as harmful. Cancer cells hide from the immune system by removing from their surface the chemical ID that says something is wrong. Some of the chemicals in cannabis are able to circumvent the disguise.

One of those chemicals is THC, a cannabinoid in cannabis. When THC meets the endocannabinoid receptors on cancer cells, they produce ceramide, which kills them. Ceramide is the agent the immune system uses to kill dead or dying cells. Once the immune system recognises that the DNA of the cancer cells is abnormal, it sends ceramide to shred the mitochondria, which provides energy to the cells. Cells without mitochondria cannot create energy to keep the cancer alive, so it dies. With cannabis oil, normal cells around the cancer remain unaffected because they don't manufacture ceramide. Another useful cannabinoid is CBD (cannabidiol), which shuts down the L1 gene that allows cancer to metastasise and divide. This one-two punch of THC and CBD kills the cancer cells and the tissue is left immune for any other cancer growth.

There is nothing else that does this and it works with all forms of cancer, no matter where the cancer is or how long you've had it for. A factor restricting positive results with cannabis oil is whether the patient has already had intense treatment such as chemotherapy that has caused too much destruction to the body. However, even some patients who have been sent home to die after conventional treatment have cured their cancer with cannabis oil. Human studies and experiments documented in Europe, the Soviet Union and Israel verify that it works.

Based on Rick Simpson's video, Dennis expected the cannabis treatment to last for three months. Searching for cannabis oil, he couldn't find any as the Bay Area dispensaries only stocked hempseed oil. A friend offered to make him cannabis butter, which he feared might be too weak to eradicate his cancer. As it was the only thing available, he started with the butter, which he used day and night for three months. At the next prostate exam, he learned that the primary tumour had been completely destroyed, but he still had metastatic lesions.

Finally, he obtained the oil with THC. At night, he took the dose recommended by Rick Simpson and slept heavily. Waking up refreshed in the morning, he felt strong enough to run daily. He would take a small dose, which enabled him to go to work as his body was accustomed to THC. He believed that the nighttime dose was doing the hard work of killing the cancer, and the small dose was keeping the cannabinoids' pressure on the cancer, preventing it from recovering. Unfatigued in the daytime, he could drive and do his two jobs safely, and live his life normally. He never once had to visit a hospital or suffered any other disruptions to his routine. Nobody had to stick needles in his veins or surgically remove any body parts. After three more months, the biopsy showed that all signs of cancer were gone. Bone scans and multiple procedures showed zero cancer. The doctors were flabbergasted. Even Dennis had a hard time believing it because it was outside of the realm of everything he had been taught, researched or worked on.

Over six months, he never took a day off work. He told some of his colleagues about the cannabis-oil cure; others, he didn't. There were members of his family he couldn't tell due to their negative attitudes towards cannabis.

Dennis has advice for anyone looking to cure cancer with cannabis oil: research on the Internet and follow Rick Simpson's instructions exactly. Educate yourself so that you have positive feelings about it. If you have a bad feeling about cannabis or consider it to be poison, your mind may interfere with the treatment. Read some of the hundreds of cannabis cancer-treatment blogs out there. If you can grow your own cannabis, it's beneficial because you can control the whole process. If not, find a convenient local dispensary or a mobile delivery service. He eventually joined a co-op, which he worked with to get his medicine. There was one grower and half a dozen cancer patients.

He believes that so many people are still sceptical of this cure because most of us have been raised with extremely strong negative conditioning about cannabis, which has tainted our perception of reality. He hopes that his story is the kind of proof that will change people's minds. Unlike other patients who used cannabis oil in association with other forms of treatment, he relied purely on cannabis oil, so there were no other factors at work that could have cured his cancer. As more patients get healed through cannabis, he hopes that the laws will be changed. Now that more information is available online, he is optimistic that cancer sufferers will do their own research and be able to get cannabis oil.

Cannabis is still illegal to many cancer patients worldwide whom Dennis is counselling, but they are finding ways to get it.

The active compounds in cannabis took so long to isolate and identify due to the suppression of cannabis research worldwide as a result of the drug laws foisted on most countries through the United Nations by Harry Anslinger, the racist drugs czar in the early 1900s, who was backed by the cabal of corporate interests described in Chapter 5. Their strategy to block the competition was successful: global pharmaceutical sales topped $1 trillion in 2014.

When googling cannabis and cancer, Dennis read about research in Israel conducted by Raphael Mechoulam, an organic chemist considered to be the grandfather of cannabis research.

Raphael was born in Bulgaria in 1930. His physician father, in addition to running a private practice, was the head of the Jewish hospital in Sofia. When anti-Jewish laws came into effect, his father decided to move them to a village, where he hoped his family would be safer, and which badly needed doctors. In 1942, he became a village doctor. For two years, they moved from village to village without any problems – until someone decided to send him to a concentration camp. Fortunately, Bulgarian Jews were not being executed. The camp ended up on fire. As his father was the only doctor, he assisted to the best of his ability. Shortly thereafter, he was released. By the end of the 1940s, most Bulgarian Jews were moving to Israel. Raphael and his family arrived in 1949. He briefly worked as a land surveyor. In the army, he researched insecticides and that's where he met his wife. The topic of his Ph.D. was Natural Products Related to Biological Problems.

As a young person at the Weizmann Institute of Science in Rehovot, Israel, Raphael wanted to investigate something that was not being pursued by major research groups around the world. Being in a small country with a tiny budget, he couldn't compete with them. Thanks to fearmongering on a global scale by drugs czar Harry Anslinger, nobody was working on cannabinoid chemistry. Raphael asked the director if he knew anyone in the police department who could provide hashish for research purposes.

The administrative director made a call to a friend. "Can you provide cannabis to one of our researchers?"

Raphael overheard the friend respond, "Is he reliable?"

Even though the director barely knew Raphael, he said, "Yes, of course, he's reliable. Let him come over and pick some hashish."

Raphael took a bus, and picked up five kilos, which he packed in a travel bag. Unbeknown to him, the police should not have handed over the cannabis because he did not have a permit from the Ministry of Health. On the return journey, the passengers started to ask, "What the hell is the unusual smell?" After arriving home safely, he contacted some of his colleagues at the Ministry of Health. He apologised for breaking the law, and agreed to get a permit. When he needed more hashish, he went to the Ministry of Health, filled out the form for a permit, drank coffee with his colleagues, took the permit to the police, drank coffee with them and left with his hashish.

In the lab, he stored five kilos in an unlocked cupboard. Nobody noticed. In order to find the structure of the compounds, he separated a dozen compounds from the cannabis. They tested them on a colony of monkeys in a nearby institute. The monkeys were only affected by one compound, which sedated them. He had identified the one major active compound: THC.

The first study on humans involved his wife baking a cake for a group of friends who had never tried cannabis. Five of his friends ate slices without THC. The rest ate slices dosed with ten milligrams of THC. The latter group were affected, and to his surprise, some reacted differently. Some sat back and enjoyed the strange feeling. Another denied any effect, but talked incessantly. Another denied any effect, but had the giggles. A female became anxious. Most felt a bit sedated and disorientated and open to discussion.

Studying the records of cannabis use in ancient civilisations, he found that it had been used in the Middle East for thousands of years. The Assyrians had used it for medicine, excitation and in religion. The Egyptians as medicine. The Greeks and Romans used it as an anti-inflammatory drug. People in India used it to free them from all worries and cares – anti-anxiety. Of particular interest was a translation of a fifteenth-century Arab story: a ruler suffering from epilepsy was visited by a physician with cannabis. It cured him, but he had to take it for his entire life. Raphael decided to try it for epilepsy.

In animal tests, cannabis worked for epilepsy, so it was time to experiment on humans. Ten epileptics in San Paulo not reacting to conventional medicine were administered high doses of cannabidiol, 200 milligrams a day. While on cannabidiol, they had no seizures. The published results were completely ignored by the medical establishment. Decades later, it remained the only publication about the effects of cannabidiol on human epileptics.

In the mid-1980s, an American researcher discovered a receptor for THC in the human brain. This posed the question as to why there were receptors in the brain for this substance. Receptors are made for compounds humans produce, not because there is a plant out there. Raphael and his team were convinced that there must be compounds in humans that mimic cannabis. They decided to experiment on pig brains because pig and human organs are considered to be closely related.

He drove to Tel Aviv and bought a few kilos of pig brains, with the butcher assuming that the brains were being cooked for a party. Every time he returned to buy more brains, the butcher increased the price. After two years, they found low amounts of an endogenous compound in the brain that acted on the receptors discovered by the American researcher. They named it anandamide. The system in the body that uses anandamide is now known as the endocannabinoid system. Teams of researchers worldwide are still investigating it.

Knowing that cannabis can reduce the harsh side-effects of drugs, Raphael decided to do a clinical trial on children with cancer in 1995. They deposited drops of THC with olive oil under the children's tongues, two or three times a day. Some received just olive oil. The latter group continued to vomit and suffer side-effects. They discovered that a small amount of THC completely blocked the vomiting and nausea. It was such a small amount of THC that the children did not get high. They published the therapeutic effects and, yet again, the medical establishment ignored the paper. Decades later, it still wasn't being used for children, adding to Raphael's disappointment in oncologists.

Eventually, other researchers caught up with Raphael and his team. A paper was published stating that the endocannabinoid system is involved in all human diseases. The cannabinoid molecules we all have are critical to our health. His vision that mother's milk contained medicinal endocannabinoids turned out to be true.

Raphael is frustrated over the lack of research about cannabis as a cancer treatment. He knows that THC in a test tube blocks the development of cancer cells. Research in Spain has explored the mechanisms through which cannabinoids act on cancer. In animals, cannabinoids exerted anti-tumour actions on a variety of tumours, including brain ones. Cannabinoids caused cancer cells to die and restrained cancer-cell growth. A trial involving nine volunteers with malignant brain cancer resulted in positive effects on survival and tumour growth. Raphael hopes there are more human trials.

Donald Abrams has worked as an oncologist in America for thirty years. His chemotherapy patients experienced nausea, pain, depression, insomnia and a loss of appetite. Instead of writing five different prescriptions with various side-effects and addictive potential, he began recommending cannabis to alleviate the symptoms.

Patients with AIDS wasting syndrome were experiencing rapid weight loss, diarrhoea, fever and death. To help stimulate their appetite, drug companies produced Dronabinol, a synthetic form of delta-9-THC, a psychoactive compound extracted from the resin of Cannabis sativa. But patients in the early '90s said that they preferred to smoke cannabis than take Dronabinol, because the drug took two to three hours to take effect and zonked them out.

Doctor Abrams set out to show that smoking cannabis was more effective in increasing appetite for these patients. The only legal source of cannabis for clinical trials was the US government. He asked twice but was declined. He approached the head of the National Institute on Drug Abuse (NIDA), who explained that NIDA has a congressional mandate only to study substances of abuse as substances of abuse, and any application to study cannabis as a therapeutic agent could never be granted by the US government. Eventually, he outsmarted the system and conducted studies. He found that the cannabis benefited the immune systems of the AIDS patients more than Dronabinol. His opinion is that the whole plant is the medicine that nature provided and that's the best medicine.

Cannabis has proven to be effective in reducing pain, especially for people with connective tissue disorders, arthritis, fibromyalgia, systemic lupus and reflex sympathetic dystrophy. On cannabis, these patients are able to decrease the amount of opiates they are taking, and in some cases, to stop taking the opiates completely. Failed back surgery, herniated discs and chronic dislocated shoulders all get relief from cannabis with fewer side-effects than opiates, which can cause confusion, constipation, withdrawal from social activities and difficulties with concentration and driving. With cannabis, patients don't get constipation and confusion and they can socialise with their children and grandchildren. For many, it can replace opiates. For others, it can be used in conjunction with lower doses of opiates, and have fewer side-effects. The main side-effects of cannabis come from smoking it. The side-effects can be minimised by eating or drinking it, or using a vaporised form.

For people with MS, cannabis treats their pain and muscle spasms. In 1999, talk show host Montel Williams announced that he had

MS. To raise money for research into the disease, he launched the Montel Williams MS Foundation. On TV, he debated his medical cannabis use with John Stossel.

"The DEA says this is anecdotal nonsense," said John Stossel, dressed like a Wall Street trader in a grey suit and tie, his dark eyes peering from a powdered face with a brown moustache, "and there is no proof that marijuana works … In fact, they categorise it as a Schedule 1 Drug, the same as heroin, which means, they say, it has no medical uses …"

In a casual grey pullover, jeans and a white shirt, Montel said that quoting the DEA is ridiculous. He cited a 1999 government study commissioned by drugs czar General Barry McCaffrey, a staunch prohibitionist, which concluded that making marijuana illegal was one of the most egregious things the US government had ever done because it is an effective pain medication.

"These aren't evil people in the DEA," Stossel said. "They have to genuinely believe the study isn't very good."

"But see, what the problem is, they've never studied it at all," Montel said. "Most people in this country have no idea why marijuana is illegal. Most people think that this government went through a process and studied the drug, and then classified it as illegal because it was dangerous." He referred to the Marihuana Tax Act of 1937, corporate interests, including William Randolph Hearst's timber investment, and racism against blacks and Hispanics. "For me, I have extreme neuropathic pain in my lower extremities, from my feet to my shins. I have pain in my side. I just got diagnosed with something that's called trigeminal neuralgia, a pain in the centre of my face." Cannabis made the pain manageable, and he didn't have to smoke it. He decried the lack of research and blamed the US government for having an exclusive patent on cannabis. "I eat it in an edible form. I take it in a pill form. I take it in a liquid form, and I also vaporise it."

"Marinol is the pill form," Stossel said. "The government could say, 'You have Marinol, and that's enough.'"

"Marinol is a synthetic drug that's not made from real

marijuana. That's part of the problem. But in London, there's a company called GW [Pharma] that has a product called Sativex that is similar to Marinol because it's a liquid form of marijuana. It's a sublingual spray. It's legal all over the world, folks. The rest of the world acknowledges the fact that that's something used for pain sensation ..." Sativex contains two chemical extracts from the cannabis plant: THC and cannabidiol. After years of Sativex use, some UK patients found that their MS stayed the same, rather than worsening, suggesting that the cannabinoids not only relieved their symptoms but also slowed the disease. "Look, this is not about your child smoking a joint ..."

"This kind of is about your child getting high because a lot of people in California have used the legal medical marijuana law to just find a way to smoke."

"There are a lot of people in this country today who are strung out on OxyContin, strung out on Vicodin, strung out on Percocet and strung out on a lot of other drugs that our government controls, and they're not doing a good job of controlling that." Montel tilted his head forward, his eyes and voice full of emotion. "I've got twenty-two years in the military. I put my life on the line for this country. Don't I have a right to pay my taxes and be a functioning member of society? Do I not?"

On June 11, 2015, Montel made an impassioned speech at the State Capitol. "I sat in a closet in my own home, in Greenwich, Connecticut, supposedly with the world in my palm, with a gun in my mouth for hours on end because I wanted to end my pain." He said he walked in front of a car in Manhattan, hoping to be killed, so that he wouldn't be blamed for committing suicide, just to stop the pain. "It wasn't until I started using medical marijuana," he said, wiping away tears, "on a daily basis, and getting my system really saturated with cannabinoids, that I started getting relief. And the reason why I'm a contributing member of society, paying taxes, the way I am right now, is because of the relief I've gotten from marijuana. What's absolutely ignorant is that we live in a country where we get to differentiate between who gets to

SHAUN ATTWOOD

have it and who doesn't ... We're trying to shove democracy down other people's throats when we don't even respect the democracy we have here." He feels it should be a doctor's right to prescribe patients medical cannabis anywhere in the world.

CHAPTER 17
PRESIDENTIAL DRUG LORDS, USERS AND HYPOCRITES

"The general public should hold our politicians accountable for saying one thing when they're not in power and doing another when they come into power," Richard Branson stated. "They disassociate themselves from their own behaviour and the public puts up with it. When they get in power they brutalise other drug users through the prison system for the same behaviour."

"President Roosevelt signed today a bill to curb traffic in the narcotic, marihuana, through heavy taxes on transactions." *New York Times*, August 3, 1937

The president who signed the Marihuana Tax Act of 1937, which destroyed the hemp industry and criminalised even the medicinal use of cannabis, was Franklin Delano Roosevelt a.k.a. FDR, whose wealth was derived from his grandfather's opium trafficking.

Since the seventh century, the Chinese had been using medicinal opium. Demand increased in the 1700s due to the popularity of smoking it with tobacco. As it devastated its users, the Chinese banned opium importation in 1729 and 1799. But the British government was only just getting started. In 1800, China imported 4,500 chests of opium, each containing 65.3kg. By 1838, on the eve of the First Opium War, the amount was 40,000 chests, which surged to 70,000 or 4,500 tons by 1858, making Queen Victoria the biggest drug lord in the world. Growing opium in places like Bengal and shipping it to over ten million addicts in China became the British Empire's most profitable business venture, generating almost 20 percent of the government's revenue. The addicts named the drug "Jesus opium" after the white Christian sailors who peddled it from "devil's ships."

Only twenty-four years old, Warren Delano – the grandfather of future president Roosevelt – sailed to China and joined the Christian smugglers on the Pearl River Delta, who sold opium under the cover of darkness. Delano wrote home that opium had an "unhappy effect" on the malnourished addicts, but he justified his dealings with statements like, "as a merchant I insist it has been ... fair, honorable and legitimate." He compared it to the importation of alcohol to America. A decade later, he was so wealthy, he returned to America before the First Opium War. Among New York's elite, he was considered one of the most eligible bachelors.

In 1838, the Chinese Emperor tried to enforce prohibition. He sent Special Imperial Commissioner Lin Zexu to Canton. Lin arrested Chinese dealers and demanded that foreign firms surrender their opium, while offering no compensation. After they refused, Lin stopped the trade and placed the foreigners under siege in their factories. The merchants were forced to relinquish their opium. Over twenty-three days, Lin destroyed 1,016 tons of it. In response, British expeditionary forces from India ravaged the Chinese coast. In 1842, the Chinese surrendered, paid $3 million in compensation and signed over Hong Kong.

While British warships bombarded the Chinese, Warren Delano was safe by New York's Hudson River. Just like the Cali Cartel would do over a century later, he invested his drug money into legitimate businesses and real estate. The financial Panic of 1857 hit his investments hard, so he once again set sail for China, at age fifty, leaving behind his pregnant wife and eight children. This time his trafficking extended to supplying opium to the US War Department to treat soldiers fighting in the American Civil War, foreshadowing the merger of drug and war profiteering that presidents such as George HW Bush would employ covertly in the next century. With his fortune rebuilt, Warren Delano returned to America, where his adventures in opium trafficking were hidden from history.

Other American families who cashed in on opium trafficking included the Cabots, who donated some of their profits to Harvard, and the Russells, who used it to finance Yale's Skull and Bones society, whose members have included many presidents and important figures. The Forbeses profited, too. Their progeny includes former US Secretary of State John Kerry, whose Kerry Committee investigated the Contra scandal highlighted by Gary Webb.

When Kevin Ives was found dead on the tracks, Linda initially suspected that criminals had murdered her son. In a sense they had, with the chief co-conspirators being President Ronald Reagan, Vice President George HW Bush and Arkansas State Governor Bill Clinton. While in private, Reagan had authorised the importation of the cocaine that had spawned the crack epidemic, in public, he was manipulating the public with lies like, "That's why I believe the tide of battle has turned, and we're beginning to win the crusade for a drug-free America."

First Lady Nancy Reagan appeared on TV in a pink outfit, surrounded by mixed-race kids in green T-shirts. "At the beginning of this year someone asked me if I wanted to make a New Year's wish and I said, 'Yes ... I'd like to see every young person in the world join the Just Say No to Drugs Club. The future of the world lies in their hands, and we must all come together in their name to end drug and alcohol abuse once and for all.'"

Under Reagan, harsh DEA tactics crushed domestic cannabis suppliers, forcing users to turn to a dangerous black market. Violence erupted as drug gangs competed. Mexico became a dominant supplier, which helped the growth of the cartels, and set the scene for the eruption of violence in Mexico.

The CIA brought so much cocaine into the USA under Reagan that the wholesale price dropped from $60,000 per kilo in 1980 to

$10,000 per kilo in 1988. The boys on the tracks had come across the importation of cocaine that pilots such as Beau Abbott and Chip Tatum were bringing in for the CIA under Reagan. That's why no one has ever been prosecuted for their murders.

The extent of Clinton's involvement was exposed by someone who worked for the Clintons for ten years. Larry Nichols eventually became the Director of Marketing for the Arkansas Development Finance Authority (ADFA), which Clinton pitched to the public as a vehicle for creating jobs and assisting churches and schools.

"I'd been there about a month," Larry said, "and I realised that I was in the epicentre of what I'd always heard about all my life … I was literally working, sitting in the middle of Bill Clinton's political machine. It was where he made pay-offs, where he repaid favours to people for campaign support."

Millions of dollars were being channelled to Clinton's election campaign, his inner circle of friends and to Hillary Clinton's law firm. Two months into the job, Larry was so suspicious that he started copying documents. "For about two months, I watched accounts accumulate money, and at the end of the month, they zero balanced. They were laundering drug money. There was a hundred million a month in cocaine coming in and out of Mena Arkansas."

According to author Roger Stone, Dan Lasater – the man posing as Dr Lasater whom Chip Tatum had delivered cocaine to – was Bill Clinton's closest and most important political contributor. Larry Nichols said Clinton had contracted Dan to launder cocaine proceeds.

"Dan Lasater, who was a best friend of Bill Clinton … He didn't sell cocaine. Nope. They were giving it away. Huge piles of cocaine in his office. Ashtray upon ashtray full at the parties, and they'd give it to young girls."

Doc DeLaughter, the police investigator in charge of Dan Lasater's cocaine case, said, "A fourteen-year-old cheerleader out of North Little Rock, she was a virgin and ultimately he [Lasater] ended up sending her to a physician of his. The physician put her on birth-control pills. He used cocaine ... and ultimately she lost her virginity. She got addicted to cocaine, and the last I heard of her when we had her subpoenaed back to the federal grand jury, she was a hooker in Lake Tahoe ...

"After Lasater was indicted, I started to receive quite a bit of harassment from my own department in the Arkansas State Police. I knew the reason behind it was because of the affiliation with the state police and the governor's office with Dan Lasater and his business associates." Lasater was convicted and sent to a minimum-security prison for six months. The day after he was released, Clinton granted him a full pardon.

Larry said, "If you think he's [Bill Cinton's] tough on crime, think about a man who pardons a man who gives cocaine to kids." The rest of the people involved in the money laundering went to Washington with Clinton when he became president.

Grand jury witness, Sharlene Wilson, said, "I lived in Little Rock, Arkansas ... I worked at a club called Le Bistros, and I met Roger Clinton there, Governor Bill Clinton and a couple of his state troopers that went with him wherever he went. Roger Clinton had come up to me and he had asked me could I give him some coke, you know, and asked for my one-hitter, which, a one-hitter is a very small silver device, OK, that you stick up into your nose and you just squeeze it and a snort of cocaine will go up in there. And I watched Roger hand what I had given him to Governor Clinton, and he just kind of turned around and walked off." This meeting led to her partying on cocaine with the Clinton brothers at Governor Clinton's mansion and at toga parties. At the toga parties, which turned into cocaine-fuelled orgies, were the Attorney General and members of the Arkansas State Police.

"They began to dance around, do the cocaine in one room, have sex in another room, 'cause in the Coachman's Inn the rooms were adjoining, you know. And to be quite truthful, you end up with somebody in particular and you, nine times out of ten, end up having sex. And there was cocaine there, I know. I'm the one that made sure it was there." Sharlene said, "I watched Bill Clinton lean up against a brick wall. He must have had an adenoid problem because he casually stuck my tooter up his nose … He was so messed up that night, he slid down the wall into a garbage can and just sat there like a complete idiot."

Sharlene admitted to having sex with Roger Clinton. She partied with the Clinton brothers until the early hours in the governor's mansion. "I thought it was the coolest thing in the world that we had a governor who got high." After she testified at the grand jury, the investigation was shut down by the Republican-appointed US Attorney Charles Banks. She told Jean Duffy that her home was under surveillance and she was petrified of the "powers that be." She felt she knew too much because she had worked, "for three or four months unloading bags of cocaine at the Mena airport."

Former 1958 Miss Arkansas, Sally Perdue, said, "He [Bill] had all of the [cocaine-snorting] equipment laid out, like a real pro."

Former model, Gennifer Flowers, had a twelve-year relationship with Clinton. After Bill denied it, Gennifer released smoochy phone conversations she had secretly recorded. In January 1998, Clinton admitted under oath that he had engaged in sex with Gennifer. She said that he had smoked pot in her presence. "I thought how foolish it was of him to carry marijuana around, but it was typical of his bulletproof attitude." Bill told Gennifer about the negative effects of his cocaine use. "He told me about the party he had been to, and said, 'I got so fucked up on cocaine at that party.' He said that it made his scalp itch, and he felt conspicuous because he was talking with people who were not aware drugs were at the party, and all he wanted to do was scratch his head."

Clinton's cocaine habit forced him to seek medical treatment, including multiple stays at a drug rehab according to Betsey Wright, Governor Clinton's chief of staff for seven years. In a YouTube video, Dr Sam Houston, the former physician to Hillary Clinton's father, says: "A Dr Suen, S-U-E-N, here at the medical centre in Little Rock, has taken care of Bill Clinton for his sinus problems, which may indeed be drug related to cocaine use as it destroys the sinus passages. Governor Bill Clinton was taken into the hospital – I believe it was the medical centre on at least one or two occasions – for cocaine abuse and over-dosage ..."

Clinton was with a state trooper when he arrived at the University of Arkansas Medical Center for emergency treatment for cocaine. Hillary was informed by phone. Unimpressed with the risks posed by his habit, she showed up. "When Mrs Clinton arrived, she told both of the resident physicians on duty that night that they would never again practice medicine in the United States if word leaked out about Clinton's drug problem," said Christopher Ruddy, the CEO of Newsmax Media who wrote an article in 1999: "Did Bill Clinton overdose on cocaine?" "Reportedly, [Hillary] pinned one of the doctors up against a wall, both hands pressed against his shoulders, as she gave her dire warning."

In 1996, the columnist R Emmett Tyrrell located and telephoned one of the nurses who had been on duty the night Clinton had ended up in the emergency room. According to Tyrrell, the nurse didn't deny the story, but said that she couldn't run the risk of losing her job by talking about it. Former Saline County criminal investigator, John Brown, said he had interviewed a lot of people who had seen Bill Clinton take drugs, but they were too afraid for their lives to speak.

A Hot Springs undercover policeman filmed Roger Clinton – Bill's younger half-brother – selling cocaine. Roger had bragged to an informant, "I've got four or five guys in uniform who keep an eye on the guys who keep an eye on me." Roger had been dealing directly with a Colombian tied to the drug cartels. After Roger's federal indictment, Bill Clinton read a statement to the media, "My brother has apparently become involved with drugs, a curse which has reached epidemic proportions and has plagued the lives of millions of families in our nation, including many in our state." He didn't take any questions. The head of the state police addressed the media. He said that when he had notified the governor of his brother's arrest, Bill Clinton had told him to handle the case like any other. Bill Clinton used his brother's arrest to pretend that the Clintons were not above the law.

The undercover policeman who had recorded Roger selling cocaine was Travis Bunn, a former military intelligence officer. Roger was caught on a police videotape in April 1984 – with undercover police detective Travis Bunn – saying he [Roger] needed to "get some [cocaine] for my brother [Bill]. He's got a nose like a vacuum cleaner." Suspecting that Roger was part of a larger criminal enterprise, Bunn wanted to "nab him, roll him over and go on up the line," in order to arrest the bigger players. His plan was foiled after an Arkansas State Police officer working in Hot Springs told his superiors. State police took over the investigation. When Dunn found out – after being on the case for a year – he told a colleague who had been investigating Roger Clinton, "We've been screwed." Dunn said that the investigation turned into a damage-control operation. The state police handed the case over to the federal government. Even though he was familiar with Roger's crimes, Dunn was never asked to testify at the grand jury or Roger's trial. "The only reason this case got as far as it did is that they knew I had Roger already," Dunn said. "I had him before they ever got into it. And that was something they couldn't undo."

In 1985, Roger served thirteen months in federal prison out of a two-year sentence. In 2001, he was granted a presidential pardon by his brother, which allowed for the conviction to be expunged from his criminal record. Roger never had to suffer the problems of reintegration into society faced by the hundreds of thousands of non-violent drug offenders incarcerated during the presidency of Bill Clinton, whose criminal records precluded them from employment, education opportunities and housing.

A few years after the arrest of Roger, his boss, Dan Lasater, was also arrested. The multimillionaire bond trader was a personal friend of Bill Clinton and one of his largest political contributors. He pled guilty to federal drug charges of cocaine possession and distribution. In December 1986, Lasater was sentenced to two and a half years. In FBI documents, he admitted to federal investigators that he used cocaine and gave it away to his friends, employees and business associates. Before being released on parole, Lasater served six months in prison, four months in a halfway house and two months under house arrest. Clinton gave him a state pardon in November 1990.

The subject of my book *American Made*, Barry Seal, was a CIA pilot in a drug-smuggling operation. He wanted to run it out of his home state of Louisiana, but they wouldn't let him. According to Larry Nichols, in 1982 Barry chose Arkansas because Governor Clinton was sleazy and hooked on cocaine. Massive amounts of cocaine were smuggled through Arkansas for almost ten years, and no one was ever arrested – except for witnesses – nor were any drugs seized.

According to Russell Welch, the Arkansas State Police Investigator in charge of the Mena investigation, "[Barry Seal] said 1983 was his most profitable cocaine smuggling period ever. The airplanes that he had placed at the Mena airport … were purchased solely for the purpose of cocaine smuggling." In addition to using Mena, small clearings were made across Arkansas to be used as drop points for cocaine and money. It was all done so blatantly that the locals knew what was happening and that criminal investigations were ongoing, yet year after year, no indictments were returned because Clinton had integrated key people as judges, high-level police and other law enforcement.

It was all going smoothly until Kevin and Don's bodies were found on the tracks. While pretending to help Linda, prosecutor Dan Harmon worked behind-the-scenes to threaten and discredit all law enforcement who wanted to bring Sharlene Wilson forward as a witness. With all of the investigations squashed, no arrests were made. According to Sharlene, the people at the tracks on the night of the murders included Dan Harmon. "I do know that the boys were watching the drop sites. OK. And they got curious as to what was being dropped there."

"The fact is we know who killed these kids," said criminal

investigator John Brown. "The whole reason this case has been slowed down and stopped ... I can't do anything with it as long as Clinton's in office because the tracks go right back to Bill Clinton being involved in the cover-up. He took care of everybody who ever covered anything up in this case. Everybody got promoted."

While Clinton got high with impunity, drug users filled Arkansas state prisons. Although many of the inmates had diseases, Clinton's associates decided to sell the prisoners' blood, creating fatal and tragic health effects. As a result of inadequate screening procedures, tens of thousands of blood recipients worldwide contracted hepatitis C, and thousands were infected with HIV. Prisoners received $7 per plasma unit, which were resold at $50 each.

One of the companies involved was Health Management Associates (HMA), run by Leonard Dunn, a banker who worked on Clinton's 1990 gubernatorial campaign. HMA was investigated, but allowed to stay in business due to Dunn's connections and lobbying. Another company was Pine Bluff Biologicals, which expanded the blood programme despite the screening problems. "In 1989, a prisoner who had been forbidden to donate on account of disease was able to sell plasma twenty-three times after he transferred from the Pine Bluff Diagnostics Units to Cummins." Arkansas was the last state to allow prisoners' blood to be sold. When Clinton was no longer governor, the programme finally ended in 1994.

In 1998, an article in *Salon* by Suzi Parker alleged that the Clinton administration had looked the other way while Clinton's cronies had profited from the tainted blood. Parker wrote, "Problems with the prison plasma program were well known to Clinton throughout the 1980s ... In 1986, Clinton's state police investigated problems at the prison and found little cause for concern, while an outside investigator looked at the same allegations and found dozens of safety violations."

According to Mike Galster, who ran orthopaedic clinics in the Arkansas state prison system, the blood programme was "a crime against humanity. Galster said that some prisoners received illegal drugs in exchange for their blood, and others "appeared jaundiced and very sick. When I would ask if they had just had a blood test, they would say, 'No, I've just given plasma.'"

During the AIDS crisis of the early 1980s, the FDA asked companies to stop obtaining blood from prisoners due to their risky behaviour. Ignoring the warnings, Governor Clinton allowed the programme to continue in Arkansas. "In so many ways it reminds you of Nazi Germany …" Galster said. "These guys had the power over a captive audience to make money from human beings. This I know: without the governor's support and protection, this disease-riddled system would have been shut down by 1982."

In 1999, a second *Salon* article written by Parker mentioned a $660 million lawsuit brought by approximately 1,000 haemophiliacs against the Canadian government and companies involved in importing and supplying tainted blood. Parker wrote that the lawyer for the Canadian victims, "said he is seeking a deposition of President Clinton into what occurred in the Arkansas prison system while he was governor during the 1980s … The suit could also name the president if evidence is found that Clinton knew about repeated FDA violations and international plasma recalls, yet failed to exercise executive power to shut down the Arkansas Department of Correction plasma industry." Tens of thousands of Canadians caught deadly diseases, and 7,000 were expected to die due to infections caused by the bad blood.

The office of the haemophiliac group behind the lawsuit was burglarised. The clinic of the whistle-blower working with the haemophiliac group was firebombed. The journalist reporting on this, Suzi Parker, claimed she was being watched and followed. After receiving intimidating phone calls, she stopped reporting, convinced that the Clintons were co-conspirators in the attacks on the haemophiliac group and clinic. Ever since, she has refused to comment.

Money-laundered cocaine proceeds helped Clinton become

the president. In private, he had no qualms about using cocaine. In his 1992 presidential campaign, Clinton advocated for drug treatment, but as soon as he became the president in 1993, he escalated the War on Drugs. "Drugs are as much a threat to our security as any outside enemy. They are a leading cause of crime and violence. They add literally billions of dollars to health care costs every year."

He rejected a US Sentencing Commission recommendation to remove the disparity between crack and powder cocaine sentences – a racist tactic the system used to mass incarcerate blacks for non-violent drug offences. He rejected ending the federal ban on funding for syringe access programmes, which increased the spread of AIDS and other diseases. He gave more federal funds to states that built prisons and housed people for longer sentences. The federal three strikes law that was introduced under his tenure mandated lengthy sentences for repeat offenders.

Under Clinton, demand for cannabis was rising, in part because the demonisation of cocaine and crack in the 1980s had led to some users switching to cannabis, which was perceived as a safer habit. Increased demand in the face of criminalisation expanded the black market and gang-related violent crime. The Mexican supply continued to increase, as did wars among the suppliers. Arms dealing and corruption flourished throughout Latin America. Every US government crackdown increased the black-market prices and provided an opportunity for criminal organisations to produce more supply. The biggest beneficiary of criminalisation was organised crime.

Under Clinton, the US prison population expanded by 487,000 – a rise fuelled by non-violent drug offenders. It was 235,000 more than under Clinton's predecessor: George HW Bush.

One of the most senior players in the CIA's cocaine importation was George HW Bush. While profiting from drugs, the interests he represented were building a prison industrial complex, so that they could profit from the drug problem they were helping to create. Arresting low-level drug users was the easiest way to fill the prisons. In particular, they targeted the black population by handing out huge sentences for crack. For each prisoner held for one year, the prisons received tens of thousands of dollars of tax-payers' money. Some contracts stipulated that they still received that money even when the bunks were empty.

George HW Bush was inaugurated on January 20, 1989. On September 5, 1989, he outlined his strategy for eradicating drug use: "This scourge will stop." He asked Congress for $7.9 billion, 70 percent for law enforcement, including $1.6 billion for jails. His focus was on reducing demand, meaning arresting more drug users, rather than prevention, education and medical treatment.

In September 1989, Bush appeared on TV. "This is the first time since taking the oath of office that I've felt an issue was so important, so threatening, that it warranted talking directly with you, the American people. The most serious problem today is cocaine, and in particular crack." Reaching to his side, the president produced a bag labelled EVIDENCE, containing chalky rocks. "Seized a few days ago by drug-enforcement agents in a park just across the street from the White House."

His claim aroused suspicion in Michael Isikoff, an NBC correspondent, who doubted that crack was being sold in Lafayette Square, an urban park north of the White House. Through his contacts in the DEA, Michael learned the truth. Bush's speech writers believed that a prop would heighten his rhetoric, so they wrote the Lafayette Square crack claim into the script. Bush loved the idea, so after his approval, the DEA was ordered to make a purchase near the White House to fit the president's words.

The assignment ended up with special agent Sam Gaye, who was asked by his boss, "Can you make a drug buy around 1600 Pennsylvania Avenue? Can you call any defendants you've been buying from?" In court, Gaye testified, "I had twenty-four hours to buy three ounces of crack."

Using informers, Gaye attempted to set up the sting. The first attempt fell through after the dealer failed to show up in the park.

During the second attempt, the agent's body microphone malfunctioned, and the cameraman about to film the transaction was assaulted by a homeless person. Finally, an informant contacted Keith Jackson, an eighteen-year-old high-school student who lived across town. Gaye asked Keith to meet him in the park.

"Where's Lafayette Park?" Keith asked.

"It's across the street from the White House."

"Where the fuck is the White House?" After being told it was the president's residence, Keith said, "Oh, you mean where Reagan lives?"

"We had to manipulate him to get him down there," said William McMullan, assistant special agent in charge of the DEA's Washington field office. "It wasn't easy."

When the DEA videotape was played in court, the jury laughed. It showed Gaye waiting on Pennsylvania Avenue with the White House and tourists behind him. Before Jackson and an informer arrived by car, an irate woman sprung up from below the camera's vision and yelling was heard.

"There was this lady," Gaye said, "who got up off the ground and said, 'Don't take my photo! Don't take my photo!'"

With no previous convictions, Keith was sentenced to ten years under federal mandatory minimum guidelines which enhanced punishment for selling crack near a school.

In November 1990, Bush signed a bill that coerced the states into suspending the driver's licenses and revoking government permits and benefits – including college loans – of those convicted of drug crimes. He advocated the heavy use of forfeiture or confiscation of property that the government believed to be drug related. It was primarily used to take cars and currency, and the money was recycled back into the state and federal government. These laws operated under presumed guilt, which did not require a trial or even a conviction.

By 1992, there were more people in federal prisons for drug charges than there were for all crimes in 1980. Twice as many people were arrested for possession than supplying. Chief Justice of the Supreme Court, William Rehnquist, said there were too many arrests. New York City jails filled to breaking point, and jail boats had to be opened. New York City abandoned the war on users to pursue traffickers. The overcrowding ended and New York City saved millions in trial and imprisonment costs. While vested interests profited, Bush's policies did nothing to stop people from buying and selling drugs.

The BBC reported that George W Bush had been secretly recorded admitting smoking cannabis. Bush had held a number of private discussions with Doug Wead, a former aide to George HW Bush. Wead had recorded conversations between 1998 and 2000 without Bush's knowledge. On the recording, Bush told Wead why he generally refused to answer questions from the media about his cannabis use:

"I wouldn't answer the marijuana question," Bush said. "You know why? 'Cause I don't want some little kid doing what I tried." He feared that any admission might have reduced his chance of becoming the president. "You gotta understand, I want to be president. I want to lead. Do you want your little kid to say, 'Hey, Daddy, President Bush tried marijuana. I think I will.'" Responding to a remark by Wead that Bush had publicly denied using cocaine, he said, "I haven't denied anything." Bush said that he would continue to refuse to comment on allegations of drug use. "I am just not going to answer those questions," he said. "And it might cost me the election."

In August 1999, the *New York Daily News* asked eleven politicians vying for the presidency whether they had ever used cocaine. The only one to refuse to answer was George W Bush. Associated Press asked twelve candidates about general drug use. Eight said no. Two admitted smoking weed. Bush refused to answer directly. He said, "I've made mistakes in the past, and I've learned from my mistakes." He said rumours about his drug use were "ridiculous and absurd," but didn't say they were untrue. At each campaign appearance, when asked about his cocaine use, he responded that he wouldn't participate in the "politics of personal destruction."

Regarding his drug use, reporters were told by Oklahoma Governor Frank Keating that Bush needed to, "address issues about private conduct. In today's world, every one of us who serves in public office needs to answer questions about conduct that is arguably criminal."

The Dallas Morning News backed Bush into a corner by posing the question as to whether he would insist that his political appointees answer drug-use questions contained in the standard FBI background check. Political appointees are required to "fully and truthfully" reveal any illegal drug use on the questionnaire for national security decisions.

With advance warning of the question, Bush discussed possible responses with his inner circle of campaign officials. One adviser said, "Imagine the ad our opponents could make if we didn't answer the question." If he became the president, George W Bush intended to maintain a double standard when it came to illegal drug use by White House employees – one for him and one for everybody else.

During a news conference, Bush responded to the question. "As I understand it, the current form asks the question, 'Did somebody use drugs in the last seven years?' and I will be glad to answer that question, and the answer is 'No.'" Again, he refused to answer about historic drug use. "Somebody floats a rumour and it causes you to ask a question and that's the game in American politics, and I refuse to play it. That is a game and you just fell for the trap." He angrily stated that his political enemies were circulating rumours. "They're ridiculous, absurd, and the American people are sick of this kind of politics."

In Virginia the next day, he extended his drug-free years by stating that at the time of his father's inauguration in 1989, he could have passed the fifteen-year background check in effect, placing his admission of drug-free years back to 1974, when he was twenty-eight and at Harvard. After an NBC journalist pointed out that the present White House appointees were required to list any drug use since the age of eighteen, he responded, "I believe it is important to put a stake in the ground and to say enough is enough when it comes to trying to dig up people's backgrounds." Voters who didn't like his answer could, "go find somebody else to vote for. I have told the American people all I'm going to tell them."

Later the same day at a homeless shelter offering treatment for drug addicts, he said that parents should discuss the dangers of drugs and alcohol with their children. "I think a baby-boomer parent ought to say, 'I have learned from the mistakes I may or may not have made, and I'd like to share some wisdom with you, and that is: Don't use drugs. Don't abuse alcohol.' That is what leadership is all about."

The editors of *USA Today* wrote, "Bush has essentially admitted to something. But he refused to say what, creating a political paradox. If his offence is trivial, why hide it? Voters have shown little inclination to punish candidates for youthful drug use, at least in the case of marijuana. And if it's substantial, why should those voters be denied the facts?"

His cryptic responses invited further media investigation. *Salon*, an online magazine, alleged that "back in the late '60s or early '70s [Bush] was ordered by a Texas judge to perform community service in exchange for expunging his record showing illicit drug use and that this service was performed at the Martin Luther King, Jr. Community Service Center in Houston."

The centre's director for thirty-one years, Madge Bush, responded that she had, "never heard of him doing community service here at the agency." She added that Bush had announced his welfare-reform programme from her agency's office. Hundreds of journalists tried to validate the story, but failed, and they lost interest. Two *Online Journal* reporters found out that Bush's Texas driver's-license number had been changed in March 1995, supposedly for security measures.

Author James Hatfield wrote in *Fortunate Son*, "the reporter's instinct in me wondered if Bush may have had something expunged from his driving record, which could have resulted in the issuance of a new license. Did Bush have something in his past that [caused him] to purge the old record?"

Hatfield went on to describe Bush's time at Project PULL, an antipoverty charity where Bush was an inner-city counsellor of young people for several months. "At the time, the 26-year-old Bush was flying planes part-time for the Texas Air National Guard on the weekends, while spending most of his days in Houston drinking heavily, chain-smoking, and, according to friends who partied with him in the early '70s, occasionally getting high on marijuana and snorting cocaine."

At Project PULL, Bush counselled black young people in Houston's third ward, played basketball with them and took them on field trips to prisons. Hatfield wondered why Bush would go from carousing to living responsibly for a few months while working at PULL, only to return to his party lifestyle after finishing his PULL work. Perhaps the *Salon* magazine article was right about his drug use, but wrong about the location of his community service. Hatfield wondered whether Bush had put his drug use on hold because he had been court-ordered to work full-time at Project PULL. Maybe that was why he refused to discuss possible drug use before 1974, and why his old driver's-license record was purged.

Hatfield called Madge Bush at the Martin Luther King, Jr. Center, which was located in the same neighbourhood as Project PULL. He posed a unique question: "Did Governor Bush perform court-ordered community service at another agency in Houston or elsewhere in Texas other than the Martin Luther King, Jr. Center?"

After pausing, Madge said, "No comment, because Madge Bush is not gonna talk to you. I'm not getting off into anything about George except he's the Governor of Texas. That's all I'm gonna say about George W Bush." She hung up. The change in her tone convinced Hatfield that she was holding out because she didn't want to lose political and financial support for the Martin Luther King, Jr. Community Service Center.

Hatfield called a former Yale classmate of Bush's, who had partied with Bush in the late 1960s and early 1970s in Houston. This source had provided him invaluable information for a year in the belief that a definitive biography of Bush should contain "both a man's halos and horns." Hatfield asked the source if Bush had volunteered to work at Project PULL or if it had been court-ordered.

"I was wondering when someone was going to get around to uncovering the truth," the source replied. "Evidently, you kind of glossed over it in the book like a lot of other reporters have done in their newspaper and magazine articles. It doesn't fit, does it? George W was arrested for possession of cocaine in 1972, but due to his father's connections, the entire record was expunged by a state judge whom the elder Bush helped get elected. It was one of those 'behind closed doors in the judge's chambers' kind of things between the old man and one of his Texas cronies who owed him a favour. In exchange for successfully completing community service at Project PULL, where Bush Sr. was a heavy contributor and an honorary chairman, the judge purged George W's record."

"Can you tell me more about the incident involving his arrest or give me a name of the police officer or, better yet, the judge?" Hatfield asked.

"I've told you enough already. There's only a handful of us that know the truth. I'm not even sure his wife knows about it. Just keep digging, but keep looking over your shoulder."

After hanging up, Hatfield contemplated the conversation. The source wasn't someone who scared easily. He wondered about the importance of his discovery and how far Bush might go to make it disappear. He wrote in the afterword to *Fortunate Son*, "Whatever I'd found had me in its grip, and short of the grave, I was willing to follow wherever it might lead."

He found another source and long-time Bush friend who stated that Bush had been arrested for cocaine possession in 1972, and had his record expunged by a Houston judge after he had worked at Project PULL. The source said, "Take this any way it sounds, but do you think George would take time out from speeding around town in his TR6 convertible sports car, bedding down just about every single woman – and a few married ones – and partying like there's no tomorrow to go to work full-time as a mentor or to a bunch of streetwise black kids? Get real, man, this is a white-bread boy from the other side of town we're talking about." The source added, "[Bush] did the community service and the judge, a good ol' Texas boy and friend of George's politically influential daddy, purged the record. It happened a lot in Texas years ago, and George damn sure wasn't the first rich kid who got caught with a little snow, and because of his family's connections, had his record taken care of by the judge."

Hatfield contacted Bush's campaign spokesman, Scott McClellan. When previously asked whether Bush had performed community service at the Martin Luther King, Jr. Community Service Center in exchange for having his illicit drug use record expunged, McClellan had told *Salon*, "We do not dignify false rumours and innuendos with a response." McClellan was a master of handling media questions.

Hatfield asked McClellan whether the expunged record had been a quid pro quo for Bush's community service at Project PULL. In *Fortunate Son*, Hatfield described what happened next: "There was a moment of electric silence, and then McClellan muttered an almost inaudible, 'Oh, shit,' and after hesitating for a moment, finally said, 'No comment.'"

Hatfield contacted a third source about the Project PULL story. Source three was a high-ranking adviser to Bush who had known Bush for several years. He requested that his name and position in the Bush campaign would remain anonymous. On a call to Hatfield, he described himself as "a close associate of the governor concerned with making sure I [Hatfield] got all the facts right in the biography." His first meeting with the source was on Lake Eufaula, the largest lake in Oklahoma with a surface area of 102,000 acres and 600 miles of shoreline. Hatfield was nervous to meet on a boat on such an expanse of water. His pregnant wife advised him to pack a gun, but the meeting, while fishing for bass for three days, went well. The information proved to be correct. Hatfield was convinced that the source was genuinely committed to helping him fill in the blanks in Bush's life in a truthful way.

The source asked never to be contacted again unless it was extremely important. Hatfield hadn't contacted him again until Project Pull had come up three months after their initial meeting. Nervous on the phone, the source promised to call back in half of an hour. Thirty minutes later, Hatfield's phone rang. After grilling Hatfield for letting Project PULL slip by the meeting on the lake, he corroborated what the other two sources had said. Hatfield asked if the judge was still alive or the arresting officer was still working for the police.

"I can't and I won't give you any new names, but I can confirm that [George] W's Dallas attorney remains the repository of any evidence of the expunged record. From what I've been told, the attorney is the one who advised him to get a new driver's license in 1995 when a survey of his public records uncovered a stale but nevertheless incriminating trail for an overly eager reporter to follow. Bush won't admit he's used drugs before 1974. Period. Because we're not talking about experimenting with a little pot like a lot of baby boomers did back then. Hell, for a significant number of us, drug use was a youthful indiscretion, a misguided rite of passage, but W got caught with cocaine in 1972 and because his daddy was oil rich and influential in Harris County politics, he got his son off with a little community service at a minority youth center instead of having to pick cotton on a Texas prison farm."

"Why didn't Bush just keep his mouth shut last month and refuse to answer questions on possible drug use, rather than establishing a statute of limitations at 1974?" Hatfield asked.

"When he admitted that he could have passed even the fifteen-year FBI background check in effect when his father was inaugurated in 1989, George, along with some other top advisers, believed his response would finally lay the story to rest. I personally advised him to stay on course and never admit anything, believing the American public would get sick of hearing about it. I said, 'George, once you start answering, you're never going to be able to stop. The press will trick you by claiming if you answer just one more question, they'll get off your ass.' But he ignored my advice and now everybody wants to know why he won't rule out drug usage prior to 1974."

As his book was almost finalised, Hatfield thanked the source and was about to say goodbye. "Be careful and watch your back every step of the way," the source said, almost whispering. "Without sounding paranoid, I think I would be amiss if I didn't remind you that George's old man was once director of the CIA. Shit, man. They named the [CIA] building after the guy not too long ago. Besides, W's raised almost a staggering $60 million for his White House run in a matter of only a few months, and his corporate sponsors and GOP fat cats aren't going to roll over and play dead when you expose the truth about their investment." Hatfield swallowed hard.

"You know what makes me sick about all this shit?" the source asked. "It's Bush's hypocrisy. Cocaine use is illegal, but as Governor of Texas, he's toughened penalties for people convicted of selling, possessing less than a gram of coke – a crime previously punished by probation – [he's] okayed the housing of sixteen-year-olds in adult correctional facilities and slashed funding for inmate substance-abuse programs. Texas currently spends over $1.4 million a day incarcerating young people on drug offenses. I've known George for several years and he has never accepted youth and irresponsibility as legitimate excuses for illegal behavior – except when it comes to himself."

From 2001 until 2009, President George W Bush allocated a record amount of money to the War on Drugs. His drugs czar, John Walters, went after cannabis users with zeal, including launching a campaign to promote student drug testing. Illegal drug use remained about the same, but fatalities from overdoses soared. It was the beginning of the militarisation of the police.

By the time Bush left office, there were 40,000 paramilitary-style SWAT raids on American homes each year, mostly for non-violent drug offenders, some even for misdemeanours.

According to Judge Jim Gray, "President George W Bush, who pretty much has acknowledged while he was young and irresponsible and a playboy used cocaine, and then when he was Governor of Texas, signed legislation mandating anyone that uses cocaine must go to jail a minimum of one hundred and eighty days. That's beyond hypocrisy."

In his autobiography, *Dreams from My Father*, Barack Obama described his drug habit: "I spent the last two years of high school in a daze, locking away the questions that life seemed insistent on imposing. I kept playing basketball, attended classes sparingly, drank beer heavily, and tried drugs enthusiastically. I discovered that it didn't make any difference if you smoked reefer in the white classmate's sparkling new van, or in the dorm room with some brother you'd met down at the gym, or on the beach with a couple of Hawaiian kids who had dropped out of school and now spent most of their time looking for an excuse to brawl."

At Punahou School in Honolulu, Obama and some of his basketball friends formed the "Choom Gang." Choom means smoking pot. In *Barack Obama: The Story*, David Maraniss documents the rituals of the Choom Gang, and Obama's innovative role. "Total Absorption" or "TA" was an Obama concept. According to Maraniss, "TA was the opposite of Bill Clinton's claim that as a Rhodes Scholar at Oxford he smoked dope but never inhaled." Basically, if you exhaled prematurely, the Choom Gang levied a penalty: you wouldn't get to smoke the joint on its next turn around. A Choom Gang member told Maraniss, "Wasting good bud smoke was not tolerated." This led to another Obama concept: "Roof hits." "When they were chooming in a car all the windows had to be rolled up so no smoke blew out and went to waste; when the pot was gone, they tilted their heads back and sucked in the last bit of smoke from the ceiling."

Obama was infamous for elbowing in on joints in circulation, yelling, "Interception!" and taking a second hit. He and his friends would take the "Choomwagon" – a Volkswagen microbus up Honolulu's Mount Tantalus where they got blazed on "sweet-sticky Hawaiian buds" in between drinking Heineken, Becks and St. Pauli Girl while listening to Aerosmith, Blue Oyster Cult and Stevie Wonder.

He and a friend were in a Toyota, racing against the Choom-wagon to the top of Mount Tantalus, when the Toyota rolled over. He was found staggering up the road, cackling. To avoid getting a criminal record, he left the driver to deal with the police. In a note in his high-school yearbook, he wrote, "Thanks Tut [his grandmother], Gramps, Choom Gang, and Ray for all the good times." Ray was a hippy who supplied the Choom Gang.

Obama came to power advocating for reforms such as reducing the crack/powder sentencing disparity, ending the ban on federal funding for syringe access programmes and supporting state medical-cannabis laws. "I will not have the Justice Department prosecute medical-marijuana users. It's not a good use of our resources." Yet once in office, he refused to shift drug-control funding to a health-based approach. He maintained strict penalties for drug users – penalties that would have ruined his White House aspirations had he ever been caught.

He had promised to end the Bush-era high-profile raids on medical-cannabis providers, yet during the first three years of his presidency, his administration launched over 100 raids on dispensaries, a crackdown that rivalled those unleashed by George W Bush. The June 2013 Americans for Safe Access Report stated that the DEA had raided 270 medical-cannabis dispensaries in the first four and a half years of Obama's presidency – more raids on dispensaries than the previous twelve years combined. On such raids, Obama outspent the Bush administration by $100 million, and in half of the time. Those who suffered the most were some of the 730,000 relying on medical cannabis, many seriously ill or dying.

In 2010, Obama renominated a right-wing prohibitionist, Michele Leonhart, as head of the DEA, a bureaucracy that had expanded to a staff of 10,000, with a budget of over \$2 billion a year, and had offices in sixty-three countries. Michele earned a reputation for using heavy-handed anti-kingpin tactics on cannabis dispensaries, and for suggesting that the deaths of 1,000 Mexican children at the hands of the cartels was a "sign of success in the fight against drugs." Immediately after her reconfirmation in January 2011, the DEA updated a paper called "The DEA Position on Marijuana" with subjects like THE FALLACY OF MARIJUANA FOR MEDICINAL USE, which reiterated the Bush administration's philosophy.

Despite its lack of toxicity and medicinal uses, cannabis remains a Schedule 1 drug under Donald Trump's administration, alongside heroin and crystal meth. Calls to decriminalise cannabis are consistently rejected at the federal level with no sound scientific or expert basis.

A president who got stoned out of his mind in Hawaii spent a record amount of taxpayers' money on raiding medicinal-cannabis facilities, preventing sick people from getting their medicine, such as those going through chemotherapy who can easily die because they have no appetite and people who suffer multiple seizures every day and are at risk of going comatose.

Robert Mueller, the FBI director under Bush and Obama (until 2013), was grilled by Tennessee Congressman Steve Cohen. "Is there a better way? And some people have suggested looking into a system of legalisation that might be effective in stemming the tide of drugs from Mexico, and the border wars, and the immigration problems from Mexico. Have you considered this as a possibility?"

"I think anybody who looks at this problem considers it," Robert Mueller said, "and ultimately, when you look at it, rejects it ... There are too many individuals, both parents and others who have lost their lives to drugs, to get a ready answer that it should be legalised."

"Name me a couple of parents who've lost their lives to marijuana."

"I can't."

"Exactly. You can't because that hasn't happened."

CHAPTER 18
LEAP

Ex-police captain, Peter Christ, worked for two decades in law enforcement, patrolling the town of Tonawanda, New York State, just below the Canadian border. After four years on the job, it became apparent that no matter how vigorously the police pursued drugs, their actions had no effect. If there were burglaries or rapes in the Tonawanda community, the culprits would be arrested, and for a while those crimes would stop. But no matter how many arrests were made, drug crimes never fell. He put that down to arrestees being willing participants in an economic transfer.

After retiring in 1989, Peter began speaking out against the War on Drugs. Attempting to challenge the one-sided coverage, he contacted mainstream media. On March 16, 2002, and with four other police officers, he became a founding member of LEAP (which originally stood for Law Enforcement Against Prohibition but has been changed to the Law Enforcement Action Partnership). LEAP gathered a solid base of members from law enforcement and the criminal-justice community, and presently has over 150,000 members and supporters. It was inspired by the Vietnam Veterans Against the War, an organisation which earned credibility by using speakers who had been on the front lines of the war they had later denounced. One of LEAP's goals was to change the typical debate on drugs, which usually involved a policeman, a judge or a nun up against a crazy hippy saying, "Hey, man, drugs are cool!" LEAP managed to replace the hippy with cops, including police chiefs.

Wearing a police-captain shirt with a gold badge and his thick brown hair pulled back into a ponytail, Peter went on WGRZ-TV in Buffalo to explain why LEAP was formed. "We see the failure of the policy of prohibition in our society. I was talking to someone earlier today and they said, 'Do you think these gangsters will just become honest people if we legalise drugs?' My answer to them was, 'No. The gangsters will stay gangsters, but most of the people that are involved in this illegal trade, you really wouldn't classify as gangsters. They're more like opportunists. To give you a quick example. In 1919, there was a homicide rate in this country. We instituted alcohol prohibition in 1920. The homicide rate in this country climbed every year until it peaked in 1933, when we legalised alcohol. And by 1937, the homicide rate in America was back down to the level it was at before alcohol prohibition started … [1937] was the deepest darkest period of the depression in this country, so there was a lot of angry people, but they weren't killing themselves anymore because we took the product away that they were killing themselves over. Legalisation of drugs is not about the drugs, it's about the gangsterism and terrorism that is supported by the illegal marketplace in this country."

"So, where do you begin? Because some people [TV viewers] just out of the gate are going, woah! They're still trying to wrap their head around that a retired police captain wants drugs … now to be made legal. It just doesn't make sense."

Peter smiled confidently. "I can understand that because they think the issue is about the drugs. It isn't. It's about the crime and violence. Law enforcement was designed by a guy named Robert Peel over in London, England in the early 1800s … He designed an organisation of law enforcement that would protect people from other people doing them harm. When you institute a prohibition like we have with drugs in this country, what you are doing is not protecting people from other people, you are attempting to use law enforcement to protect people from themselves. Protecting you from yourself is a function of family, church, education and the healthcare system. It never is and never should have been intended to be a law-enforcement function. We are out there enforcing morality when we enforce drug laws and that is not our job. We were not trained to do it. We are not capable of doing it, and if anything else, you see the failure of it. We've been doing this for over forty years since Nixon kicked it off, and the drugs are more available, purer quality and cheaper than they've ever been before on the streets of America. And we've had 40,000 deaths in Mexico over the last five years fighting over this drug trade, plus we've destroyed more lives than the drugs have by incarcerating people and hanging felony convictions on them and denying them college educations, denying them jobs for no good reason. And one other thing I want to point out just in case people think that if we do it hard enough this is actually going to be doable and make drugs go away: we have the largest prison system on the planet and … one of the most efficient prison systems on the planet, and in that huge efficient prison system, we do not have one drug-free prison in America. And if you cannot keep drugs out of prison, who is going to be delusional enough to think you can keep them out of our free society?"

"I think President Nixon declared a War on Drugs over thirty years ago. How are we doing on that war?"

"We're losing. I speak to a lot of Rotary clubs … and I start off my presentation by asking them a question: 'Do you think we can win the War on Drugs?' Now, let's define what winning war means. We won the Second World War. We don't fight the Germans and the Italians and the Japanese every once in a while. The war is over. We won it. It's done … So if we win the War on Drugs that means we've taken the words marijuana and heroin out of the dictionary because we've defeated the drugs. They're gone. And I ask people to raise their hands and nobody ever puts their hand up to think that's possible. So, now, let's change the discussion. If instead of talking about things like drug-free and winning the War on Drugs, we start saying things like drugs are always going to be in our society … Which group of people do you want to run the marketplace? Do you want it run by gangsters, thugs and terrorists who have thirteen-year-old children selling drugs on street corners or do you think a licensed regulated marketplace in which we can set age limits, distribution points and control the purity of the drugs is a better system? Call me crazy, but I'm not a prohibitionist. I think that a better system is a regulated and controlled marketplace … I am not implying that if we legalise drugs that is going to solve our drug problem. Just like when we legalised alcohol in 1933, that didn't solve our alcohol problem … We have to deal with our drug problem as an educational and healthcare issue."

"If you're legalising drugs, doesn't that promote more usage?"

"I don't know. Does it? How many people do you think there are in America that are not using cocaine because they can't get it?"

The flustered female TV presenter responded, "Every single person who wants to get it is getting it."

"[The legality] of the drug is not what makes people decide to use it."

The male TV presenter asked the female, "Well, if heroin were legalised, would you go out tomorrow and do heroin?"

"Of course not," she said, "because I know what the effects are."

"One of the comments I get from people all of the time is, 'If we legalise drugs, what kind of message does that send to our children? It's condoning. It's saying that drugs are really OK.' I like to use tobacco, and if you ask any tobacco smoker who's been smoking more than twenty years if they ever felt condoned in the society, they'll tell you, 'Oh, yeah, ten years ago, fifteen years ago, I felt absolutely condoned. Every place I walked into there was an ashtray. I could smoke on an airplane all the way from New York to Los Angeles.' You ask cigarette smokers today if they feel condoned, and they'll tell you no. They feel barely tolerated by the rest of society. And let's also point out another victory. We've got 50 percent of the adult cigarette smokers to stop smoking in the last ten years without banning one cigarette, without burning or poisoning one tobacco field. Just by simply making it less easy for people to smoke and also by talking against it and pointing out the errors of it. That's the things that work. The drugs czar said the other day at a press conference ... 'This drug issue in America is fundamentally a healthcare and an educational problem.' And nobody asked him: what other healthcare and educational problems do you think we should use the criminal justice system as our main approach to? Because I can't think of any."

"We've been talking about how alcohol prohibition led to homicide rates increasing. So you said do away with all the laws and rules and regulations. Again, you can drink alcohol out in public. I don't know if I would want to see someone shooting up heroin next to me somewhere ... How do you combat that?"

"Well, you set regulations. We are setting different regulations than we've ever had in this country for tobacco use. We are now preventing people from smoking in the park, and in some places from smoking on the street ... Those are the things we have to do. I just want to remind you. In 1933, when we legalised alcohol, the federal government didn't legalise alcohol and set up a regulatory system for the whole country ... They basically got out of the prohibition business and said to the states: regulate it any way you want to ... Those are local things to do. What we're trying to do is get the federal government out of the prohibition business, and let the law enforcement go back to doing what they're supposed to be doing, and that's protecting people from each other.

"You know twenty years of police work, working in the town of Tonawanda, a community of about 80,000 people, I remember two incidents. One was a father who found out his son had committed a rape, and he turned his son into the police for that rape. Another was a mother who'd found out her son was committing burglaries, and she turned her son in for committing burglaries. Not once, in twenty years, did a parent ever turn their child in for drugs. Not once. And I can't believe that out of 80,000 people some mother or father didn't find in the sock drawer a little baggie with something in it. When it was their child, the last thought in the world was to turn it over to the police. They found other ways to deal with that problem. And we as a society should find other ways.

"Four hundred and fifty thousand deaths a year due to tobacco. A hundred and fifty thousand deaths a year due to alcohol. Now my question is when you look at all of the illegal drugs and you only have 30,000 deaths a year from all illegal drugs combined, first question is: if prohibition is such a good idea, why don't we bring back alcohol prohibition and prohibit tobacco? If it's a good idea, let's do it for all the things that we don't like. And the reality is when I say that, the people they look at me and say, 'Well, that doesn't work.' And that's absolutely right. Prohibition doesn't work."

A viewer sent in a comment: "There are places in Asia that have no drugs. They execute people who sell, use or manufacture drugs. Extreme, but effective."

"[A guy said to me,] 'Well, you know what they do in Saudi Arabia if they catch you with drugs?' And I said, 'Yeah. They take you down to the town square and they chop your head off.' And he said smugly, 'Yeah. That's right.' And I answered him with two answers. One was, 'Call me crazy, but when I think of countries that I want America to be more like, Saudi Arabia is not one of the first ones that pops into my head. And two: do you know what they do every year in Saudi Arabia when they catch people with drugs? They take them down to the town square and they chop their head off. And do you know why they do it every year? Because it doesn't work. If it worked, the rest of the people would see that head rolling through the courtyard, and that'd be the end of the drug problem. But even that doesn't work. People choose to do this. The first attempt at prohibition that we have any historical record of started with these words: do not eat the fruit of the tree of knowledge of good and evil. It was in the Garden of Eden. And the reason why it didn't work was told to you in Genesis, and it's because the creator after creating the two people granted them free will. And that's what we're trying to outlaw."

Asked about legalisation and taxation, Peter responded, "We are spending $70 billion a year in this country trying to win this drug war. We could revert that to using that in our prison systems, in the treatment community. We can spend that money in other ways. Plus if we legalise it, I'm sure we're going to tax it ... We're gonna generate income from it. Plus, we'll create jobs. Plus, we'll bring the hemp industry back, which was also outlawed in the 1930s when they outlawed cannabis, and the hemp industry is a very strong industry."

Peter finished with, "[Ending the drug war will] let law enforcement get out of this work and let us focus on paedophiles, people who are robbing from people, people that are harming other people, instead of going after people who are doing what they choose to do."

Another co-founder of LEAP is Jack Cole, a retired detective lieutenant who spent twenty-six years in the New Jersey State Police. For fourteen years, he was undercover in narcotics. Upon retirement, he felt bad about his role in the War on Drugs, which he classified as "a self-perpetuating and constantly expanding policy disaster."

In 1964, Jack joined a state police force of 1,700 troopers and a seven-man narcotic unit, which he believed was enough to address crime. Six years later, the force had approximately the same amount of employees as in 1964, which worked fine because there wasn't much of a drug problem. The only drugs in circulation were cannabis, hashish and small amounts of hallucinogenics such as LSD and magic mushrooms. Heroin, cocaine and methamphetamine were virtually unheard of.

"The likelihood of anyone dying [in 1970]," Jack said, "in that year in the United States as the result of the drug culture was less than the likelihood of them dying from falling down the steps in their own house. It was less than the likelihood of them dying from them choking to death from their own food at dinner ... So you've got to wonder: what was really the purpose behind this [War on Drugs]?"

In 1970, he was assigned to narcotics. Overnight in October, the narcotic unit expanded from seven men to a seventy-six-person narcotic bureau thanks to funding from the federal government.

This was replicated across the country as Nixon commenced his War on Drugs.

"When you increase the number of cops with one job to do," Jack said, "by eleven times its size, you set up a great deal of expectation. The expectation with us in that coming year was that we were going to make at least eleven times more drug arrests than we did the year before ... That's how this thing became a numbers game with the police."

After training for two weeks, all seventy-six had to line up. Every third person, including Jack, was selected to be an undercover agent and instructed to arrest dealers. Hitting the streets, the agents couldn't find any dealers. There were none in the suburbs or rural America or in the schools. Instead of targeting dealers, the agents were told to target young people, including high school and college kids.

Jack weaselled his way into small friendship groups of ten to fifteen young people. On Friday night, the groups would be out of school or off work for the weekend. Sometimes, someone would suggest that they get high. If they didn't, it was Jack's job to suggest it. Jack would say something like, "Hey, do you wanna get high tonight?" Some might reply, "No. I'm studying for a test tonight. I'll catch you next time." Others might say, "Yeah. While you're in the city, pick me up a couple of joints would you." Or they might say, "I hear there's some really good blotter acid out there. If you run across any, pick me up a hit of blotter acid." Whoever had access to a car would go to the city, return an hour later and hand out those drugs to their friends.

These social drug-use situations typically involved the group sitting in a circle. A person would spark up a joint, take two tokes and hand it to the person on the right. When it came around the second time, people were high and losing concentration on what was going on. Jack would be handed a roach. He improvised smoking it, while knocking the flame off the end and sticking the roach in a pocket. That night, he would submit it as evidence.

"When they handed it to me," he said, "they became a big-time

234

drug dealer because that's what we labelled them. And that's what stuck."

At any time, he had infiltrated up to ten friendship groups in the suburbs. He would stay until he got every single friend in the group involved in drug activity, which was easy to do because they weren't dealers. They were young people experimenting with drugs and accommodating their friends. Not only were they not making any money on the drugs, they weren't even covering their travel expenses to the city. Every two months, he had up to 100 people ready to be arrested.

At around 5 AM, hundreds of police would sweep into the neighbourhoods, kick doors down and drag the young people out in chains. When they were at the police station, the media would be ready – alerted by the police – to take photos, which were splashed all over the front pages of local newspapers, annihilating the credibility and respectability of the arrestees. When they were all lined up against a back wall, Jack's boss would appear, and say to the reporters, "Do you see that? There's 100 major drug dealers we took out of your community. This is the worst thing that's ever happened in America! This is going to destroy society as we know it! And your only hope is that thin blue line of police. We need more money, so we can hire more police. We need faster cars and better equipment and radios and guns that shoot a whole bunch of bullets and bulletproof vests. We need harsher laws and mandatory minimum sentences. We need three-strikes-you're-out laws."

After reading the horror stories in the newspapers, the public would demand the police be given everything Jack's boss had requested. The next year, the police would have the resources to arrest even more young people.

"We've been doing that now for forty-four years," Jack said in 2014. "Every year worse than the year before."

Back in 1970, drug offenders were sentenced under one law: it was illegal to distribute a controlled dangerous substance. Money didn't even need to have changed hands. Everybody police raided received a sentence of seven years in the state prison, with parole eligibility after one third or two and a half years. A hundred people going in meant a hundred coming out at a time. They had been snatched off the streets at the prime of their lives when they were trying to get an education. Now, they didn't have an education or even if they did, they were unhirable. Most of them ended up turning right back to the drug culture that the police purported to be saving them from. Except now, they would become real dealers, having made connections in prison and becoming hardened to the world. Every one that became a dealer actively recruited young people and spawned more users. That's how the War on Drugs self-perpetuated.

"When Mr Clinton was smoking, but not inhaling," Jack said, "was exactly when I was doing this to those young people, and he was college age at that time ... If I would have infiltrated his group, it would have been curtains for Mr Clinton ... So if Mr Clinton had been in that circle, it wouldn't have mattered if he'd inhaled or not. Handing that joint to me would have confirmed that he would never be an attorney much less the President of the United States."

CHAPTER 19
NARCO JOURNALIST INTERVIEW

Born in the UK, Ioan Grillo moved to Mexico to put himself on the front line of narco journalism. Over the years, he inspected cartel massacres, met international kingpins and ended up in court with El Chapo. After watching Ioan on the Joe Rogan Podcast (available on YouTube: Joe Rogan Experience #1253 – Ioan Grillo), I read both of his books: *El Narco: The Bloody Rise of Mexican Drug Cartels* and *Gangster Warlords: Drug Dollars, Killing Fields, and the New Politics of Latin America*. In August 2019, when Ioan was briefly back in the UK, I interviewed him for almost three hours (available on YouTube: Mexican Cartels, Mafia and Gangster Warlords: Ioan Grillo Narco Journalist | True Crime Podcast 40). Towards the end of the interview, we discussed the War on Drugs:

Ioan: Covering all this violence in Mexico and Latin America, I saw a lot of regular people suffer really badly. Now, seeing people – mothers whose kids have been dragged away in front of them; people just being brutalised – it makes me think as well: *How do you solve that?* And like here in the UK … it's easy to criticise the police. But then you think, *Oh well, here in England, there's so much safety in comparison. Here, you can walk down the street and people aren't worried about their kids being kidnapped violently.* The US has got a very brutal … hard system and still a lot of violence in some places but a lot of security in other places. So, it's kind of a mix as well there.

Shaun: Well, you've brought me to what I was going to conclude with. I watched your podcast with Joe Rogan where he's [saying,] "How do we end this?" These cartels just get bigger and crazier and more violent and it just moves from one country to the other ... So, from researching Escobar, he was sourcing a kilo of coca paste for $60. This was in the '70s, when cocaine's going for $60,000 a kilo in America. Weed was called weed because it grew at the sides of roads. It was a worthless plant. Opium's [from] a plant. Cocaine's [from] a plant. They're worthless plants at the end of the day, but when politicians made drugs illegal, those plants became more valuable than gold, so it doesn't matter who they arrest. The root cause is never addressed. If plants are worth more than gold and the only people who can sustain the mass production of them is the Mafia. It's the biggest incentive in the world for the Mafia to keep flooding the entire world with drugs and it just gets bigger every year in the illegal black market because of drug laws.

Ioan: Sure, so I agree with you totally, however, how do we actually move forward? I believe ... we have to reform drug policy. The idea of prohibition doesn't work. We have to look at damage limitation, but if you look as well, going back, people had this belief, I mean, go back to Richard Nixon when he was kind of launching the War on Drugs and he had this kind of belief, he said, "We can abolish heroin from Americans' lives. We can abolish this ... It won't exist. There won't be any heroin around." And there was even a United Nations conference in the '90s with the slogan, "A drug-free world. We can do it." Because he believed there could be a drug-free world ... Imagine that. We're here now, you know, you go out in any city in the UK, how many drugs can you find in any city in America, anywhere around in the world? I mean, they actually believed we can do this. It's got to be damage limitation.

Well, what does it really mean? OK, marijuana we can legalise ... It's already become legal ... With health stuff ... there is an issue with schizophrenia ... [that's] something that you know I've seen ... If you legalise it, it might be easier to try and lower the doses and for people to be more aware of not having the super-strong stuff when they're teenagers or whoever and if they do suffer from any mental-health issues ...

Then we get to the issues. OK, cocaine, heroin, crystal meth, ecstasy. I mean so exactly how are we going to treat these drugs? Now, you could ... legalise everything or we could say, "OK, first of all ... decriminalise it ... We're not going to send you to prison for simply possessing this stuff." But you still have the trade being illegal and then being controlled by criminals [and] organised crime. So, say if we get to heroin, are we ever going to be able to really legalise? Imagine if you legalise heroin and somebody dies of a heroin overdose, they're going to go and sue whoever sold it them right away. It's quite hard to legalise it ... That's one of the difficulties now of how you deal with some of those harder drugs. The issue of cocaine. I mean, can you legalise cocaine? Can we allow shops to sell cocaine? Well, what do you think?

Shaun: Oddly enough, out of all the towns and cities in this country, in my town, Widnes, there was a programme set up by a doctor because heroin use was off the scale, shoplifting was off the scale and burglaries. Out of all of the drug users, heroin users commit a disproportionate amount of acquisitive crime. [There was] the spread of AIDS as well from sharing needles. To try and address that, this doctor said, "We're just going to give them medicinal-grade heroin for free." It doesn't cost much – like I said: it's a worthless plant – if ... it's not black-market-sourced. It saves the taxpayers a lot of money, if these people aren't creating all the crime and going to prison and all those costs and the health cost of the diseases. What happened was in Widnes, the addicts were no longer afraid of getting arrested. They were going in and getting this medicinal-grade heroin, so the diseases weren't getting transmitted. They were talking to the health teams because they weren't going to get arrested. They were helped with counselling to get off the drugs. They weren't shoplifting. They weren't stealing cars and they weren't robbing people's houses, and this was so successful in my town, it started to make news headlines ... The shops, the chains like Woolworths or WH Smiths back then or whatever they were called, they wanted it rolled out across the entire country and it started to make news headlines. The Americans found out, the DEA found out, and a call to Downing Street ensued and that programme was completely closed down.

But, years later, Portugal had over 100,000 heroin problem users and they adopted that programme and they got the heroin users halved again because they weren't afraid of getting arrested and they spoke to the health teams and all of the crime, the theft and the disease transmission collapsed as well.

Ioan: Yes, that's one thing that's interesting. I might say you're totally open-minded about trying to expand those programmes. One of the things or questions that I always have about those programmes ... Where are they making the heroin? Like who is it that is actually making the heroin itself? Where are they buying the opium poppies from?

Shaun: Well, we went into Afghanistan to stop the growth of the opium, but it's up a thousand percent!

Ioan: I wonder whether the government is buying ... I agree I'm totally open-minded to see and try these and expand these and see if that stops money going to drug cartels. Like in the United States, there's still a lot of money being made from Mexico, from the cartel selling heroin to the United States. So, if the United States started ... creating heroin and giving it out to people, it would be interesting to question where they are making the heroin from ... We have weird things with opium that certain countries under the UN treaties like, I think Turkey is allowed to legally produce more opium poppies which then go to this kind of legal market. You don't really hear much about this do you? How's the legal market of opioids? We have opioids used in certain medicine. How's that working and you know, why is it that these peasant farmers in Mexico are not allowed to make any opium for these legal markets? You go and talk to these people and they're like, "Well, I'm only doing this because there's nothing else." How can they get access to these legal markets?

The other thing is ... a lot of the time, people overdose on heroin because the level is so inconsistent in the illegal market and I believe that heroin, the level of overdose is much closer than the other drugs. So, people overdose much more on heroin than say cocaine because [with] cocaine you can take this amount and it's like way, way, way more to overdose on a lot of cocaine … So people, because they're inconsistent … they're used to taking bad heroin and they think it's that amount and suddenly they take pure heroin and they overdose. So, maybe … you could reduce overdoses by having a really regulated amount. However, if someone's kid dies of heroin they got from a government programme, are they going to resist the pressure of a parent saying, "Wow! The government gave my kid heroin and my kid died of heroin."

Shaun: If it were legalised in theory, kids would be educated and it would be sequestered from kids. Adults have got a right to do it to their own bodies without getting arrested. It would be adults that would still be doing it and those guys, hopefully, will be getting counselled by the health teams to get off it, which will be the purpose of [legalisation] versus doing it through the black market.

Ioan: Sure, yeah. I mean I'm open-minded, but you see it's a discussion we need to keep having about heroin … The other thing right now … the overdoses are crazy in the United States … So, you've got like in 2018 or 2017, I think it's over 70,000 overdose deaths … Heroin was high, but the highest numbers were from the actual pharmaceutical drugs and obviously fentanyl and these drugs. So again, how do you deal with a lot of people who are getting doctors prescriptions and stuff in the medical system? I just talked to a friend yesterday over here … whose mum was an alcoholic. She then suffered from cancer. It was during cancer treatment that she was given opioids and has now kind of gone into opioid addiction …

Yeah, I agree I'm totally in favour of drug-policy reform. All I'm saying is that it's complicated and it's not like one button and everything is legalised and the whole problem goes away. There's complicated issues over each of these drugs … You were talking about the legalisation of heroin where doctors give free heroin or the government makes heroin and gives it for free, so it's not really legalisation in the same way of legalising cannabis.

Shaun: As a scheme to get people off it: give it free to the existing addicts.

Ioan: That's still not letting a shop sell heroin. It's not allowing, for example, the way that B&H makes cigarettes and then advertises them.

Shaun: But I would prefer that as well as opposed to people getting it from the black-market. If an adult person has got to take risks doing it in a shady drug transaction [during] which somebody might rob him or stab him and [he might] get a substance that could be toxic, I would rather that person went to a government-approved shop to get a fixed amount that they knew exactly what it was in the purest level instead of all those other risks that they would have to take.

Ioan: But ... if we allow a company to start making heroin ... what are the rules going to be there? Can they advertise their heroin?

Shaun: It's a very murky world.

Ioan: Yeah ... it's going to be like picking up your mobile phone and it's going to get a flashing, "Buy new PNH heroin!"

Shaun: Well, that's the problem we touched on in America: it's capitalism run amuck. The amount of money [the drug companies] spend on advertising versus drug development ... When I was watching the TV: "You're feeling depressed, call your doctor. You're upset about something, call your doctor." It's constantly bombarded. Americans are indoctrinated to think that a pill is the solution to all of your problems. Now, [prescription pills are] a leading cause of death.

Ioan: Yeah, back to these legal companies that made all this oxycodone. So, this was in a legalised system, but a badly legalised system ... In America, you've had – going back a long time – an overuse of drugs ... Everyone's like, "You're depressed, take a drug. You're hyperactive ..." If they're giving drugs to every hyperactive kid ... when I was a kid, I definitely would've been on a lot of drugs. I was certainly hyperactive as a teenager. So, there's an over prescription of drugs as well [from] the pharmaceutical industry and the way they're pushing out and making money from all of these drugs.

So, this kind of raises the question [of] drug-policy reform ... Start from the point of view that prohibition has not stopped people taking drugs and it's created this terrible black market and now we've got this chance to reshape the world, reshape the policies, but what is it going to be and how should we classify drugs? With opiates? With crystal meth? With legal drugs? They're already legalised now the opioids, so [there's] a lot of questions out there.

Shaun: I think that people will always harm themselves and people will always die from using drugs and we can't stop it and all we can do is reduce the harm. I think that the drug laws have created more harm than they were intended somehow to stop. The other thing is I'm a member of an organisation called LEAP ... and [their members say,] "We joined the police to arrest paedophiles, murderers, rapists and I was assigned to infiltrate a student group, get them smoking weed and arrest them all at the end of the month. This is not what I signed up for."

If you look at all the arrests under the War on Drugs [there were] almost a million arrests a year and the peak of it was weed possession [for] private prison interests and all the legal fees. [The prison] industrial complex is built around that. There's this massive incentive not to stop it. So, it's turned society against a lot of the police because half of the young people in this country experiment with drugs, then they're thinking, *The police could arrest us for this.*

I know a lot of good police officers like Neil Woods ... He wrote the book *Good Cop, Bad War*. He did join up to take down the bad guys and he said he became so disillusioned because the amount of money that the drug traffickers were making was enough to put people in the police force and tell them who the undercover cops were, and also the vast majority of his arrests were just low-level drug users and he felt really sad he was going undercover with these heroin users, pretending he was one of them and hearing the heartbreaking stories of how they're living on the streets and thrown away as kids and molested as kids and seeing [their] parents die. It just broke his heart to have to arrest all these people ... and now seeing them all in court [thinking,] *I was the guy that did this to you.*

Ioan: It's amazing how the UK is so slow about marijuana legalisation and I thought it might be further ahead on this ... If you're caught with weed these days, you're not going to get done for it, but I'm surprised they haven't [legalised] and there aren't already marijuana dispensaries like in the US or coffee shops. Why has it been so slow about moving on this?

Shaun: Politicians have got to be tough on crime to get votes. That's what they've believed ever since Nixon, even though they've all done these drugs themselves. People like [Bill] Clinton; his brother Roger was arrested dealing coke, and he said Bill had a nose like a vacuum cleaner. [Bill] put more non-violent drug users in prison than anyone else before him and every other president has done [the same]. So, that model has been [adapted] all over the world by politicians: I've got to appear to be tough on crime even though I've done these drugs myself, otherwise I'm going to lose votes.

Ioan: Going back [to] the '80s and '90s, there was still a "be tough on drugs" [attitude]. It was a big issue from the '70s onwards. Now I don't think people really care about this anymore.

Shaun: Young people. I've been in the schools and the young people are thinking like us. There is a generation of people who were brought up on Nancy Reagan's Just Say No [campaign] and they're stuck in that mentality.

Ioan: But one thing, when marijuana was legalised in Washington State and Colorado, I think that was in 2012. It was the same day that Obama won re-election. I talked to the person who ran the campaign in Washington State and that was fully legalised marijuana. It already had this kind of build-up of medicinal cannabis ... I talked about how it happened, and one of the interesting things now looking back, it's like a kind of dominoes toppling, so it came as a surprise to me that now we're in 2019, seven years after this, then you had Uruguay, the whole country legalised, and now you've got Canada, basically you've got dominoes toppling, but why's the UK being so slow to follow? The US kind of leads in some of these things ... For a long time, conservative arguments have been there, and they collapsed and really suddenly they weren't there, suddenly they went.

I actually remember going on *The Charlie Rose Show* a few months before that year. I talked to a couple of people about the Mexico thing and they brought up the drug thing and I said, "Let's talk about it." Somebody said, "Our drug-policy reform's a non-starter. Our legalisation is a non-starter." I said, "No. We have to talk about this stuff. We've got to talk about these issues," and a few months later that year they legalised. So, again it was kind of a mantra repeated by a lot of journalists. I think older journalists ... and that has been blown out but now we're in a funny place because now I feel like in some ways the arguments about this have already been won, especially with marijuana, and in fact most people are not, even the people who are kind of pursuing the drug war, are not really pursuing it in the same way as before anymore. Now they don't even use the phrase War on Drugs mostly anymore. That's more like we use it to criticise them for it. You don't really hear people say "We need a War on Drugs" anymore but the policies keep on, the prohibition keeps on, so how do you actually move the ball forward? How do you actually change things, change the reality? That's where we're at now, I think.

Shaun: It's the people that have voted for it in America at state level that have got the ball rolling all over the world presently, and that's not the US federal government, [which has] maintained weed as a Schedule I substance more harmful than coke and crystal meth with no medicinal value whatsoever. If you look at the

Partnership for a Drug-Free America that's financed by alcohol, tobacco and Big Pharma. The politicians are in a deal with these big corporations to try and hold the flood water back, but the flood water's getting stronger every single day because politicians can't go up against families who've got sick kids who are having hundreds of seizures a month and can go into a coma and die and all the pharmaceutical pills in the world won't stop it, but they get on the cannabis oil and it completely stops it or minimises it and can save their lives. Like Charlotte Figi in America; that case has been used now across states for medicinal use.

Ioan: I guess why the UK has been slow compared to the US is [that] the US does have this that states can change it. If in the UK, counties could change the law themselves or if cities could change it, Brighton would legalise cannabis for a start. Bristol might do it. But because it's all national laws here, you have to have a whole change with parliament doing it. So maybe that's why it's kind of been slow. California was resisted and then it went and now you've got like how many states legalised?

One of the really sad things, I wrote op-eds supporting marijuana legalisation and arguing [that it] would reduce the violence in Mexico, and this is sad to say now, to concede that after marijuana has been legalised in large parts of the United States [that] the violence in Mexico has not gone down. In fact, it's only increased and that's for a whole bunch of reasons. I don't think because of marijuana legalisation. I just think they've got deep problems in Mexico and that marijuana was only one part of it – in terms of drugs, heroin, crystal meth, cocaine, fentanyl and other issues as well. Why do fourteen-year-old kids commit murders? I talked to kids in Mexico who committed murders for $100 or even less. So, how do you change that mentality? I guess there's kids of that age in England or pretty close to that age who commit murders for nothing; you know, some of the stabbings and stuff.

CHAPTER 20
JEFFREY EPSTEIN

After his presidency, Bill Clinton achieved new heights of debauchery in the company of the now deceased child sex trafficker, Jeffrey Epstein, who ran a paedophile island and owned a Boeing 727 known as the Lolita Express. The flight logs show that Clinton took almost thirty flights on the Lolita Express, without taking his Secret Service bodyguards on at least five of them. On one he was accompanied by a girl called Tatania.

Epstein and his crime partner, Ghislaine Maxwell, were luring teenage girls to Epstein's mansion by offering them $300 to perform massages. Over time, the girls were manipulated into doing increasingly sexual acts, including threesomes, penetration with sex toys such as vibrators, strap-ons and plastic penises, and participation in orgies with high-profile individuals. According to a victim, Epstein demanded up to three orgasms a day from underage girls, a physical requirement that he compared to eating food. Assisted by Maxwell, they built a pyramid scheme whereby girls were paid to recruit their schoolmates. Some victims alleged that Prince Andrew took part in the abuse. Jean-Luc Brunel, a French model-agency kingpin, supplied Epstein with girls from desperate families in Europe, including twelve-year-old triplets, whom he gave Epstein as a birthday present. According to one victim, Epstein bragged about the triplets giving him oral sex.

Flight logs show that Clinton was accompanied by ten bodyguards on some Epstein flights, but on a five-leg Asia trip in 2002, no bodyguards were recorded. Epstein's bizarre art collection included a portrait of Clinton in a blue dress and high heels, pointing a finger directly at the viewer. It seemed as if Clinton had found a friend similar to the financier Dan Lasater, who according to Larry Nichols, had laundered money for Clinton and handed out free cocaine to underage girls. Some behavioural patterns are hard to change.

In March 2005, a woman filed a report with the Florida Palm Beach Police. She was concerned about her fourteen-year-old stepdaughter, who had been recruited by another girl to give massages for $300 per session to a wealthy man who lived in a mansion. Investigations by the police and FBI found evidence that Epstein and his co-conspirators had abused girls as young as fourteen. Epstein's powerful friends closed ranks and the sex offender was granted a sweetheart non-prosecution deal, which the lawyer Alan Dershowitz helped to arrange. Victim Virginia Roberts alleged that Dershowitz had participated in the abuse.

Epstein pled guilty to procuring a prostitute under the age of eighteen and felony solicitation of prostitution. His plea deal granted him, four named co-conspirators and any unnamed potential co-conspirators immunity from prosecution by the federal government. The deal had been approved by former Florida state attorney Alex Acosta, who years later was forced to resign under public pressure from his position as Labor Secretary under President Trump. Acosta claimed that he had cut the sweetheart deal for Epstein because he had "been told" to back off as Epstein was above his pay grade. "I was told Epstein 'belonged to intelligence' and to leave it alone," Acosta said.

No friend of Bill Clinton's and Prince Andrew's would be doing hard time. Instead of going to a state prison, Epstein ended up in a private wing of the Palm Beach County Stockade, according to ex-Florida-cop John Mark Duggan, who fled to Russia with some of the Epstein case files and video evidence of powerful people at orgies organised by Epstein. My entire interview with John Mark Duggan is available on YouTube: Meet The Ex Cop Who Fled To Russia: John Mark Dougan Interview. After three and a half months, Epstein was allowed out for half a day, six days a week, for work release, during which it is alleged that he abused more girls. According to the sheriff's rules, sex offenders were ineligible for such privileges.

Epstein's non-profit organisation donated $120,000 to the sheriff's office, ostensibly for the extra costs of the services being provided during his work release. Initially, his cell door was unlocked, granting him access to a legal-visit room, where a TV had been installed for him. After getting moved to the Stockade's infirmary, he worked at the office of a charitable foundation he had established shortly before entering the jail. In his office, he was supervised by permit deputies, whose overtime he paid. He required them to wear suits and to screen guests at the check-in desk. His chauffeur drove him back and forth and to other appointments.

After thirteen months, he was put on house arrest. While on probation, he travelled by corporate jet to his paedophile island and his Manhattan residences, where victims alleged that more abuse took place. As a Level 3 sex offender, he was required to check in with the New York Police Department every ninety days, but that was unenforced.

The lenient sentence, the immunity for the co-conspirators in the child-sex trafficking and Epstein's conviction for procuring a prostitute under the age of eighteen outraged the victims. In 2015, Virginia Roberts filed a civil lawsuit stating that Epstein and Maxwell had sexually abused her and pimped her out as a sex slave to powerful people including Prince Andrew and Alan Dershowitz. Everyone she accused denied her claims and counter-suits were filed. Dershowitz called his accusers liars and prostitutes. An out-of-court settlement was reached with Epstein.

The court document filed in 2015 by Virginia Roberts stated:

Epstein made me have sex with Prince Andrew several times. Prince Andrew, Maxwell, and I are shown in the photograph below. I had sex with him three times, including one orgy. I knew he was a member of the British Royal Family, but I just called him "Andy."

One day when I was in London (specifically in a townhouse that is under Maxwell's name), I got news from Maxwell that I would be meeting a prince. Later that day, Epstein told me I was meeting a "major prince." Epstein told me "to exceed" everything I had been taught. He emphasized that whatever Prince Andrew wanted, I was to make sure he got.

Eventually Prince Andrew arrived, along with his security guards. The guards then went out of the house and stayed out front in their car. It was just Epstein, Maxwell, and me inside alone with Andy. I was introduced to the prince, and we kissed formally, cheek to cheek.

There was a lot of legal discussion about Andy and his ex-wife ("Fergie"). Then the discussion turned to me. Maxwell said "guess how old she is." Prince Andrew guessed 17.

Then we all went to a Chinese restaurant for dinner and then to Club Tramp, a fancy "members only" nightclub in central London. Andy arranged for alcohol to be provided to me at the club. Eventually we left. I rode with Epstein and Maxwell back to the townhouse.

On the way there, Epstein and Maxwell informed me that the prince wanted to see "more of me" that night. Andy traveled in a separate car with his guards.

We all arrived back at the townhouse and went upstairs. Epstein took a picture of me and Andy with my own camera. The picture above is that picture, which has been widely circulated on the Internet. Andy has his left arm around my waist and is smiling. The picture was developed on March 13, 2001, and was taken sometime shortly before I had it developed. I was 17 years old at the time.

I wanted a picture with the prince because I was keeping in contact with my family. I had told my mom and my grandma that I was meeting Prince Andrew and that I'd take a picture for them. They told me to "be careful."

After the picture, Epstein and Maxwell kissed me and said to "have fun." They left Andy and me alone upstairs. We went to the bathroom and bedroom, which were just steps away from where the picture was taken. We engaged in sexual activities there. Afterwards, Andy left quickly with his security.

I chatted with Epstein about this the next day. I told him, "It went great." Epstein said something to the effect of, "You did well. The prince had fun." I felt like I was being graded. It was horrible to have to recount all these events and have to try to meet all these needs and wants. I told Epstein about Andy's sexual interests in feet. Epstein thought it was very funny. Epstein appeared to be collecting private information about Andy.

When I got back from my trip, Epstein paid me more than he had paid me to be with anyone else – approximately $15,000. That money was for what I had done and to keep my mouth shut about "working" with the prince.

The second time I had sex with Prince Andrew was in Epstein's New York mansion in spring 2001. I was 17 at the time. Epstein called me down to his office. When I got there, Epstein was there, along with Maxwell, Johanna Sjoberg, and Andy. I was very surprised to see him again. Epstein and Maxwell were making lewd jokes about "Randy Andy."

I had the impression that Andy had come there to see Epstein and to have sex with me. There was no other apparent purpose for Andy to be there. I was told to go upstairs with Andy and to go to the room I thought of as the "dungeon" (the massage room, but it is really scary looking). I had sex with Andy there. I was only paid $400 from Epstein for servicing Andy that time.

The third time I had sex with Andy was in an orgy on Epstein's private island in the U.S. Virgin Islands. I was around 18 at the time. Epstein, Andy, approximately eight other young girls, and I had sex together. The other girls all seemed and appeared to be under the age of 18 and didn't really speak English. Epstein laughed about the fact they couldn't really communicate, saying that they are the "easiest" girls to get along with. My assumption was that Jean-Luc Brunel got the girls from Eastern Europe (as he procured many young foreign girls for Epstein). They were young and European looking and sounding.

Afterwards we all had dinner by the cabanas. The other girls were chatting away among themselves, and Epstein and the prince chatted together. I felt disgusted, and went quickly to my own cabana that night and went to sleep. Prince Andrew must have flown out early the next morning, as I did not see him when I got up.

I have seen Buckingham Palace's recent "emphatic" denial that Prince Andrew had sexual contact with me. That denial is false and hurtful to me. I did have sexual contact with him as I have described here – under oath. Given what he knows and has seen, I was hoping that he would simply voluntarily tell the truth about everything. I hope my attorneys can interview Prince Andrew under oath about the contacts and that he will tell the truth.

I also had sexual intercourse with Jean-Luc Brunel many times when I was 16 through 19 years old. He was another of Epstein's powerful friends who had many contacts with young girls throughout the world. In fact, his only similarity with Epstein and the only link to their friendship appeared to be that Brunel could get dozens of underage girls and feed Epstein's (and Maxwell's) strong appetite for sex with minors.

Brunel ran some kind of modeling agency and appeared to have an arrangement with the US Government where he could get passports or other travel documents for young girls. He would then bring these young girls (girls ranging in age from 12 to 24) to the United States for sexual purposes and farm them out to his friends, including Epstein.

Brunel would offer the girls "modeling" jobs. A lot of the girls came from poor countries or poor backgrounds, and he lured them in with a promise of making good money.

I had to have sex with Brunel at Little St. James (orgies), Palm Beach, New York City, New Mexico, Paris, the South of France, and California. He did not care about conversation, just sex. Jeffrey Epstein has told me that he has slept with over 1,000 of Brunel's girls, and everything that I have seen confirms this claim.

On July 6, 2019, Epstein was arrested at a Florida airport. During a raid on his mansion, the FBI found numerous nude photos, which included ones taken of underage girls. Charged with sex trafficking and conspiracy to traffic minors for sex, he offered to pay a $600 million bail bond, but was denied because he was a flight risk, an acute danger to the community and he could threaten witnesses.

With his case under intense public scrutiny, his former protectors – some of whom he was attempting to compromise in a blackmail scheme – began to pull away. Facing a life sentence, he hoped to win a double-jeopardy motion or to cut a deal with the prosecutor, which would have required him naming accomplices. As his legal difficulties intensified, so did the risks to his associates, including Bill Clinton. If their activity was documented in court, certain government agencies would be forced to take action. No matter how wealthy, it had become apparent that Epstein had to go.

Having started writing this book five years ago, I had become familiar with all of the methods that the Clinton and Bush crime families employed to eliminate any risk to themselves. On August 3, 2019, I posted a video on YouTube: Has Bill Clinton Scheduled Jeffrey Epstein For Prison Death To Cover Lolita Scandal? In the video, I stated that Epstein would be killed and that it probably would be made to look like a suicide. On August 10, 2019, the news reported that he had been found dead in his cell at 6:30 AM.

I believe that the first attempt on his life had occurred on July 23 in the Metropolitan Correctional Center, New York, where he was found unconscious with injuries to his neck. He had been assigned a cellmate called Nicholas Tartaglione, a muscle-bound ex-cop turned gangster who was accused of killing four men in his brother's bar after a drug deal went bad. Facing the death penalty, Nick had access to the outside world through an illegal cellphone. Under normal circumstances, sex offenders would never be housed with murderers and gangsters because the convict code dictates that they should be killed on sight. Epstein complained to one of his lawyers that he had been attacked by Nick, who told investigators that he had nothing to do with it.

Whatever had prevented the first attempt on his life, Epstein was placed on suicide watch. On July 29, he was taken off suicide watch and put in a special housing unit with another prisoner. Every thirty minutes, a guard was supposed to check on him. The night before his murder, his cellmate was conveniently removed. The cameras monitoring the area malfunctioned and the guards on duty had supposedly fallen asleep. Although it is documented that individual guards have fallen asleep from time to time, no records exist that show that two guards have ever fallen asleep simultaneously in the entire history of the Metropolitan Correctional Center, which opened in 1975.

According to Nick's lawyer, "Nobody heard anything. It was a silent act."

The autopsy revealed that various neck bones had been fractured, including the hyoid, which most medical experts have stated is more common in homicide than suicide. Life is cheap in prison. A small amount of heroin is enough to have somebody killed. To get away with murder, the victim would have to die in a way that would look like suicide.

Out of all of the methods that prisoners commit suicide or die accidentally, a professional killer would probably go with hanging or a hotshot. Guards who have killed prisoners have been known to rope them up. Gang members often employ the hotshot because a prisoner found overdosed on heroin appears to be just another dead addict, which requires no further investigation.

In 2008, a teenager named Ronnie White, who had been charged with killing a cop, was found dead in a Washington jail. After the medical examiner found a broken hyoid, the cause of death was changed from suicide to homicide. The examiners suspected that he had been strangled with a sheet, towel or the crux of an elbow. The guard who had moved his body was found guilty of obstruction, but no charges were brought for his murder.

In 2013, a federal judge declared the cause of death a mystery.

One of Epstein's victims' lawyers, Spencer Kuvin, spoke to a staff member at the jail and told the media:

"I received a call from a supervisor at the MCC, which is the jail that Mr Epstein was held. The first words out of his mouth to be honest were, 'Don't believe what you are hearing in regards to Epstein's death.' I had a lengthy conversation with him about the issue of security within MCC and he gave me a fairly detailed description of the interior of the jail, which led me to believe that he was credible. He told me how the SHU (special housing unit) where Mr Epstein was kept was basically designed to be a jail within the jail. And then there was a separate, even more secure unit, inside the SHU where the highest value targets were kept. He said every square inch of that place is covered by cameras. It was designed that way because of super high-value targets that are kept there such as terrorists, drug dealers and other extremely high-value targets or suspects like Mr Epstein.

"If reports that there is no CCTV are true it would mean that they'd either shut the cameras off or they were not functioning in some way. He says there's no way that they would not have been able to see what was going on. What my source found very suspicious was that his cellmate was pulled the day before. The purpose of a cellmate for someone who either was on suicide watch or is on suicide watch is to notify guards if something is happening. So the fact that they pulled the cellmate is not only one level above negligent, it also appears intentional. Really he should have been on suicide watch. Not only was he not on suicide watch, they pulled the one person that could have notified guards if something untoward was about to occur. It was almost as though they did it so that no one could see what was going to happen the following day.

"I met [Epstein] on three separate occasions and he never seemed to me to be a remorseful individual. He always seemed highly intelligent, arrogant, self-assured, confident; never thought he did anything wrong, even in light of all the evidence against him. He basically just blamed the victims and had an incredible ego about himself and someone with that type of ego just never struck me as someone that could possibly commit suicide. I didn't think he was that brave to be perfectly honest. He always hid behind lawyers upon lawyers upon lawyers in his civil and criminal cases. I mean you can't even count the number of people he hired to protect him from any allegations, both civil and criminal. This type of an act requires a certain amount of resolve, and he just never struck me as someone that could do that.

"I think the most likely scenario if it's not suicide is that somebody on the inside of the prison was paid essentially to make it look like a suicide, and the guards were paid to disappear and not be there, and his cellmate was taken away on Friday, so there'd be no witness. So someone went in there in the early morning hours, tied him around the neck with a bed sheet, tied the bed sheet to the bed and pushed him down effectively and held him down until he choked to death.

"For something like this, you would expect to see some type of bruising or whatever around his shoulders if he's being held down against his will. So that would be the most likely scenario to make it appear as though he had done the act himself. With the fracture of the bone in his neck it suggests a high amount of force pushing down on him. I think the most likely scenario if it is not suicide is that there were too many people that were afraid that he would talk about what he may have done with them and others. They just paid off someone to go into the jail and take care of him."

Even with the most baffling assassinations, those responsible sometimes reveal themselves during the cover-up. The person assigned to investigate Epstein's death was Attorney General William Barr, whose headmaster father had hired Epstein in 1974 to teach teenagers mathematics and physics at the exclusive Dalton School on the Upper East Side of Manhattan. From 1973 to 1977, Barr worked for the CIA, starting out as an analyst and then becoming the Assistant Legislative Counsel. From 1991 to 1993, he was the Attorney General for George HW Bush.

According to the journalist Whitney Webb, while Barr was in the CIA's Office of Legislative Counsel, he stonewalled the Church and Pike Committees, which were investigating the wrongdoing of the CIA, including sexual blackmail operations carried out in the 1970s. While working for the Bush administration, he pardoned several controversial Iran Contra figures, including people linked to sexual blackmail operations involving children. Barr worked for Kirkland & Ellis, a law firm that defended Epstein. Stating that he didn't specifically work on the Epstein case, Barr refused to recuse himself from the investigation. His history of covering things up for the CIA suggests that the Agency was used to coordinate the assassination.

In October 2019, I interviewed Charlie Robinson, author of *The Octopus of Global Control*. The interview is available on YouTube under Epstein Clinton Maxwell Interview | Charlie Robinson. From the interview:

Charlie: Trump is an amateur criminal compared to [the Clinton and Bush crime families] ... They are high-level criminals with a trail of dead bodies behind them. So, is anyone surprised that Jeffery Epstein running a child-trafficking operation and an intelligence gathering operation and probably a money-laundering operation has ties to the Clintons? Of course not! I mean they're in the same industry. They're in the same business. They're colleagues.

So this is how it kind of goes: the Clintons would have been building a network of captured politicians and high-ranking people that were indebted to them or just straight up fearful of them and would do whatever they said. [Bill Clinton] would've been a perfect person for Epstein to get close to because for one: he's just a compromised human being incapable of saying no to anything; and plus, he has all of the money of the Clinton Foundation, which Charles Ortel and Jason Goodman will tell you, is the largest criminal charity fraud in the history of the world.

So [Clinton's] got access to all this money through that ... and once you've got Bill Clinton on camera doing some bad things … I would imagine Bill Clinton would respect it: "Hey [Epstein], I respect the fact that you got me on camera. I was gonna do that. That's my move!" You've got to just wonder what the conversations at the [paedophile] island were like. It must've been a mutual appreciation society where they were just patting each other on the back for their level of criminality and cleverness.

Shaun: What did the Clintons get up to in Haiti and was there a child-sex-trafficking component?

Charlie: So this is really disturbing in general when you talk about child trafficking. But, to do it to Haiti, a country that has just had some really bad luck: it's been economically pillaged; they cut down all their trees to use as firewood; just a really sad situation to begin with. Then they get hit by a gigantic earthquake and the Clinton Foundation is put in charge of distributing all the funds. Everything comes in through them and then filters out. Which is fine if it's an organisation that people trust like the Red Cross (although I'm not totally convinced, they're not up to no good), but when it's the Clinton Foundation, you just have to wonder because they're such shim-sham people; that they're constantly lining their pockets and stealing money from organisations and there'd be no way to track it in Haiti, and Americans in general are just very generous when something like that happens. So when the earthquake hit, it was all over television. They would have these big telethons, "Hey, call in. Send in what you can. Help these people," and they raised billions of dollars and they built like a dozen houses and it's still just a tent city there.

But one of the most despicable things that happened was that a lady named Laura Silsby was arrested in Haiti. She's an American. She was in Haiti and she was caught trying to steal thirty-three children. I'm not sure if the significance of the number thirty-three plays into this, but we understand that that is a very particular number. Anyway, she was arrested and jailed in Haiti for six months or so, trying to steal these kids and take them out of the country. When asked, she said, "They're orphans. They didn't have parents and we were a charity organisation. We're trying to get them adopted out to other parents," and their parents were coming forward saying, "I'm alive. These aren't orphans. That's my kid. You stole my kid."

So, it was a huge problem, and she, by all rights, should die in a Haitian prison, but that isn't what happened. Bill Clinton personally came to Haiti and got her out because she was working for the Clinton Foundation at the time that she was doing this. He got her out. I don't know what the arrangements were, but no doubt someone received something in exchange for this. Now, Laura Silsby went back to the US, changed her last name and then got herself a job with a company that does the amber alert system [which is] what happens when a child goes missing, they send out a mass alert to people. They do it over television. They do it over sometimes now cellphones. If you're in the area, your phone will just start squawking. It'll say, "Missing child this age, last seen wearing this."

So, the lady who went to jail in Haiti for stealing thirty-three children, got out by Bill Clinton, now works for the amber alert system. Something is wrong here. And to take this one step further, when reporters that had gone to the US Virgin Islands had talked to the people at the airport, they'd asked them, "When Jeffery Epstein was coming and going all these years, did you ever see kids?" and they said, "Yeah, yeah, yeah. We saw a lot of kids," and they said, "Where were the kids from?" They said, "Well, a lot of the kids were from Puerto Rico and the Dominican Republic and Haiti." And so you have to wonder, and it's speculation, but I think it's a logical step to make, was Laura Silsby taking kids out of Haiti through the Clinton Foundation and taking them to Epstein somehow?

The [paedophile] island is not that far from Haiti if you look geographically on a map. It's a quick plane ride or a boat ride and there's mysteries about Epstein's island. What's going on in that temple, or more specifically what's going on *underneath* that temple? Is that a place where they were housing people? Is this a child-trafficking operation? Was this the midway point where they were then taken and sent other places? It could be that the kids that were being taken out of Haiti were taken to Epstein. I don't know that for sure, so that's speculation on my part, but I think it's worth taking a look at because they were going somewhere right. She was planning to take them somewhere and the Clinton Foundation does have this connection with a guy who is a child trafficker, so it's something worth investigating. Maybe the information that comes out from the guy in Russia who was formerly at the West Palm Beach Police. Maybe there's information regarding that, too, because I would imagine that it'll blow the lid off of quite a bit of the scams that they were running.

CHAPTER 21
GARY, RICK AND LINDA

Even while he was riding high on *The Montel Williams Show*, Gary Webb's enemies were scheming to annihilate him. On October 3, 1996, in an article titled "The CIA and Crack: Evidence is Lacking of Alleged Plot" *The Washington Post* railed against "Dark Alliance," citing errors in the story according to various unnamed sources. Having hoped that the other newspapers would build upon their story, the staff at the *San Jose Mercury News* were devastated and they defended Gary. A tip came in that one of the authors of the article had been featured in a *San Jose Mercury News* story in 1967. In the newspaper's library, Gary found the story: "How I Travelled Abroad on CIA Subsidy."

On October 20, the *Los Angeles Times* started a three-day series attacking Gary's story. The *LA Times* journalist who had two years earlier described Rick Ross as the biggest crack dealer in the history of LA, selling half a million crack rocks per day, now claimed that Rick was not central to the story. On October 21, *The New York Times* weighed in with "Pivotal Figures of Newspaper Series May Be Only Bit Players."

With the support of his editors, Gary believed that the backlash would blow over. When the media started to attack the credibility of the *San Jose Mercury News*, Gary flew to Costa Rica, interviewed more people and returned emboldened with a new story that backed up his claims. He flew to Miami to interview a former CIA pilot, and returned with a story about the DEA protecting a CIA agent who had trafficked drugs.

Under relentless pressure, Gary's editors eventually turned against him and announced they were going to print a letter

SHAUN ATTWOOD

acknowledging that errors had been made in his story. Enraged, he went on a radio broadcast and vented about the betrayal. Sensing a division at the newspaper, the media challenged Gary's entire career. Even with large offers from publishers to write a book, he refused up to $100,000 because he didn't want to quit his job. His loyalty was repaid by the newspaper offering him a relocation to the San Jose office, where his work would be closely supervised, or he could move to Cupertino, which had a small regional bureau. Before moving to Cupertino, he sobbed.

One hundred and fifty miles away from his family, he lived in a furnished apartment and wrote stories about lost pets and car crashes, while praying that the union would help him to fight his transfer. On November 19, 1997, he resigned. Within weeks, the media announced that the CIA's investigation into itself had absolved the Agency from contributing to the LA crack epidemic. Gary wrote a book proposal which the major publishers rejected, but he managed to get a contract with Seven Stories Press. He obtained a well-paid job as an investigator for the California Joint Legislative Audit Committee and wrote in the evenings. His book, *Dark Alliance*, received little publicity, but it sold and launched Gary on a nationwide speaking tour.

Noticing him upset one night, his wife asked what was wrong. He said a source had reported that he was going to be killed. It might not happen for five or ten years and it wouldn't be done in an obvious way. The source gave an example of him driving down a steep slope and his brakes failing.

On February 10, 2004, now divorced, depressed and on medication, he sent an email to his ex-wife to commemorate the twenty-fifth anniversary of a marriage that no longer existed. He said that remembering their marriage made him happy and sad. Two hours later, he lost his job, which he had not attended properly. Eventually, he got a job at a small newsweekly and wrote an article about the military's interest in violent videogames.

Relying more on smoking cannabis, he stopped taking his medication. Struggling to pay his mortgage and child support, he put his house up for sale. A week before he planned to move in with his mother, he read his daughter a Dr. Seuss book, *Green Eggs and Ham*, and insisted on his son helping him fix a bike in the garage.

On December 10, 2004, he was found dead with two gunshot wounds to the head, which was ruled a suicide. Inundated by calls asking about his death, the Sacramento County Coroner Robert Lyons issued a press release stating that it had been a suicide. Lyons told reporters, "It's unusual in a suicide case to have two shots, but it has been done in the past, and it is in fact a distinct possibility."

People are still debating whether it was suicide committed during a worsening depression or if the CIA had eliminated him.

After learning to read at the age of twenty-eight, Rick Ross shed enough sweat over the law books in prison to challenge the life sentence he had received under the three-strikes law. The Federal Court of Appeals ruled that the three strikes had been applied erroneously, and he was re-sentenced to twenty years. On September 29, 2009, he was released.

In 2010, he sued a former prison guard called William Leonard Roberts II, who had stolen his name to help promote his career as a rap artist. On December 30, 2013, the court decided that the rapper Rick Ross could keep the name based on a First Amendment ruling. In videos for songs such as "Hustlin'," the former prison guard glamorises drug dealing, encouraging young people to commit crimes that would help to expand the prison system.

Meanwhile, the real Rick Ross turned to educating young people by talking at schools and published a book, *Freeway Rick Ross: The Untold Autobiography*. In September 2019, he was interviewed by the broadcaster Alex Jones, who had visited him during his incarceration:

Alex Jones: Freeway Rick Ross. He's one of the biggest cocaine kingpins ever busted in this country and it turned out that he was working for the CIA. That's all declassified. That's all admitted and Gary Webb who got shot twice in the back of the head with a shotgun – he had his new book coming out that was going to vindicate him – but he got killed. Well, the film came out a few years ago, *Kill the Messenger*, and I actually got physically sick watching it because I knew Gary Webb and I knew how accurate the film was. It blew me away ... *Kill the Messenger* goes so deep. The real Rick Ross is here.

There was a big fat jail guard who basically stole his identity and then said he was the kingpin. But Rick Ross is a really nice guy. He'll tell you how he got into it. I'm sure you didn't know why he was the biggest coke dealer in the United States 'cause the CIA was delivering it to him. But it's good to see you again ... What was it like watching *Kill the Messenger* because, you know, I'd interviewed you and I knew Gary pretty good? We built a website together. He'd been on the show a lot and all of a sudden he was executed. I mean he was really excited before he died ...

Rick Ross: Yeah, I'd spoke to him about a month or two before he got killed or died or whatever ... I don't know what happened ... I was also working at that time [with] Kevin Booth [on] a documentary ... and he's the one that told me the first time that Gary had gotten killed and/or that he was dead, committed suicide. I don't know which.

Alex Jones: Well, the police say two gunshots is pretty normal: shoot yourself twice in the head.

Rick Ross: Yeah ... they had a doctor to say that ...

Alex Jones: If I ever get shot twice in the head, it wasn't me. If I get shot once in the head, it wasn't me.

Rick Ross: (Laughs) Remember when you interviewed me in jail? That's ... one of the first things you asked me. You were like, "Rick, how do you feel?" and I was like, "What do you mean?" And, I was trying to figure out what you was getting at and you was like, "You don't feel suicidal do you?" And I was like, "Hell no! I'm enjoying life. Even though I'm in prison, I still like life," and you was like, "Oh. I just wanted to check and make sure, you know? We don't want nothing happening to you in here." You don't remember that?

Alex Jones: Hey man, they threaten to kill me all the time ... So we'll get more into things that are currently happening: fentanyl, the drug wars, all of it with Rick Ross here. But again, he was good friends with Gary Webb, who was an award-winning journalist, absolutely vindicated, who was executed, assassinated ... He said they tried to assassinate his character, broke in his house, threatened him. That was all on record. He was so excited to get ready to come on the show. His [new] book was coming out in a month. He'd sent me a CD with all his info to put up a website and they killed him ... and then his good friends came out and said, "Oh no. He committed suicide." Those are the type of friends you don't need.

But Rick Ross is here with us. Recap what happened to you and the hypocrisy of it and I don't like illegal drugs. I don't like drug dealing because of all the stuff that goes with it and happens with it ... Big Pharma with all the hillbilly heroin and all the Ritalin for kids, I mean really they're bigger drug dealers than you ever were.

Rick Ross: Oh absolutely ... Even like you was just saying now with the opioids addiction, you know all the doctors ... and dentists who've been prescribing people opioids and got us hooked on opioids right now. It's crazy, you know the epidemic that we're going through right now and it's worse than the cocaine epidemic.

Alex Jones: Plus, Hollywood glamourises it.

Rick Ross: Absolutely, I didn't even think about that part. Hollywood: when you talk about some of the movies: *Super Fly*, *Tequila Sunrise*, *Scarface*, *The Godfather*, you see people who come over to this country and they basically have nothing and then with the help of drugs, they start to control the whole world or the country and I mean who doesn't want a part of that?

Alex Jones: But when did you start discovering the reason you were being left alone and were you dealing $15 million a week or whatever at some point of cocaine, that the CIA was using you as one of their … major capos in distribution?

Rick Ross: Well, I didn't know that until after I got arrested, after Danilo Blandón set me up. So Gary came down [to the prison] and let me tell you, Gary was a very cool guy, somebody that you feel comfortable being around, not threatening, not boastful, just a down-to-earth, jeans-wearing, tennis-shoe guy … He came down maybe about four or five more times. Gary didn't give me much information. The deal was when we talked on the phone that he was gonna help me with my case and he had information for me, but really what he did on those first interviews was just decipher what I had, the information that I knew.

Alex Jones: Why'd you think they burned you?

Rick Ross: Well, if I would've been out on the street, free and this case hit the fan, I would've been more credible. Because what they tried to do is … make this story as if I created this story. One of the things that Gary did with them is he said that I would've had to have been really creative to create the paper trail that went along with the story and you know, just for the record, I didn't create the story. I'm not the one that came up with the idea about the CIA. I knew absolutely nothing.

Alex Jones: Well, they now, as you know, years after even Gary Webb's death, that [after] Iran Contra they had hearings confirming it all in the Congress.

Rick Ross: Absolutely, I saw the paperwork. I got a photo from the CIA themselves and I read it in the newspaper when the paper came out and I was like, "Aha. No, not me with the CIA! No way. Impossible. I'm a rebel." I was against the government. I didn't want to be with the government. So then when the CIA themselves said that, "Yes, we knew these guys were selling drugs, but we didn't sanction it, we didn't sanction them selling drugs, but we knew they were selling drugs and they were part of our army and we went to the Attorney General to write a letter and asked her that we not have to report these guys selling drugs."

So when I saw that it was kind of like, hold up now, if you go with your same conspiracy theory, you know that I was in prison on, because I never got [caught] with drugs. The only thing that I got caught with was guys saying, "Oh, well. Yesterday Rick had ten kilos ... A year ago, I saw him sell twenty kilos to this guy. I saw him sell ten kilos. I saw him with $50,000. I saw him with $100,000," and that's the kind of evidence I was convicted on. So, if you went with that same type of evidence with this conspiracy for the Iran Contra Nicaragua connection, then these guys could've been convicted, under those same circumstances ... That was my theory.

Alex Jones: So basically, to try to cover up the larger story, they claimed you were the guy with the story: you were just a drug dealer that concocted it.

Rick Ross: Right. That was the *LA Times.*

Alex Jones: Which turns out was being run by the CIA.

Rick Ross: Yeah, Jesse Katz, who was a friend of mine, had written stories before about me. They hired him to go against Gary Webb. You know you see in the documentary, he's apologising for what he did to Gary. He felt that he probably was one of the ones that drove a knife through Gary's heart by writing the story that he wrote.

Alex Jones: Well, they just had the hearings confirming [Oliver] North or as you say Northie, but Oliver North, the whole thing, Gary Webb, and he had that new book coming out that never got published proving he was right and then that's when he conveniently dies. It's a real tragedy.

Rick Ross: Well, we know that the CIA confirmed Gary's story ... Now they didn't say, "Well, this particular agent or this particular president or this vice president or this general OK'd it," but they said that, "We as a whole knew that these guys were selling drugs."

Alex Jones: And how it works was to buy the weapons from the US clandestinely. They let them ship the drugs in and have you and others sell them.

Rick Ross: Congress had outlawed them giving money to the

Contras, so what they needed was a source where this money was coming from where Congress couldn't tell that the money was being given or was being raised, so what better way to do it than to raise it on the black market.

Alex Jones: Absolutely, I go back to Iran Contra and all of that. Of course, it all later came out in Congress not just in the '80s but in the '90s and more of it's come out today and then we see China trying to ship in 25,000 tonnes ...

Rick Ross: My birth certificate says Rick Ross, so for everybody who don't know that, I didn't change my name. I was born Rick Ross and I made Rick Ross famous by going to court. I wish he would've went to court and come in to the judge and said, "Oh, I'm Rick Ross. He's not Rick Ross," when I was going to court, but he didn't do that.

Alex Jones: And he's a jail guard, the fake Rick Ross.

Rick Ross: Yeah, a jail guard.

Alex Jones: What's his real name?

Rick Ross: William Roberts, but that's not the worst part ... I got a judgement against me for $700,000 because I tried to sue to stop him from using my name and to stop Universal and Warner Brothers from using my name.

Alex Jones: And they went back with the court fees against you?

Rick Ross: Right, and made me pay attorney fees. I don't know how I lost the case, but you know how that goes when you're fighting with big corporations.

Alex Jones: How's ol' Rick Ross doing today, the fake one?

Rick Ross: I don't know. I don't really keep up with him. I mean he's still making fake music, selling it to the kids, telling them what a great drug dealer he was and that you can go out and sell drugs and parlay that into a record career and live happily ever after.

Alex Jones: What do you want to tell kids? You travel the country. I should've said that up front, helping kids and keeping them away from drugs ...

Rick Ross: Selling drugs, you really got two ends to that. There's no pot of gold at the end of that rainbow. Usually, it's a set of handcuffs or the graveyard. Very few people are able to get into the drug business, the black market and come out on top. It's usually the other way round. You usually come up dead or injured for a really long time ... With drugs you can't just say that this is for blacks or this is for whites. Now in the crack epidemic: blacks were targeted by the police to get arrested.

Alex Jones: And longer sentences?

Rick Ross: And longer sentences, but whites used cocaine just as much or more than blacks did ... As for the heroin epidemic, if it's whites that are doing it now. It's not gonna stay that way. It's gonna trickle down to the rest of society because that's just the way drugs work. It may start with one person, but it's like a virus. It has its way of getting introduced.

Alex Jones: Well, I've been down to skid row in LA and it's about half white, maybe like 40 percent black and maybe 10 percent Asian. There's a lot of black folks on heroin down there.

Rick Ross: Yeah, it affects everybody. I mean it's an epidemic and when you're dealing with epidemics, we have to try to get out of the black-and-white concept because it's a universal epidemic.

Over the years, bad things happened to the insiders and police who blew the whistle on the Bush and Clinton cocaine-trafficking operation in Arkansas. Federal agent Bill Duncan, a fifteen-year IRS veteran with a gun permit, was arrested for possessing a weapon and handcuffed to a pipe in the basement of the Washington, DC police station. His kidnapping ended the investigation into how the cocaine money was laundered. His bosses ordered him to lie to a federal grand jury. After refusing, he lost his job.

Arkansas State Police investigator Russell Welsh nearly died after being poisoned with military-grade anthrax – only available through the US government. Arkansas State Police investigator Julius "Doc" Delaughter, who successfully led the investigation against Clinton's launderer and cocaine distributor, Dan Lasater, was forced to resign after attempting to re-open the cocaine-trafficking investigation into Don Tyson, another Clinton contributor.

John Brown, the Saline County homicide detective in charge of the boys on the tracks investigation, was removed from the case after providing Congress with information linking the Clinton administration to drug trafficking. His superiors ordered him to remain silent about Clinton's connection to the case. After he refused, he was forced to resign.

In February 1994, the journalist LJ Davis was beaten in a hotel room. The assailant tore pages from his notebook, which had information about the inner workings of Hillary Clinton's Rose Law Firm and the Arkansas Development Finance Authority.

On August 3, 1994, Larry Nichols – who had exposed the Arkansas Development Finance Authority's laundering of cocaine money for Clinton – was falsely arrested for writing two bad cheques and failing to obey a yield sign seven years earlier. After the Arkansas Police admitted that the cheques and traffic violations were fabricated, the charges were dropped. After participating in a video called the Clinton Chronicles (available on YouTube), Nichols survived three attempts on his life.

It's now been thirty-two years since the murders of Kevin Ives and Don Henry. In August 2012, a vigil took place at the Saline County Courthouse in honour of the twenty-fifth anniversary. More than a hundred people – family, friends and other supporters, solemn-faced and teary-eyed – gathered behind a white gazebo to release red, white and blue balloons. One banner held up to a news camera read Justice for Kevin and Don 25 years too long.

"It's something that you'll never forget," said Laura Patton, Don Henry's high-school girlfriend, "cause back then, you know, as a teenager, [it's] a shock like that someone your age could actually be murdered. It's something that you never get over."

"I followed this case from day one in 1987," said Amy Burnett, a high-school friend of Kevin Ives. "It hit me really hard for someone I knew to be murdered."

Amid emotional words were demands for justice. Supporters were upset with the authorities for their inaction and the lack of attention the case had over the years. At the time of the vigil, the lone person in charge of the investigation was Lieutenant Frost, who was having difficulty making any progress because crucial files were missing from the police department, including witness testimonies, and many of the witnesses were dead.

Linda Ives expressed gratitude for the outpouring of support and the effort for a renewed investigation. She was humbled by the numerous strangers who had offered help over the years. "I think that we were kind of naïve common ordinary people that got up, went to work every day, came home and went to bed, and assumed that everybody else did the same thing, and tried to do what was right. Kevin's death has been the greatest awakening that anyone could ever have to see what really goes on."

The death of her son made Linda realise that the War on Drugs is one of the world's biggest lies.

GET A FREE BOOK:

JOIN SHAUN'S NEWSLETTER

HTTPS://SHAUNATTWOOD.COM/ SHAUN/NEWSLETTER-SUBSCRIBE/

REFERENCES

Bowden, Mark. *Killing Pablo*. Atlantic Books, 2001.

Bowen, Russell. *The Immaculate Deception*. America West Publishers, 1991.

Castaño, Carlos. *My Confession*. Oveja Negra, 2001.

Caycedo, Germán Castro. *In Secret*. Planeta, 1996.

Chepesiuk, Ron. *Crazy Charlie*. Strategic Media Books, 2016.

Chepesiuk, Ron. *Drug Lords: The Rise and Fall of the Cali Cartel*. Milo Books, 2003.

Chepesiuk, Ron. *Escobar vs Cali: The War of the Cartels*. Strategic Media, 2013.

Cockburn, Leslie. *Out of Control*. Bloomsbury, 1988.

Cockburn and Clair. *Whiteout*. Verso, 1998.

Don Berna. *Killing the Boss*. ICONO, 2013.

Escobar, Juan Pablo. *Pablo Escobar: My Father*. Ebury Press, 2014.

Escobar, Roberto. *Escobar*. Hodder & Stoughton, 2009.

Grillo, Joan. *El Narco*. Bloomsbury, 2012.

Gugliotta and Leen. *Kings of Cocaine*. Harper and Row, 1989.

Hari, Johann. *Chasing the Scream*. Bloomsbury, 2015.

Hopsicker, Daniel. *Barry and the Boys*. MadCow Press, 2001.

Leveritt, Mara. *The Boys on the Tracks*. Bird Call Press, 2007.

Levine, Michael. *The Big White Lie*. Thunder's Mouth Press, 1993.

MacQuarrie, Kim. *Life and Death in the Andes*. Simon & Schuster, 2016.

Márquez, Gabriel García. *News of a Kidnapping*. Penguin, 1996.

Martínez, Astrid María Legarda. *The True Life of Pablo Escobar*. Ediciones y Distribuciones Dipon Ltda, 2017.

Massing, Michael. *The Fix*. Simon & Schuster, 1998.

McAleese, Peter. *No Mean Soldier*. Cassell Military Paperbacks, 2000.

McCoy, Alfred. *The Politics of Heroin in Southeast Asia*. Harper and Row, 1972.

Mollison, James. *The Memory of Pablo Escobar*. Chris Boot, 2009.

Morris, Roger. *Partners in Power*. Henry Holt, 1996.

Noriega, Manuel. *The Memoirs of Manuel Noriega*. Random House, 1997.

North, Oliver. *Under Fire*. Harper Collins, 1991.

Paley, Dawn. *Drug War Capitalism*. AK Press, 2014.

Porter, Bruce. *Blow*. St Martin's Press, 1993.

Reed, Terry. *Compromised*. Clandestine Publishing, 1995.

Rempel, William. *At the Devil's Table: Inside the Fall of the Cali Cartel, the World's Biggest Crime Syndicate*. Random House, 2011.

Ross, Rick. *Freeway Rick Ross*. Freeway Studios, 2014.

Ruppert, Michael. *Crossing the Rubicon*. New Society Publishers, 2004.

Salazar, Alonso. *The Words of Pablo*. Planeta, 2001.

Salazar, Alonso. *Born to Die in Medellín*. Latin America Bureau, 1992.

Saviano, Roberto. *Zero Zero Zero*. Penguin Random House UK, 2013.

Schou, Nick. *Kill the Messenger*. Nation Books, 2006.

Shannon, Elaine. *Desperados*. Penguin, 1988.

Stich, Rodney. *Defrauding America* 3rd Ed. Diablo Western Press, 1998.

Stich, Rodney. *Drugging America* 2nd Ed. Silverpeak, 2006.

Stokes, Doug. *America's Other War: Terrorizing Colombia*. Zed Books, 2005.

Stone, Roger. *The Clintons' War on Women*. Skyhorse, 2015.

Stone, Roger. *Jeb and the Bush Crime Family*. Skyhorse, 2016.

Streatfield, Dominic. *Cocaine*. Virgin Publishing, 2001.

Tarpley and Chaitkin. *George Bush*. Progressive Press, 2004.

Tomkins, David. *Dirty Combat*. Mainstream Publishing, 2008.

Valentine, Douglas. *The Strength of the Pack*. Trine Day LLC, 2009.

Vallejo, Virginia. *Loving Pablo, Hating Escobar*. Vintage, 2018.

Velásquez Vásquez, Jhon Jairo. *Surviving Pablo Escobar*. Ediciones y Distribuciones Dipon Ltda, 2017.

Woods, Neil. *Good Cop Bad War*. Ebury Press, 2016.

SHAUN'S BOOKS

English Shaun Trilogy
Party Time
Hard Time
Prison Time

War on Drugs Series
Pablo Escobar: Beyond Narcos
American Made: Who Killed Barry Seal? Pablo Escobar or George HW Bush
The Cali Cartel: Beyond Narcos
The War Against Weed (Expected 2020)

Un-Making a Murderer: The Framing of Steven Avery and Brendan Dassey
The Mafia Philosopher: Two Tonys
Life Lessons

Pablo Escobar's Story (4-book series 2019-20)
T-Bone (Expected 2022)

SOCIAL-MEDIA LINKS

Email: attwood.shaun@hotmail.co.uk
YouTube: Shaun Attwood
Blog: Jon's Jail Journal
Website: shaunattwood.com
Instagram: @shaunattwood
Twitter: @shaunattwood
LinkedIn: Shaun Attwood
Goodreads: Shaun Attwood
Facebook: Shaun Attwood, Jon's Jail Journal,
T-Bone Appreciation Society

Shaun welcomes feedback on any of his
books and YouTube videos.

Thank you for the Amazon and Goodreads reviews and to all of
the people who have subscribed to Shaun's YouTube channel!

OTHER BOOKS BY SHAUN ATTWOOD

Pablo Escobar: Beyond Narcos

War on Drugs Series Book 1

The mind-blowing true story of Pablo Escobar and the Medellín Cartel beyond their portrayal on Netflix.

Colombian drug lord Pablo Escobar was a devoted family man and a psychopathic killer; a terrible enemy, yet a wonderful friend. While donating millions to the poor, he bombed and tortured his enemies – some had their eyeballs removed with hot spoons. Through ruthless cunning and America's insatiable appetite for cocaine, he became a multi-billionaire, who lived in a $100-million house with its own zoo.

Pablo Escobar: Beyond Narcos demolishes the standard good versus evil telling of his story. The authorities were not hunting Pablo down to stop his cocaine business. They were taking over it.

American Made: Who Killed Barry Seal?
Pablo Escobar or George HW Bush

War on Drugs Series Book 2

Set in a world where crime and government coexist, *American Made* is the jaw-dropping true story of CIA pilot Barry Seal that the Hollywood movie starring Tom Cruise is afraid to tell.

Barry Seal flew cocaine and weapons worth billions of dollars into and out of America in the 1980s. After he became a government informant, Pablo Escobar's Medellin Cartel offered a million for him alive and half a million dead. But his real trouble began after he threatened to expose the dirty dealings of George HW Bush.

American Made rips the roof off Bush and Clinton's complicity in cocaine trafficking in Mena, Arkansas.

"A conspiracy of the grandest magnitude." Congressman Bill Alexander on the Mena affair.

The Cali Cartel: Beyond Narcos

War on Drugs Series Book 3

An electrifying account of the Cali Cartel beyond its portrayal on Netflix.

From the ashes of Pablo Escobar's empire rose an even bigger and more malevolent cartel. A new breed of sophisticated mobsters became the kings of cocaine. Their leader was Gilberto Rodríguez Orejuela – known as the Chess Player due to his foresight and calculated cunning.

Gilberto and his terrifying brother, Miguel, ran a multi-billion-dollar drug empire like a corporation. They employed a politically astute brand of thuggery and spent $10 million to put a president in power. Although the godfathers from Cali preferred bribery over violence, their many loyal torturers and hit men were never idle.

Pablo Escobar's Story (4-book series)

"Finally, the definitive book about Escobar, original and up-to-date" – UNILAD

"The most comprehensive account ever written" – True Geordie

Pablo Escobar was a mama's boy who cherished his family and sang in the shower, yet he bombed a passenger plane and formed a death squad that used genital electrocution.

Most Escobar biographies only provide a few pieces of the puzzle, but this action-packed 1000-page book reveals everything about the king of cocaine.

Mostly translated from Spanish, Part 1 contains stories untold in the English-speaking world, including:

The tragic death of his youngest brother Fernando.

The fate of his pregnant mistress.

The shocking details of his affair with a TV celebrity.

The presidential candidate who encouraged him to eliminate their rivals.

The Mafia Philosopher

"A fast-paced true-crime memoir with all of the action of Good-fellas" – UNILAD

"Sopranos v Sons of Anarchy with an Alaskan-snow backdrop" – True Geordie Podcast

Breaking bones, burying bodies and planting bombs became second nature to Two Tonys while working for the Bonanno Crime Family, whose exploits inspired The Godfather.

After a dispute with an outlaw motorcycle club, Two Tonys left a trail of corpses from Arizona to Alaska. On the run, he was pursued by bikers and a neo-Nazi gang blood-thirsty for revenge, while a homicide detective launched a nationwide manhunt.

As the mist from his smoking gun fades, readers are left with an unexpected portrait of a stoic philosopher with a wealth of charm, a glorious turn of phrase and a fanatical devotion to his daughter.

Party Time

An action-packed roller-coaster account of a life spiralling out of control, featuring wild women, gangsters and a mountain of drugs.

Shaun Attwood arrived in Phoenix, Arizona, a penniless business graduate from a small industrial town in England. Within a decade, he became a stock-market millionaire. But he was leading a double life.

After taking his first Ecstasy pill at a rave in Manchester as a shy student, Shaun became intoxicated by the party lifestyle that would change his fortune. Years later, in the Arizona desert, he became submerged in a criminal underworld, throwing parties for thousands of ravers and running an Ecstasy ring in competition with the Mafia mass murderer Sammy 'The Bull' Gravano.

As greed and excess tore through his life, Shaun had eye-watering encounters with Mafia hit men and crystal-meth addicts, enjoyed extravagant debauchery with superstar DJs and glitter girls, and ingested enough drugs to kill a herd of elephants. This is his story.

Hard Time

"Makes the Shawshank Redemption look like a holiday camp"
– NOTW

After a SWAT team smashed down stock-market millionaire Shaun Attwood's door, he found himself inside of Arizona's deadliest jail and locked into a brutal struggle for survival.

Shaun's hope of living the American Dream turned into a nightmare of violence and chaos, when he had a run-in with Sammy the Bull Gravano, an Italian Mafia mass murderer.

In jail, Shaun was forced to endure cockroaches crawling in his ears at night, dead rats in the food and the sound of skulls getting cracked against toilets. He meticulously documented the conditions and smuggled out his message.

Join Shaun on a harrowing voyage into the darkest recesses of human existence.

Hard Time provides a revealing glimpse into the tragedy, brutality, dark comedy and eccentricity of prison life.

Featured worldwide on Nat Geo Channel's Locked-Up/ Banged-Up Abroad Raving Arizona.

Prison Time

Sentenced to 9½ years in Arizona's state prison for distributing Ecstasy, Shaun finds himself living among gang members, sexual predators and drug-crazed psychopaths. After being attacked by a Californian biker in for stabbing a girlfriend, Shaun writes about the prisoners who befriend, protect and inspire him. They include T-Bone, a massive African American ex-Marine who risks his life saving vulnerable inmates from rape, and Two Tonys, an old-school Mafia murderer who left the corpses of his rivals from Arizona to Alaska. They teach Shaun how to turn incarceration to his advantage, and to learn from his mistakes.

Shaun is no stranger to love and lust in the heterosexual world, but the tables are turned on him inside. Sexual advances come at him from all directions, some cleverly disguised, others more sinister – making Shaun question his sexual identity.

Resigned to living alongside violent, mentally-ill and drug-addicted inmates, Shaun immerses himself in psychology and philosophy to try to make sense of his past behaviour, and begins applying what he learns as he adapts to prison life. Encouraged by Two Tonys to explore fiction as well, Shaun reads over 1000 books which, with support from a brilliant psychotherapist, Dr Owen, speed along his personal development. As his ability to deflect daily threats improves, Shaun begins to look forward to his release with optimism and a new love waiting for him. Yet the words of Aristotle from one of Shaun's books will prove prophetic: "We cannot learn without pain."

Un-Making a Murderer: The Framing of Steven Avery and Brendan Dassey

Innocent people do go to jail. Sometimes mistakes are made. But even more terrifying is when the authorities conspire to frame them. That's what happened to Steven Avery and Brendan Dassey, who were convicted of murder and are serving life sentences.

Un-Making a Murderer is an explosive book which uncovers the illegal, devious and covert tactics used by Wisconsin officials, including:

– Concealing Other Suspects

– Paying Expert Witnesses to Lie

– Planting Evidence

– Jury Tampering

The art of framing innocent people has been in practice for centuries and will continue until the perpetrators are held accountable. Turning conventional assumptions and beliefs in the justice system upside down, *Un-Making a Murderer* takes you on that journey.

The profits from this book are going to Steven and Brendan and to donate free books to schools and prisons. In the last three years, Shaun Attwood has donated 20,000 books.

ABOUT SHAUN ATTWOOD

Shaun Attwood is a former stock-market millionaire and Ecstasy supplier turned YouTuber, public speaker, author and activist, who is banned from America for life. His story was featured worldwide on National Geographic Channel as an episode of Locked Up/ Banged Up Abroad called Raving Arizona.

Shaun's writing – smuggled out of the jail with the highest death rate in America run by Sheriff Joe Arpaio – attracted international media attention to the human rights violations: murders by guards and gang members, dead rats in the food, cockroach infestations...

While incarcerated, Shaun was forced to reappraise his life. He read over 1,000 books in just under six years. By studying original texts in psychology and philosophy, he sought to better understand himself and his past behaviour. He credits books as being the lifeblood of his rehabilitation.

Shaun tells his story to schools to dissuade young people from drugs and crime. He campaigns against injustice via his books and blog, Jon's Jail Journal. He has appeared on the BBC, Sky News and TV worldwide to talk about issues affecting prisoners' rights.

As a best-selling true-crime author, Shaun is presently writing a series of action-packed books exposing the War on Drugs, which feature the CIA, Pablo Escobar and the cocaine Mafia. He is also writing the longest ever Escobar biography: *Pablo Escobar's Story*, a 4-book series with over 1,000 pages. On his weekly true-crime podcast on YouTube, Shaun interviews people with hard-hitting crime stories and harrowing prison experiences.

CPSIA information can be obtained
at www.ICGtesting.com
Printed in the USA
LVHW080416071120
671022LV00004B/7

9 781912 885060